The Encyclopedia Shatnerica

The Encyclopedia Shatnerica

Robert E. Schnakenberg

BOOKS

RENAISSANCE BOOKS
Los Angeles

Library of Congress Cataloging-in-Publication Data

Schnakenberg, Robert E.
    The encyclopedia Shatnerica / Robert E. Schnakenberg.
      p. cm.
    Filmography: p.
    Includes bibliographical references and index.
    ISBN 1-58063-039-1 (trade paperback : alk. paper)
    1. Shatner, William. 2. Actors—Canada—Biography.
PN2308.S52S36 1998
791.45'028'092—dc21
   [B]   98-27718
                                              CIP

10 9 8 7 6 5 4 3 2 1

Design by Tanya Maiboroda

Distributed by St. Martin's Press
Manufactured in the United States of America
First Edition

For my Miramanee,
You have made me . . . soooo . . . happeeee!

KIROK

"Possibly there are aspects to me which people see that I'm not aware of…"

—WILLIAM SHATNER,
attempting to explain his mystique

Contents

∿

Acknowledgments

~

The author would like to thank the following for their assistance: Archive Photos (Michael Shulman), Jane Klain, Karen and Karma Lurie, Alvin H. Marill, Bob Mould and Grant Hart, The Museum of Television & Radio (Jonathan Rosenthal), my incomparable editor James Robert Parish, Photofest (Howard Mandelbaum), Rena and Hannah Rosenthal, Jonathan Samet, J. Trusk, and, of course, my captain, William Shatner, for making it all possible.

Introduction

⁓

Welcome to the final frontier of Shatnerology. If you've come this far, then you, like me, are a wayfarer in the Shatnerverse. You have struggled with the riddle that is Shatner, squeezed your hands around this unruly Rubik's Cube of a man and failed to put the colored sides together properly. However, I am here to tell you there is a solution. It starts with the magic book you now hold in your hand.

The Encyclopedia Shatnerica is the world's first comprehensive guide to the complex, multidimensional universe of William Shatner. Other books may cover his life and career, or the fictional universe of TV's **Star Trek** (1966-69), his most celebrated professional achievement, but in *no one place* can you find A to Z coverage of the whole wide world of William Shatner, performer and private citizen. All his television series, TV movies, and feature films are annotated herein, along with selected Shatner stage productions and notable TV guest appearances. Special emphasis is given to trends, recurring themes in his life and work, and revealing personal anecdotes. What Shatner says about himself, and what others say about him, are given a full and fair airing.

If you are a fan—and there are millions worldwide—you will look upon the amount of information in this volume and the many layers to it as evidence of your hero's lasting impact on popular culture. On the flip side, Shatner's detractors—and there are many—will no doubt find much to gnash their fangs about between these covers. However, I do not seek to judge this man. Some of my fondest childhood memories involve waiting up late at night to watch him work, in midnight TV re-airings of *Star Trek*, or guest appearances on such classic television anthology shows as *Twilight Zone* or *Alfred Hitchcock Presents*. If sometimes William Shatner has provided unintentional amusement to myself and others, then so be it. All performers should be so lucky, to provoke such a response in an audience as vast as this personality has commanded for decades.

So come with me into the Shatner chamber. Sit down on the toilet seat shaped like a captain's chair and discover what I have uncovered. Without a guide to shed light on the shadowy places, this dark forest of a man will swallow you whole. Our mission here is a simple one: to boldly go where no book has gone before. To unlock the secrets of Shatnerica...

Entries

~

NOTE: Items in boldface are cross-references to entries in *The Encyclopedia Shatnerica*. For Shatner films and television appearances, a handy "Six Degrees of ***Star Trek***" guide has been included to alert fans of that TV show to appearances by ***Star Trek*** regulars and notable guests in the particular film entry under discussion. (These appearances are also noted as "Friends of Bill" under each ***Star Trek*** episode listing in Appendix 2: A Shatnercentric Episode Guide.) For Shatner features and television films, we are employing a rating guide of "Lucky Horseshoes" ∪ (in acknowledgment of Shatner's affinity for horses). Four horseshoes is the highest—and rarest—rating. One horseshoe indicates the only thing to be said for the movie is Shatner is in it so it can't be all bad... can it? When the answer to that question is YES, we have no choice but to rate it a bomb 💣. For more details on Shatner's many works, see Appendix 1: A Shatnerography. Appendix 2: ***Star Trek***: A Shatnercentric Episode Guide offers further data on his landmark sci-fi TV series.

Acting

"I don't have a technique for acting," Shatner told the *New York Daily News* in 1982. That revelation will come as a surprise to some, but Shatner has never had any formal acting training. He views his craft as a visceral endeavor in which learned responses have no place. "An actor's emotions are just below the magma of his sophistication," he has said. As a result, Shatner has little use for elaborate performance rehearsals. Despite this idiosyncratic approach, he has influenced a number of other talents, including **Jason Alexander** of *Seinfeld* TV sitcom fame. When comic dervish Jim Carrey is asked what other actor makes him laugh, he says, unhesitatingly, William Shatner.

What do Jason and Jim see that others don't? Let's observe William Shatner at work. His most notable contribution to the art of acting may be his mannered, readily identifiable style. Often imitated, but never duplicated, the "Shatner approach" is marked by his use of urgent, hurried phrasing, an emphasis on unexpected words and syllables, a tendency to linger on words in the middle of a sentence, and a curious habit of overrunning logical voice stops and careening into the next sentence. Another characteristic is his trademark shrug, usually accompanied by open arms, bent at the elbows, upturned palms, and very wide eyes. This works especially well when, as Captain Kirk, he must confront an adversary appearing on the Starship *Enterprise's* viewer.

The origin of this performance style can be traced to one of Shatner's earliest professional experiences. While serving as an understudy at the **Stratford Shakespeare Festival** in Ontario, Canada, Shatner had to play the title role in Shakespeare's *Henry V* on a few hours' notice *without* benefit of rehearsal. His hastily cobbled performance—full of abrupt stops and inappropriate pauses where he could not remember the dialogue—was acclaimed by critics as remarkably intuitive and full of passion. Always quick to respond to positive feedback from his audience, Shatner began to incorporate these techniques into subsequent performances.

The apotheosis of the Shatner acting style came in his most famous role, Captain Kirk, which he played on TV's ***Star Trek*** from 1966 to 1969. In a 1989 interview with *Playboy*, Shatner explained his thinking in employing these devices. "There were two things at work. One was what I do naturally. Because it [***Star Trek***] was a series, and because fatigue means you have no time to separate yourself from the character, I tried to retain in Captain Kirk what was the essential me, I guess. I'm dimly aware that Captain Kirk phrased things in a certain way, and *I'll* do that on occasion. But I try not to be deliberate or even cognitive about it. It's all just part of me."

"I sometimes think of myself as an acting machine."
                                        —SHATNER, in 1967

Airplane II: The Sequel   RATING: U U

The 1982 comedy feature, a PG-rated sequel to the popular *Airplane!* (1980), features Shatner in a supporting role to coleads Robert Hays and Julie Hagerty. As Buck Murdock, the commander of a moonbase where a distressed space shuttle must land, Shatner mugs shamelessly and spoofs his heroic Captain Kirk persona. However, to the distress of the audience, the film, which boasts cameos by Raymond Burr, Sonny Bono, Chuck Connors, et al., is *not* very funny. If the thought of Shatner playing a pompous ass is a stretch, how about Jack Jones as an oleaginous lounge singer? Little man Hervé Villechaize (who played in *The Man with the Golden Gun* [1973], starring Roger Moore as James Bond) has a small role (forgive the pun),

As moonbase commander Buck Murdock, Shatner chews the scenery in Airplane II: The Sequel *(1982). [photo courtesy of Archive Photos]*

making this the second time Shatner worked on screen with a James Bond villain (the first was Harold "Oddjob" Sakata in **Want a Ride, Little Girl?**). Video and TV versions contain additional footage, none of which helps.

Alexander, Jason (B. 1959)

Best known for his portrayal of pint-sized, super paranoid George Costanza on the sitcom megahit *Seinfeld* (1990–98), this multitalented, five-foot-six-inch performer maintains a profound—and largely unexplained—reverence for Shatner and his body of work. "I became an actor because of Shatner," Alexander told *Entertainment Weekly* in 1994. "Everywhere I went as a kid, I was doing the best Shatner you've ever seen." The two performers bumped into each other for the first time that same year (1994) on a crowded elevator at an entertainment industry convention in Miami. "I broke into a huge sweat," reported Alexander. "I don't know if he knows who I am." Shatner has had no reported comment on the brief encounter. Prior to landing his signature comedy role on *Seinfeld*, Alexander worked in television commercials and musical theater. Jason began in feature films in *The Burning* (1982), and enjoyed a large-sized role in the movie adaptation (1997) of Terrance McNally's play *Love, Valour, Compassion!*

Alexander the Great

No, not the same entry as Jason Alexander. Actually a one-hour television pilot, filmed in 1963, starring Shatner as the Macedonian conqueror (356–333 B.C.). The "epic" program sat on a shelf in the ABC-TV network vaults until January 26, 1968, when it earned a one-time-only airing in the wake of *Star Trek*'s success. The all-star (if that is the proper term) cast includes a pre-*Batman* (1966–68) Adam West as Cleander, Alexander's lieutenant, a pre-*Faces* (1968) John Cassavetes as Kronos, and a post-everything Joseph Cotten as the venerable Antigonus. All the actors wear extremely short togas—a shameless attempt to divert viewer attention from the bad acting. Filmed on location in Utah (substituting for Syria), it was the first of many **costume dramas** in which Shatner would boldly partake.

The telefilm met with a negative reception from critics. None was harsher than that notorious voice of reason, TV's own Adam West: "It just didn't work. The audience and Madison Avenue just weren't ready for orgies with Shatner and West lying there on their backs, eating grapes, with belly dancers beside them." Apparently, overseas audiences *were* ready for such an advanced entertainment concept, as *Alexander the Great* later met with success as a European theatrical release.

Shatner, at least, found a silver lining in this misbegotten small-screen project. "The nine months I spent working on *Alexander the Great* came in handy for **Star Trek**," he said. "Captain Kirk is in many ways the quintessential hero, and the Greek heroes in literature have many of the same qualities I wanted to explore."

Alfred Hitchcock Presents

Shatner appeared twice on the legendary director's anthology black-and-white TV series (1955–65), each time in a memorable installment. The first, "The Glass Eye," aired on October 6, 1957, on CBS-TV, and is justly considered a classic of the suspense show. Shatner plays Jim Whitely, the brother of a spinster recently buried. In a cool monotone, he narrates certain unnerving events regarding his late sibling, a dwarf, and a ventriloquist named Max Collodi. The final scene of this under-stated half-hour shocker is a must-see for fans of the genre.

Almost three years later, on April 10, 1960, Shatner made his second *Hitchcock* appearance in "Mother, May I Go Out to Swim?" The thirty-minute format gave him ample opportunity to showcase more of his acting acumen. He plays John Crane, a weak-willed mama's boy whose fiancée urges him to do away with his meddling mother. Again, there is a surprise thrust to the ending in the usual Alfred Hitchcock tradition.

Alien encounter

"I believe in UFOs," Shatner enunciated in 1968. "The time is long past when the Air Force or the scientists or the government can say what people are seeing in the sky are nothing but hot air balloons or the planet Venus. That kind of double-talk won't wash any longer. There has been too much evidence over the years that UFOs exist."

"And," he added ominously in a separate interview, "there's a strong possibility that these UFOs may be scouting our earth."

Shatner provided testimony in support of that hypothesis when, in the summer of 1967, he reportedly had a personal encounter with an unidentified flying object. The setting was the Mojave Desert in California, where the actor frequently went on weekend motorcycle rides with a clique of Harley-hugging bike buddies. With nothing but the sand and the sun to occupy his mind, Shatner often turned his thoughts to the heavens above him. "I'd say to myself, 'Well if I were a little green man in a flying saucer and wanted to get publicity, who would I contact faster than Captain Kirk of the Starship *Enterprise*?'" In subsequent interviews, he coyly denied trying to send telepathic messages to space aliens.

Shatner in macho mode in full motorcycle regalia. [photo courtesy of The Everett Collection]

On one particular afternoon in 1967, however, his random transmission apparently got through. During a cycle ride, Shatner got separated from his pals—who later reported an unidentified stranger had replaced him in their convoy, then mysteriously disappeared. Shatner hit a ditch and wiped out, the bike collapsing on top of him. When he awoke a minute or so later, he experienced a weird apparition—"like when you have a nightmare and you feel something crawling over your body or wrestling with you"—but he was unable to pinpoint its source. He freed himself from his immediate predicament underneath the cycle, but found that he could not start his road hog. He tried to push the motorcycle along but was unsure of the direction. Disoriented and dehydrating in 130-degree heat, Shatner seemed in dire straits. Just then he saw, or thought he saw, another cyclist in the distance beckoning to him. He struggled to lug the heavy Harley toward this vision, eventually coming upon a gas station and the chance to get a drink and recuperate. Finally, he observed an object "glistening in the heavens"—an object he would neither confirm nor deny was a flying saucer. No matter what its origins, however, Shatner remained convinced the unknown force saved his life.

In fact, he was so moved by this experience he planned to make a half-hour film about it. While that project never came to fruition, Shatner used the alien encounter as a point of departure for many future works, including his 1968 album *The Transformed Man* and a series of **one-man shows** in the late 1970s.

SO SAYETH SHATNER

ON THE POSSIBILITY OF EXTRATERRESTRIAL LIFE:

"I can't prove UFOs exist. But anyone who denies they exist is as foolish as the person who denies that God exists."

Alley, Kirstie (B. 1955)

This buxom Scientologist played Lieutenant Saavik, a Vulcan crewmember, in the film *Star Trek II: The Wrath of Khan* (1982). Formerly married to TV's "Hardy Boy" Parker Stevenson from *The Hardy Boys Mysteries* (1977–79), the actress allegedly endured the amorous advances of "hard boy" Shatner during filming in 1982. At one point, during production, playful Shatner stepped on a round styrofoam prop and shouted "I've crushed a ball." Outspoken Alley lamented that it wasn't one of his own! She reportedly found the experience of working with Shatner so distasteful she refused to appear in *Star Trek III: The Search for Spock* (1984) unless she was paid as much as he was. Paramount refused to give in to her salary demands and they replaced her with lesser-known actress Robin Curtis. Alley went on to star on the popular TV sitcom *Cheers* (1987–93) and *Veronica's Closet* (1997–).

"Captain Kirk, this is Xenu. Xenu, Captain Kirk"

Kirstie Alley gave up on science fiction after her appearance in *"Star Trek II"*—except where her religious beliefs are concerned. "I'm a Scientologist all the way!" Alley proclaimed to *USA Today* in 1997. A controversial self-improvement cult started by pulp science fiction writer, novelist, and short story writer L. Ron Hubbard in 1950, Scientology derives many of its adherents—and a lot of its financial backing—from the California celebrity community. Scientologists believe humans are made of clusters of spirits (or "thetans") who were banished to earth

---

Star Trek Sings: Collect All Seven!

Shatner is the only *Star Trek* crew member whose record album *The Transformed Man* places consistently on critics' lists of the Fifty Worst Rock 'n' Roll Albums of All Time. But that's only because so few people have heard the abominable LPs released by **Leonard Nimoy**, **Nichelle Nichols**, and **Grace Lee Whitney**. Even Brent Spiner of *Star Trek: Generations* (and TV's *Star Trek: The Next Generation*) has chimed in with an album of pop standards. Behold the roundup of misguided solo projects:

Nichelle Nichols

• *Uhura Sings* (1986)
Have you heard "Ode to the Space Shuttle"? Seen the video? Don't worry, you have plenty of company.

Leonard Nimoy

• *Leonard Nimoy Presents Mr. Spock's Music from Outer Space* (1968)
Gene Roddenberry tried to stop Nimoy from using the Spock name on this turkey. Nimoy should have considered removing his own moniker.

• *Two Sides of Leonard Nimoy* (1969)
An album of original tone poems set to music. If it weren't so consistently boring, it might actually be worse than *The Transformed Man*.

some seventy-five million years ago by a cruel galactic ruler named Xenu. As yet there are no plans for a *Wrath of Xenu* motion picture featuring the *Star Trek* crew.

Andersonville Trial, The   RATING: ∪ ∪ ∪

The 1970 television film stars Shatner, Martin Sheen, and Richard Basehart. Directed by legendary actor George C. Scott, who starred in the 1959 Broadway adaptation, *The Andersonville Trial* dramatizes MacKinlay Kan-

- *The Way I Feel* (1969)
  This time, Nimoy breaks up the poetic tedium with cover versions of famous tunes. "If I Had a Hammer" is a real lowlight.

- *The New World of Leonard Nimoy* (1970)
  Yet another album of pop classics disemboweled by the master. This one features a positively constipated rendition of "Proud Mary."

- *Outer Space, Inner Mind* (1976)
  God help us, it's a double album. Need I say more?

Brent Spiner

- *Ol' Yellow Eyes Is Back* (1991)
  Spiner can actually carry a tune (he starred in the 1997 Broadway revival of *1776*). But did he have to invite his *Next Generation* costars to warble backing vocals on "It's a Sin to Tell a Lie"?

Grace Lee Whitney

- *Disco Trekkin'* (1976)
  Actually a 45 r.p.m. (backed with "Star Child"), this one just *feels* like an LP.

tor's Pulitzer Prize-winning book (1955) about a notorious Civil War prison camp in Georgia where barbaric conditions resulted in the deaths of nearly 15,000 Union soldiers. As Colonel Chipman, the smarmy prosecutor at a Nuremberg-like war crimes trial, Shatner gives one of his most powerful TV performances. Broadcast by PBS on May 17, 1970, *The Andersonville Trial* earned rave reviews and won Emmys for Outstanding Single Program and Best Adapted Teleplay. Shatner met his future wife, **Marcy Lafferty**, on the set of this production.

Shatner gives one of the most powerful performances of his career as a passionate prosecutor in The Andersonville Trial *(1970). [photo courtesy of Photofest]*

Archery

This outdoor sport is one of Shatner's longtime hobbies. For an early 1970s segment of the ABC-TV outdoor sports series *The American Sportsman*, Shatner hunted bear armed only with his bow and arrow. He eventually killed a nine-foot-tall Kodiak bear and kept the skin for use as a rug in his Los Angeles home. In a separate expedition, Shatner led a large wild boar hunt on Southern California's Catalina Island and, again relying only on his bow and arrow, bagged both a huge boar *and* a wild goat.

As with horsemanship, flying, and numerous other activities (see **sexuality**), Shatner finds in archery a profound sexual metaphor. "What could be more sexual than archery as a phallic symbol?" he has said. "I mean, it's like an act of sex." Perhaps this explains why, on the ***Star Trek* blooper reel** (1969), Shatner can be seen clowning around with an arrow sticking out of his crotch.

"Looking back on the things I've done, I must be a little crazy. But I'm constantly testing myself, both in athletics and acting. I've always believed that if you don't define your limits by trying everything, you'll never know your capabilities."

—SHATNER, on his passion for adventure

Shatner ponders the plight of the American eagle—and of his own endangered career—as the host of ABC's The American Sportsman. *[photo courtesy of Photofest]*

Ardrey, Robert (1908–1980)

This American anthropologist and writer had a profound effect upon Shatner. Ardrey's two most important books, *African Genesis* (1965), and *The Territorial Imperative* (1966), greatly influenced the actor's thinking about society and the male ethos. The author believed man is an innately aggressive creature, driven by a desire to protect his property and hold sway over others. "His theories are illuminating, and—dazzling to me," Shatner has said.

Captain Kirk in civilian clothes. [photo courtesy of Photofest]

Originally a playwright, Ardrey became fascinated in the late 1950s with the theories of Raymond Dart (1893–1988), which held that man's earliest ancestor was both aggressive and violent. Ardrey soon developed his own thesis based on this idea. "Man is a predator whose natural instinct is to kill with a weapon," Ardrey wrote in *African Genesis*. "The sudden addition of the enlarged brain to the equipment of an armed already-successful predatory animal created not only the human being but also the human predicament." Shatner dabbled in this kind of theorizing when he offered biographers his dream for the achievement of **world peace**, a vision grounded in the judicious use of that self-same enlarged cerebellum.

Ardrey's theories have been used by fundamentalist Christians and other traditionalist thinkers as an apologia for male dominion over society. "The time will come when the male will lose all interest in sex; but he will still fight for his status," Ardrey wrote. This male instinct for dominion reveals itself in animals in three ways: first, in territoriality, i.e., a property instinct and drive; second, in status, a drive to establish dominion in terms of rank in a rigidly hierarchical order; and third, in survival, using order as a means of survival. In the male, Ardrey claims, dominion leads to increased sexual potency and longevity. Shatner has applied these ideas to the ongoing war over screen parts in Hollywood, which may explain his obsession with **line counting** and his other territorial drives. "I loved Ardrey's stuff about males stamping out a little territory there, fighting other males off, and the females coming because the males have a little area," Shatner once said.

SO SAYETH SHATNER

ON MANKIND'S PRIMAL NATURE:

"We wear Halston clothes, but we're still dressed in sheepskin rags—and still—wolves."

Ashes of Eden

This 1995 *Star Trek* novel was penned by Shatner, with help from veteran sci-fi authors Judith and Garfield Reeves-Stevens. Not surprisingly, Captain Kirk is the focal point of the narrative, which finds the aging *Enterprise* commander chasing the secret of eternal youth on a mysterious planet. "I'd had this idea for a number of years," Shatner confided to *Entertainment Weekly* in 1995, "a scenario to do with Kirk and age and a young lady." In fact, he originally pitched the idea to Paramount Pictures back in 1992 as a scenario for the pending *Star Trek VII*, but was rebuffed by studio executives. Three years later, he jumped at the chance to become the first original TV crew cast member to author a *Star Trek* novel. Writing for *Booklist*, critic Karen Simonetti called *Ashes of Eden* "a satisfying, commercial-free, escapist episode to the apparently endless *Star Trek* series." The same crew of writers teamed up on 1997's *Avenger*.

Asheton, Ron (B. 1948)

Born in Washington, DC, this guitarist for punk rocker Iggy Pop's band claimed that, in the summer of 1975, Shatner made a pass at him in a Los Angeles bar. According to Asheton's allegations, a seemingly inebriated

Shatner supposedly approached him in the Hyatt House pub, where the axe-man had gone to listen to some jazz. "He wanted me to sit down, and then he got kind of grabby," Asheton claims. Horrified at the prospect that Captain Kirk might be anything less than one hundred percent straight, Asheton promptly fled the scene. "Probably if I'd been drinking I would have sat down just for the weirdness of seeing what would happen," the reluctant boy toy concluded. Asheton's aggressive musical chops can be heard on such seminal albums as The Stooges' *Fun City* (1970) and *Raw Power* (1973).

Asimov, Isaac (1920–1992)

The legendary science fiction author of such sci-fi classics as *Foundation* (1942) and *I, Robot* (1950), was consulted by **Gene Roddenberry**, creator of TV's **Star Trek** (1966-69), about resolving the growing tension between Shatner and **Leonard Nimoy** on the set. The two biggest stars of this outer space series were constantly competing over lines and screen time. Their tinkering with scripts resulted in awkward on-camera exchanges in which Kirk often completed Spock's sentences for him, and vice versa. Asimov advised Roddenberry to accentuate the closeness of the Kirk/Spock relationship—to make the two seem inseparable and, hence, make the byplay believable. The idea reached fruition in the **Star Trek** episode "Obsession" (December 15, 1967) in which Spock saves Kirk's life while he is in the grip of monomania surrounding the pursuit of a malevolent gaseous cloud. While Asimov never wrote a **Star Trek** teleplay, he is widely credited with saving the television show from ruination by its egocentric costars.

Ass-kicking

Shatner received his first proper butt-whupping while a child at summer camp on a farm in French-speaking Canada. "I got my ass, literally, kicked—*hard*—for pulling up carrots out of a farmer's field," he told biographers in 1979. "I couldn't make it over the fence like the other kids did and dive over the top. The farmer caught *me* with a good kick. That was his way of teaching children not to steal." The pain was severe and it lingered, although Shatner ranked its intensity "somewhat short of getting kicked in the balls"—an experience for which he has yet to relate a comparable anecdote.

> *"Very few people have actually gotten their ass kicked with a hard,*
> *hobnailed boot by a strong, angry man. That hurts."*
>
> —SHATNER, on his first ass-kicking

Atomic Submarines

Shatner says he learned a lot about the "loneliness of command" through discussions with the captains of atomic submarines. "[I] talked to those guys about it, the skippers.... I said, what about... when you're alone? I mean, you can only be so familiar with your executive officers. There comes a point when you come back to this little cubicle—you're really *alone*, man." Shatner claims he used his experience of loneliness in his portrayal of Captain Kirk, the archetypal commander married to his ship, the *Enterprise*.

Auto Racing

Shatner took up auto racing for a brief time in the late 1970s. Reportedly, he was asked to try his hand at driving a Formula One car after a friend saw him racing go-carts on a TV special. Never one to back down from any challenge, Shatner took classes to learn race driving and actually competed in a grand prix race in Long Beach, California. It wasn't until he was on the course going 110 miles per hour that Shatner came to a crucial realization. "You know, I could get hurt. Killed." That ended his brief love affair with the track pits forever.

Avenger

This 1997 **Star Trek** novel was written by Shatner, with help from **Ashes of Eden** co-authors Judith and Garfield Reeves-Stevens. In this space epic, Kirk and Spock join forces to save the universe from a deadly virus that has pushed the Federation to the brink of apocalypse. The improbable plot also features Captain Jean-Luc Picard of TV's syndicated *Star Trek: The Next Generation* (1987–94).

Babysitter, The   RATING: U U

This 1980 ABC-TV movie was directed by Peter Medok and stars Shatner
and Patty Duke Astin as parents tormented by a psychotic babysitter
(Stephanie Zimbalist). Quinn Cummings, the delightful gamin nominated for an Oscar for *The Goodbye Girl* (1977), graduates to obscurity
here as Shatner's on-camera daughter. Venerable John Houseman makes
a special guest appearance as the ancient family physician.

Bacchus

At the 1987 Mardi Gras Parade in New Orleans, Louisiana, Shatner
assumed the role of King Bacchus, the mythical Roman god of wine. The
"Bacchus krewe" is one of the most spirited parade organizations in the
Mardi Gras. Spectacular floats, a massive supper dance with Las Vegas-

*Shatner lets the good times roll away as "King Bacchus," the ceremonial monarch of
the Mardi Gras, in 1987. [photo courtesy of AP Worldwide Photos]*

type entertainment, and the choice of a national celebrity as its monarch are a few of the signatures of the Bacchus organization. Other celebrities who played the giddy god of the grape through the years include Bob Hope, Jackie Gleason, Dom DeLuise, Charlton Heston, and Kirk Douglas.

> *"Bacchus is anything you want him to be. I want him to be wild and woolly and to have a great time."*
>
> —SHATNER, on his role as the god of wine
> at the 1987 Mardi Gras Parade

Bacon, Kevin (B. 1958)

The prodigious cinematic output of this hard-working actor and musician has inspired the popular parlor game *Six Degrees of Kevin Bacon*. The game, usually played by World Wide Web surfers, links other celebrities, by either direct or tortuous means, to the ubiquitous Bacon. According to the "Oracle of Bacon" at the University of Virginia (http://www.cs.virginia.edu/~bct7m/bacon.html), one of the leading Internet authorities on such matters, Shatner has a "Bacon number" of two, calculated as follows: Shatner was in **Star Trek VI: The Undiscovered Country** (1991) with Christian Slater, and Slater was in *Murder in the First* (1995) with Kevin Bacon. And so it goes....

Barbary Coast, The

This short-lived TV western series (1975–76) starred Shatner as Jeff Cable, a master of disguises. Set in the lawless Barbary Coast district of San Francisco in the 1870s, the hour-long ABC-TV network program followed two special agents who spent their time collecting information on local criminals. Dennis Cole (pilot film) and then Doug McClure played Cable's partner, Cash Conover.

Loosely derived from the very popular *Wild Wild West* (1965–70), which was itself a kind of sagebrush **Star Trek**, *The Barbary Coast* debuted with a two-hour pilot on May 4, 1975. Bill Bixby (later TV's *Incredible Hulk*) directed, with a script from **Twilight Zone** veteran Douglas Heyes. In this showcase, Shatner donned a variety of disguises, including a pirate, a Ku Klux Klansman, and a sightless vagrant. The pilot did well enough to warrant a network series commitment. However, critics decried the lack of chemistry between the two stars (despite the switch to McClure) and the show's obvious and torturous plots.

Ideally, ABC-TV would have given the struggling *The Barbary Coast* the time to grow and find its audience, but instead, did all it could to undermine the already floundering show. Programming it in a family hour time slot (opposite CBS's popular sitcoms *Rhoda* and *Phyllis* and NBC's adventure show *The Invisible Man*), the network then insisted that violence and conflict on camera be kept to a very discrete minimum. For a show that was

Playing a master of disguises, Shatner got to wear many different hats on the ABC series The Barbary Coast *(1975). [photo courtesy of Photofest]*

supposed to be about two-fisted western action, this executive decision was a death sentence.

"We can't have any man-to-man combat, even for the fun of it," Shatner wailed."We're throwing mud pies at each other in an effort to get in some action.... However, mud in the face works only for a while. We need more tension in the stories and that comes from conflict between stalwart people."

Unfortunately, ABC never heeded Shatner's urgings. It canceled *The Barbary Coast* as of January 9, 1976, after only thirteen episodes. All that remained to remind Shatner there had even been a series were his scratches and bruises, the painful consequences of doing all his own stunts.

"[It] took me months to recover from *Barbary Coast*," Shatner later recalled. "I mean physically, literally physically. I had to stop working. I'd get out of bed tired. I'd have nine hours sleep and I'd get up—I couldn't *move*. Took me three months."

Six Degrees of *Star Trek*

Michael Ansara (Diamond Jack Bassiter in the pilot film of *The Barbary Coast*) played Kang the Klingon in the third-season **Star Trek** episode "Day of the Dove" (November 1, 1968).

Bastard, The   RATING: UUl

This bizarrely cast two-part TV movie (1978) is based on the John Jakes potboiler (1972) about life during the American Revolution. Always dreamed of seeing Tom Bosley play Benjamin Franklin? You can find it here. How about Shatner as Paul Revere? Look no further! Made under the auspices of Operation Prime Time (like **Testimony of Two Men**), a joint endeavor by independent TV stations to create highfalutin' dramatic programs, *The Bastard* emphasizes soap opera shenanigans over history in its marathon four-hour running time. Andrew Stevens struts as the eponymous bastard, Phillipe Charboneau, a hunky French nobleman who assumes a new identity as Philip Kent and meets all the leading figures in colonial America. William Daniels, who previously capered as John Adams in the Broadway musical *1776* (1969), plays his brother Samuel here. Peter Bonerz, the wacky dentist from TV's *The Bob Newhart Show* (1972–78), spouts a homily in *The Bastard* on the benefits of democracy. "Haven't we seen all this before?" asked a cynical *Variety*. Yes, the year before in **Testimony of Two Men**. Shatner passed on the popular telefilm sequels, *The Rebels* (1979) and *The Seekers* (1979), also based on Jakes' novels of the same names.

Six Degrees of *Star Trek*

Kim Cattrall (Anne Ware of *The Bastard*) went on to play Valeris, the treacherous Vulcan, in **Star Trek VI: The Undiscovered Country** (1991). John DeLancie (Lieutenant Stark) would bedevil the *Enterprise* crew as the mischievous Q Entity on *Star Trek: The Next Generation* (1987–94) and *Star Trek: Voyager* (1995–).

Beck (B. 1970)

This doe-eyed, elfin alternative rocker (born Beck Campbell) parodied Shatner's 1978 performance of **"Rocket Man"** in a 1996 music video. In the video for the song "Where It's At," from Beck's critically acclaimed album *Odelay* (1996), the singer mimics the "three Shatner" motif from the actor's misbegotten performance at the 1978 Science Fiction Film Awards. Never pausing to explain this obscure visual cue, Beck leaves it to the initiated to recognize the insider's reference.

Believe

This historical novel was written by Shatner and *Voice of the Planet* author Michael Tobias, and published in 1992. The speculative tale concerns an imagined battle of wits between world-renowned American magician Harry Houdini (1874–1926) and British physician, novelist, and detective-story writer Sir Arthur Conan Doyle (1859–1930). (Doyle was most famous for his creation of the intrepid crime-solver, Sherlock Holmes.) Ambitious Shatner hoped to produce a stage version of *Believe* with himself as Houdini and **Leonard Nimoy** as Doyle, but he could not conjure up enough money to cover the cost of production. (It should be noted that, in September of 1994, a playhouse owner in Allentown, Pennsylvania, attempted to sue Shatner because he reportedly failed to appear, as he had allegedly agreed to do, in a play based upon this book.)

Belle Reve

This sprawling 360-acre farm is found in the lush bluegrass country near Versailles, Kentucky, where Shatner raises his **horses**. In French, the name of the spread means beautiful dream. Beginning in the early 1980s, Shatner started breeding American Saddlebreds, and, by the close of this century, now owns over one hundred of the expensive high-stepping horses. "You might say I put myself pretty deep into the business," he said of his passion for breeding. "When I'm not acting or directing, I'm at the farm."

Bicycle Story

See **Practical Jokes**.

Big Bad Mama

RATING: U U

This trashy 1974 feature film stars Shatner and shapely Angie Dickinson. She is the machine-gun-toting, bank-robbing mom in Depression-era Texas. Shatner plays William J. Baxter, an effete Southern drifter who takes up with Mama and her gang. Tom Skerritt, who went on to play Shatner's brother in *The Devil's Rain* (1975), is his rival for Angie's affections. Although given star billing, Shatner really has little to do in the eighty-three minutes of low-voltage shenanigans. This *Bonnie and Clyde* (1967) knock-off is notable only for Shatner's three **nude scenes** with Dickinson, stills of which were subsequently published in men's magazines. Produced by B-movie impresario Roger Corman, the film also features Joan Prather, Dick Miller, and Royal Dano. The British *Monthly Film Bulletin* (February, 1975) judged that, "All five principals appear nude in bed scenes, all looking excruciatingly embarrassed." The Shatnerless and shameless sequel *Big Bad Mama II* appeared in 1987.

Shatner appears to be eating his cigarette in this publicity still for Big Bad Mama *(1974). [photo courtesy of Photofest]*

Bill and Ted's Bogus Journey   RATING: U ℄

The 1992 comedy, a sequel to the 1989 movie hit *Bill and Ted's Excellent Adventure*, features Shatner in a cameo as Captain **James T. Kirk**. The lowbrow romp stars Alex Winter and Keanu Reeves as the eponymous nitwit dudes, who travel back and forth in time and meet up with a gaggle of strange characters—including the commander of the *Enterprise*. The general critical consensus: not as good as the first movie.

Blooper Reel

This notorious reel of foul-ups, bleeps, and blunders was caught by cameras on the **Star Trek** TV series set during its filming in the late 1960s. The first blooper reel began circulating in 1969. Shatner has admitted that seeing the blooper reel for the first time alerted him to the growing popularity of **Star Trek** after its cancellation in 1969. Among the highlights for Shatner were the numerous scenes in which he would keep

Hold on to Your Shatner Collectibles!

Item	Vintage	Approximate Value
25th Anniversary Kirk coin	1991	$200–225
Captain Kirk plastic bank	1975	$100–125
Captain Kirk novelty stamp	1979	$70–80
William Shatner—Live! LP	1978	$55–75
Captain Kirk collectible plate	1985	$55–60
Mego Captain Kirk action figure	1975	$55–60
Captain Kirk Dr. Pepper drinking glass	1976	$50–55
Captain Kirk Halloween costume	1967	$40–55
Captain Kirk jump suit	1975	$25–30
Captain Kirk vinyl model kit	1994	$20–25
Captain Kirk pewter figurine	1991	$18–20
Captain Kirk punch-out birthday card	1976	$5–7

kissing a guest star long after the cameras had stopped rolling. He also initiated a number of famous bloopers. In one instance, Spock shoots an arrow and the next scene calls for Kirk to be carried into a cave. Unaware that the cameras are rolling, playful Shatner walks through the sequence with the offending arrow sticking out of his crotch.

Broken Angel
RATING:

This 1988 ABC-TV movie, directed by Richard T. Heffron, starred Shatner and Susan Blakely as the shocked parents of a teenage gang leader. The alarmist melodrama features pretty Erika Eleniak as the couple's wayward daughter, who entices other affluent suburban kids into a hedonist cult called "Live for Now." Enter Shatner as the obsessed dad, who descends into a seamy underworld of gangbangers and runaways to haul his little princess back from the abyss. "Shatner struggles," observed the *Variety* critic kindly, going on to lament the film's "cardboard characters cut out to fit a thesis." There's a thesis here?

Brothers Karamazov, The
RATING: ♆ ♆ ♆

This 1958 MGM prestige movie is based on the classic Fyodor Dostoyevsky novel (1880), and features Shatner in support of Yul Brynner, Oscar-nominated Lee J. Cobb, and Claire Bloom. Producer Pandro S. Berman cast Shatner in the role of Alexei, the monastic youngest of the three Karamazov siblings. At a meeting to discuss the part, Berman reportedly took one look at the handsome young actor and proclaimed "Yes, he's the one." Shatner's performance earned strong notices in the trade press. "William Shatner has the difficult task of portraying youthful male goodness," *Variety* reported in its review, "and he does it with such gentle candor it is effective." Less effective was the ludicrous wig Shatner wore in this 147-minute Russian-set movie. The helmet-like "rug" looks to have been modeled on a Hummel figurine.

Burmese sailor

No stranger to portraying **racial stereotypes**, Shatner played a Burmese sailor on an episode of the TV drama *Naked City* (1958–63). This hour-long episode, "Without Stick or Sword," aired on March 28, 1962, on the ABC network. As Maung Tun, a devout Buddhist seaman lately returned to shore, Asian Shatner stabs several people to death in revenge for the killing of his brothers. However, he is wracked by guilt and turns himself in during the funeral of one of his victims.

"Wig? What wig?" Shatner shows off a new lid for The Brothers Karamazov *(1958). [photo courtesy of Photofest]*

To research his character, Shatner visited the Burmese consulate and talked at length with natives of the southeast Asian nation (now known as Myanmar). However, his principal contribution to the role—aside from wearing racially offensive eye makeup—was an overly exaggerated Charlie Chan accent. In addition, in his *Native City* gig he sports a black wig very much like the one he would later wear as Paul Revere in **The Bastard** (1978). In 1968, Shatner labeled the Burmese sailor the one part he played "that was completely and utterly foreign to me."

Butt Tightening

Demanded by Shatner, an airbrush technique helped make his rump look narrower in **Star Trek VI: The Undiscovered Country** (1991). Shatner was especially distressed by the width of his caboose during a screen scene in which he walks across the *Enterprise* bridge in full view of the widescreen camera.

Camp

The man whose career offers such camp value learned to value camps from an early age. Summer camp was a childhood staple for Shatner while growing up in Canada. However, Shatner's summer camp was no *Meatballs*-style idyll (1979). He spent his months off from school on working farms in French-speaking Quebec. These children's activities included tending to the animals and watching the farmer slaughter his pigs. Also, it was here that Shatner received his first **ass-kicking**, an experience he would not soon forget.

Perhaps his most important experience at camp came in 1937, at the age of six. The setting was another farm, this one belonging to Shatner's aunt, in the Laurentian Mountains about two hours north of Montreal. He starred in *Winterset*, a camp production about a persecuted Jewish family (not the better-known 1935 Maxwell Anderson play of the same name). In a poignant moment, Shatner, playing a young boy, bids goodbye to his beloved dog. Desiring a canine of his own in real life, but forbidden by his parents to own one, Shatner was able to conjure up actual tears that left the audience bawling along with him. "I looked out, and they were weeping. I thought, something I did made them weep. And I got a little crazy. Wow, I did that!" It was a big turning point in the impressionable boy's life.

Shatner excelled in other camp activities as well. He was an accomplished swimmer and won many boxing matches with other boys. As a teenager, Shatner became a counselor at the same camp. Over campfires, he regaled his companions with dazzling improvisational performances, including his personal specialty—the mad scientist. When he was nineteen, Shatner and eight other counselors took a canoe trip from Montreal to New York. Their two-week paddle over Lake Champlain and down the Hudson River was covered by a local TV station in New York.

> *"We'd milk cows—the feeling of warm milk being squirted into my face postdated my mother's."*
> —SHATNER, on his experience in summer camp

Campus, Jake

Original name for **Jake Cardigan**, protagonist of Shatner's *Tek* book series.

Canada

While Shatner has never shied away from his Canadian heritage, many people don't know he hails from the Great White North. Part of the reason is his complete lack of a Canadian accent, something he worked hard to eradicate after making the decision to pursue a career in American television. Shatner joins an impressive list (see below) of Canadians who have made it in the world of the performing arts in the United States, Canada, and other countries. Interestingly, many of these individuals are comedy performers, an indication, maybe, that Shatner missed his true calling. Still, he has carved out a niche for himself as one of Canada's most accomplished dramatic actors—and he believes he knows why. "I think we Canadians do well in acting because we have the technique of the English and the virility of the Americans," Shatner once remarked to an interviewer. "We're in an advantageous position by being in the middle of the two."

Coincidence or Conspiracy?:
A List of Prominent Canadians in Show Business

Dan Aykroyd	Rick Moranis
Raymond Burr	Mike Myers
Neve Campbell	Leslie Nielsen
John Candy	Mary Pickford
Jim Carrey	Walter Pidgeon
Yvonne De Carlo	Christopher Plummer
Dave Foley	Jason Priestley
Glenn Ford	Keanu Reeves
Michael J. Fox	Norma Shearer
Lorne Greene	Donald Sutherland
Arthur Hill	Kiefer Sutherland
Ruby Keeler	Alex Trebek
Raymond Massey	Fay Wray

Canadian National Repertory Theatre

This touring theatre company, based in Ottawa, is where Shatner appeared from 1952 to 1954. Relying on a professional reference from the

Mountain Playhouse, Shatner secured a job as the assistant manager for $31 a week. However, he quickly moved out from behind the scenes and onto the stage, often playing children and teenagers. During the summer months, Shatner returned to the **Mountain Playhouse** in Montreal to appear in stock productions.

Cardigan, Jake

This character is the hero of Shatner's popular *Tek* book series, set in the twenty-first century. Originally called **Jake Campus**, Cardigan is a hard-boiled ex-cop turned private eye who is falsely convicted of trafficking the mind-altering brain stimulant called **Tek**. He spends four years in suspended animation for this crime, then emerges to find his private life turned upside down and the world in the grip of the drug-dealing Teklords. Cardigan signs on with the mysterious philanthropist Walter Bascom, in a bid to clear his own name and rid the planet of **Tek**.

Cardigan is played in the **TekWar** cable television series (1994–95) by hunk Greg Evigan of *My Two Dads* (1987–90). As in the books he is in his mid-fifties and bears more than a passing resemblance to several of Shatner's own on screen creations. "In the beginning I planned *TekWar* as a screenplay for myself to star in," the actor/author told *Entertainment Weekly* in 1993. "I had this idea of putting *T. J. Hooker* into a futuristic milieu." Shatner later developed the concept during production holdups on **Star Trek V** (1989) caused by a writers' strike. Cardigan's many travails in the **Tek** cycle include wrestling robot bulls, deactivating android doubles, and staving off homicidal hockey players. His loyal partner through it all is Sid Gomez.

Cat on a Hot Tin Roof

Shatner was in the running to play Brick Pollitt in the 1958 MGM film version of Tennessee Williams' 1955 hit Broadway play, which won the Pulitzer Prize that year. Newspaper reports even had Shatner the top choice for the lead opposite Elizabeth Taylor. The prime role, however, went to Paul Newman, marking the onset of a trend in which Shatner lost choice movie parts to more bankable film actors. "My dream of success was hollow," Shatner confided to *TV Guide* in 1968. "I started losing parts—something that had never happened to me before." Shatner's failure to establish a foothold as a big-screen actor eventually led him to accept the part of Captain Kirk on TV's **Star Trek** in the mid 1960s.

Columbo: Butterfly in Shades of Grey   RATING: U U

This two-hour TV movie (1995) stars Peter Falk as the rumpled, intrusive Lieutenant Columbo. Shatner is the villain, Fielding Chase, a very pompous radio talk show host clearly based on conservative firebrand Rush Limbaugh. Shatner gets to wear a comical wig (some would say a wig even more laugh-provoking than the one he reputedly normally wears) and a false mustache that changes position from scene to scene. Shatner's dirty deeds on camera include murdering one of his assistants and framing the deceased's gay lover for the homicide. Shatner previously tangled with the veteran Los Angeles police detective in the 1976 *Columbo* series episode "Fade in to Murder."

A forlorn Shatner fights a losing battle with Peter Falk and his own false moustache in the TV movie Columbo: Butterfly in Shades of Gray *(1994). [photo courtesy of Photofest]*

C.O.R.E. Digital Pictures

This Toronto-based computer animation firm boasts Shatner as chief executive officer. Started in September of 1994, the company has provided special effects for both theatrical films and television, including the Canadian-made *Johnny Mnemonic* (1995) with Keanu Reeves. The organization was founded by a group of animators hired to work on effects for the mid-1990s **TekWar** cable TV movies. Shatner is not involved in the day-to-day operations of the firm, but he sits on its board of directors, offers advice, and serves as a marketing resource in dealing with Hollywood.

Costume Drama

Over the decades, Shatner has excelled at playing heavily-costumed characters in both period movies and television specials. Some of the actor's memorable portrayals in this vein include Paul Revere in *The Bastard* (TV, 1978); a nineteenth-century Pennsylvanian in *Testimony of Two Men* (TV, 1977); a colonial Satanist in *The Devil's Rain* (1975); an ex-Army captain on TV's *How the West Was Won* (1977); and Jo March's husband in a 1978 television adaptation of Louisa May Alcott's classic *Little Women*.

Shatner models the sport coat that earned him People *magazine recognition as one of the worst dressed people of 1993. [photo courtesy of Photofest]*

One of Shatner's most instructive costume roles, however, was **Alexander the Great**, which he essayed for a failed ABC network pilot in 1963.

"One day we were on location in the wilds of Utah where the geological formations, mesas, and fauna and flora were remarkably similar to Syria where Alexander conducted his military campaign. The director and I were alone, off in the distance from the company. We discussed a great dilemma we had, namely, what to do about the creaking of the leather uniforms." After all, Shatner ruminated, wouldn't the noisy duds give the soldiers away as they crept forward to surprise the enemy?

"There I was, dressed in the costume of ancient Greece with my horse beside me and the panoramic view around me. I was discussing a problem that Alexander must have discussed with his own soldiers. Suddenly, in a flash, I came to the awareness of how bound we are to history and how universal our problems are.

"That insight was also the solution to the problem of the creaking uniforms. I realized that Alexander could do nothing about it, so why should we! Anything we feel, they felt. This fact makes me understand men anywhere, any time."

> *"It was like* Combat *in drag."*
> —SHATNER, describing the experience
> of filming *Alexander the Great*

Crash of Flight 401, The   RATING: U ℂ

This made-for-television airline disaster movie, directed by Barry Shear, starred Shatner, Adrienne Barbeau, Sharon Gless, and jazz bandleader Artie Shaw. Released to video as *Crash*, the 1978 quickie film is based on the real-life crash of a jet plane into the Florida Everglades in December, 1972. Shatner played Carl Tobias (the narrator), an FAA investigator who has been sent to study the disaster which killed 103 of its 171 passengers. This was the second of two 1978 TV movies based on the same incident. Ernest Borgnine starred in the other, *The Ghost of Flight 401*. Just to confuse things further, Shatner and Borgnine had previously locked horns in the 1975 devil cult theatrical feature **The Devil's Rain.**

"Crash" of the Titans:

OK, it's four in the morning and you can't sleep. You crack open the *TV Guide* and find out that *The Ghost of Flight 401* and *The Crash of Flight 401* are playing on different channels. Which one would you watch? Think carefully, they each have an all-star cast. Here are your starting lineups:

CRASH	GHOST
William Shatner (**"Toughy"**)	Ernest Borgnine ("Marty")
Adrienne Barbeau ("Maude")	Kim Basinger ("Mrs. Alec Baldwin")
Ron Glass ("Barney Miller")	Howard Hesseman ("Dr. Johnny Fever")
Sharon Gless ("Cagney & Lacey")	Russell Johnson ("Professor Roy Hinkley")
Artie Shaw (famous bandleader)	Meeno Peluce (brother of Soleil Moon-Frye)

Cross Country Journey

Together with a friend from **McGill University**, Shatner hitchhiked across the United States and Canada in 1951 when he was twenty years old. The pair left Toronto with only $200 between them and a sign that read "Two McGill Students Seeing America." Hitchhiking the entire way, they proceeded down the eastern seaboard to Washington, DC. From there, it was due west to Los Angeles, north to Vancouver, and back east to Chicago. The trip ended in Canada in Shatner's native Montreal.

Dead Man's Island   RATING: U L

This 1996 CBS-TV movie stars Shatner, Christopher Atkins, and a diverse trio of blondes: Barbara Eden, Morgan Fairchild, and former porn queen Traci Lords. Shatner wanders listlessly through the proceedings as Chase Prescott, a wealthy businessman whose journey to a remote Pacific island retreat helps him discover which one of nine guests staying in his mansion is trying to kill him.

Deathdream   RATING: U U L

This 1972 Canadian-made horror flick features Shatner in a small role. Also known as *Dead of Night*, the film reworks the W. W. Jacobs' classic horror story "The Monkey's Paw" (1902) in modern dress. Richard Backus plays a dead soldier who returns from Vietnam after his mother wishes him alive again. Not surprisingly, he begins killing everyone in sight. Shatner appears briefly as a family friend. The director, Bob Clark, went on to create the inexplicably popular *Porky's* (horny teenagers) film series in the 1980s.

Defenders, The

This legal drama TV series concerns a father/son team of attorneys. Ralph Bellamy and Shatner played the roles in a 1957 CBS-TV *Studio One* production of the story (then titled "The Defender"). However, when the concept was adapted as an hour-long series by CBS in 1961, E. G. Marshall and Robert Reed were picked for the new coleads. The revamped *The Defenders* ran on the network until 1965, at which time a buoyant Shatner had already moved into his own legal drama, playing feisty attorney David Koster on the short-lived CBS show *For the People* (January 31–May 9, 1965).

Delta Search

This is the first of Shatner's *Quest for Tomorrow* novels, published in 1997. *Delta Search* begins the odyssey of Jim Endicott, a teenager who carries in his DNA the secret to transforming the human race into a huge organic supercomputer. This unique attribute naturally makes him the target of an array of nefarious forces, including his spymaster father. Shatner claims the idea for the book, on which he was "assisted" by writer Bill Quick, was grounded in his own adolescent fantasies. "But I didn't kill my father," he affirmed to reporters after the book's release. "I was going for this Oedipal thing."

Shatner's target audience with *Delta Search* was teenagers. However, he received a harsh reception from some young readers during a conference call to promote the novel. "I found it very insulting to my level of intellect," complained a seventeen-year-old intern from the *Richmond Times-Dispatch*. A reporter for the *Allentown* (Pennsylvania) *Morning Call* slammed the work as too male-oriented. "Well, this is the story of a boy, which I'm much more comfortable writing because of my testosterone," Shatner responded.

A weird amalgam of sci-fi, espionage, and social commentary, *Delta Search* was the opening salvo in Shatner's 1997 campaign to stimulate interest in literature and encourage **literacy** among teens. It was followed with almost indecent haste by a sequel, ***In Alien Hands***.

Dentistry

Rumors have abounded for years that multi-talented Shatner has a background in dentistry. The probable source of the confusion is *New York* magazine movie critic David Denby, who inexplicably began referring to Shatner as a dentist in his movie reviews. For example, in his critique of ***Star Trek V: The Final Frontier*** (1989), Denby wrote: "William Shatner, that muscular dentist who unaccountably wandered into acting, has now wandered into directing." Shatner has never studied dentistry—honest! He has a business degree from **McGill University** in Montreal, Canada.

Devil's Rain, The   RATING: ∪ ∪ ∪

This grisly 1975 horror movie is directed by Robert Fuest and features Shatner, Eddie Albert, and Tom Skerritt. Shatner plays Martin Fife, a pony-tailed Puritan Satanist who is burned at the stake in the seventeenth century. Then, as Mark Preston, Fife's modern-day descendant, he is set upon by a cadre of devil worshippers who include a very young

Shatner as an eyeless, soulless zombie under the Satanic dominion of Ernest Borgnine in the 1975 cheapie The Devil's Rain. *[photo courtesy of Photofest]*

John Travolta. Ernest Borgnine is the vindictive Corbis, the leader of the ritualistic cult, who crucifies Shatner, removes his eyes, and makes him atone mightily for betraying the group in his past life. Keenan Wynn and Ida Lupino are among the other victims. "Satanic effects are piled on at every possible juncture," opined *Variety*, "with gore virtually used to plaster over every gaping loophole." Providing technical advice on the Satanic effects was Anton Lavey, a real-life devil worshiper. This celluloid burnt offering was shot on location in Mexico.

> *"Blasphemer! Blasphemer!"*
> —single line uttered by JOHN TRAVOLTA as Danny
> the Satan Worshiper in *The Devil's Rain*

Directing

"Directing has been a lifelong dream," Shatner once admitted. "My business is to entertain people, and to communicate my feelings to them, so I find the best way is to direct. Directing is the pinnacle of our business....I'm under the impression that I can gather all my skills around me to make people laugh and cry."

Actor Nichelle Nichols saw a less altruistic motive behind Shatner's passion for directing. "Bill needs to control the action and be the center of attention," his **Star Trek** TV series costar once observed. In fact, it was Shatner's pronounced tendency to direct *even* when he was acting that irked his fellow crew members the most on the *Trek* set. Nonetheless, for whatever reason, Shatner has not pursued directing as aggressively as his acting career. His directorial efforts comprise a handful of stage and television credits and one notable feature film—the 1989 embarrassment **Star Trek V: The Final Frontier**.

Shatner has talked often about the complicated relationship between writer, director, and performer. "A director must know the spines, or cores, of all the characters and see how they mesh or entwine or go against each other. And, of course, neither the actors nor the director can find them unless the playwright has put them there in the first place. As a writer, I've found from acting what I have to put in my plays to make them come alive for the persons who direct and act them so they'll come alive for the audience."

The creative failure of **Star Trek V: The Final Frontier** has often been laid at the feet of Shatner the director. However, as Leonard Nimoy has noted, the film's problems went way (!) beyond the man behind the lens. "He was riding a bad script," Nimoy championed, "and as I've said at other times and places, when you're riding a bad script, there's not much that can be done to salvage a film." In fact, while they went into the theatrical project with grave apprehensions about their colleague's newfound status as director, Shatner's costars emerged with nothing but praise for his directorial style. "Bill turned out to be among the finest, most respectful directors I've ever worked with," Nichelle Nichols concluded, to her own astonishment.

> *"I love the idea of having a dream, bringing it to fruition, and putting it on the screen. I still think directing is the best job in entertainment."*
> —SHATNER, on his love of directing

Disaster on the Coastliner   RATING: U U

This 1979 ABC-TV movie, directed by Richard C. Sarafian, headlines Shatner as a con artist onboard one of those typical runaway passenger trains. TV heavyweights Lloyd Bridges and Raymond Burr also appear, with E. G. Marshall and curvaceous Yvette Mimieux in support. As Stuart Peters, Shatner places his own precious life on the line to save his fellow passengers while performing some of his own stunts when a deranged engineer sets two trains on a deadly collision course.

Dobermans

Shatner is a dedicated breeder of Doberman pinschers, those fiercely loyal short-haired dogs of German origin. He began acquiring the daunting canines soon after achieving his first success as an actor in the 1950s.

"The first thing I did when I got married was I bought a dog," Shatner told biographers in the late 1970s. As a child, he had always wanted one, but for a long time his parents resisted on the grounds that a canine creature would mess up their house. "They'd say, 'You can have a hobby horse, but you can't have a dog!'" Shatner once recalled. "I did

Shatner with one of his prize Dobermans. He later had one buried in a celebrity pet cemetery. [photo courtesy of Archive Photos]

have dogs as I got older but never for any length of time ... [and] not the *kind* of dog and the *way* I wanted a dog in some inchoate way."

One anecdote from Shatner's TV days on **Star Trek** illustrates the special place his Dobermans have in his daily life. Paramount TV's Business Affairs office became concerned after Shatner submitted an expense account containing a $15 bill for breakfast. Producer Fred Freiberger was dispatched to confront his star with the then-exorbitant food charge. Shatner calmly listed the items in his breakfast, which totaled $7.50. When Freiberger reminded him he had billed Paramount for twice that amount, Shatner was non-plussed.

"Right. $7.50 for me and $7.50 for my dog. My dog and I always breakfast together and we usually order the same things."

For the record, Freiberger approved the special expense.

The Shatminster Dog Show:

Shatner has had a number of beloved Dobermans over the years. A round-up of some of the more notable:

- DUNHILL. One of Shatner's early favorites, Dunhill would accompany him and his first wife to expensive restaurants. Shatner even made sure the pooch was provided its own place at the table.

- STIRLING. A strapping male Doberman, Stirling once devoured a twenty-pound Thanksgiving turkey; Shatner was forced to serve cheese and crackers to his bewildered dinner guests.

- **KIRK.** In the 1970s, Shatner named one manly dog Kirk after his most famous character.
- **CHINA.** The so-called "Beauty Girl," this bitch loved to lie in the shade and was a special favorite of her master. Shatner had China interred alongside other celebrity canines at the **Los Angeles Pet Memorial Park** following her demise in 1988. (Not included on most guided tours of the City of the Angels, the **Los Angeles Pet Memorial Park** is located in Calabasas in the San Fernando Valley, some twenty-two miles from downtown Los Angeles.)

Dr. Kildare

Shatner turned down the title role in this hour-long medical drama series, which ran on the NBC-TV network from 1961 to 1966. Stolid but handsome actor Richard Chamberlain instead won the plum role of Dr. James Kildare, an intern at metropolitan Blair Hospital who turns for counsel and advice to the more experienced Dr. Leonard Gillespie (Canadian native Raymond Massey). The series helped make Chamberlain a star, while Shatner had to wait in the wings for the 1966 debut of **Star Trek** for his next crack at a network series lead. Ironically, Shatner agreed to six guest appearances on *Dr. Kildare* over the course of its five-year run, often playing a physician.

Doohan, James (B. 1920)

The burly character actor played Chief Engineer Montgomery Scott (or, as he was affectionately termed, "Scotty") on TV's **Star Trek** from 1966 to 1969. A native of Vancouver, British Columbia, Canada, Doohan was a master of dialects who had worked steadily in television throughout the 1950s and 1960s. His facility with a Scottish accent impressed **Gene Roddenberry**, who created the role of Scotty to accommodate Doohan's dialectic talents.

Doohan, who has been featured in such recent movies as *Double Trouble* (1992) and *Amore!* (1993), has long been one of Shatner's harshest and most outspoken critics. In fact, he was the only member of the original cast of the original *Star Trek* to refuse to be interviewed by Shatner for the latter's 1993 memoir *Star Trek Memories*. The long-brewing antipathy came as big news to Shatner, who, for decades, had remained blithely unaware of Doohan's dislike for him.

Captain Kirk even took credit for launching Doohan's show business career with the TV sci-fi show. "I believe I was instrumental in getting him his job [on *Star Trek*]," Shatner told biographers in 1979. "I can't remember exactly whether I first suggested his name or they mentioned it to me and asked me if I knew him. But I knew him as a fine actor from Toronto and I had worked with him. I recommended him."

Scotty Pops Off:

Here are just a few of the verbal grenades Jimmy Doohan has lobbed at his longtime nemesis, William Shatner:

> "Bill has a big, fat head. To me, Bill is selling Paramount a bill of goods which is rotten. I don't know why. He's got power somewhere. He shouldn't have it."

> "There is really only one person on the show that nobody can stand.... He can't even act. He doesn't act: he makes faces. He'll wrinkle his nose like a rabbit and that's supposed to mean, 'Oh look, I'm about to cry.'"

> "Bill doesn't like anyone to do good acting around him."

SO SAYETH SHATNER

(RESPONDING TO CHARGES BY *STAR TREK* CAST MEMBERS THAT HE HOGGED THE SHOW)

"I was never rude, I was never angry at anybody—I love them all. They can't be angry at me, because I love them. So how can you be angry with someone who loves you?"

Dual Roles

Shatner has always relished playing dual roles and split personalities on camera. "It gives the viewers twice as much of me!" he has gleefully observed. More often than not, the two sides of Shatner's character war with one another, providing dramatic conflict, as in the otherwise forgettable feature **White Comanche** (1968), in which he plays feuding Indian twins.

Some of Shatner's most memorable dual performances occurred in **Star Trek** TV episodes. In "What Are Little Girls Made Of?" (October 20, 1966) a deranged scientist bent on populating the universe with androids creates a perfect duplicate of Captain Kirk. The lookalikes have a very civilized dinner conversation thanks to a surprisingly well-executed split-screen effect.

Shatner gives one of his best **Star Trek** interpretations in "The Enemy Within" (October 6, 1966), wherein a transporter malfunction splits Kirk into two physically identical individuals. In one scene, Shatner must play both halves of Kirk as they fight for control of his personality. When the star finished filming the sequence, the entire crew gave him a standing ovation.

Finally, in "Turnabout Intruder" (June 3, 1969), the last episode of the original **Star Trek** series, Shatner took on the ultimate acting challenge. He played a woman inhabiting Kirk's body for purposes of taking over the Starship *Enterprise*. However, Shatner's portrayal was hardly a valentine to feminism. His idea of representative female characteristics were nail-biting, hysterical outbursts, and chronic indecision. The folks at NOW (National Organization for Women) may have cringed, but Shatner received kudos from some TV critics for his versatility.

Part of Shatner's attraction to dual roles comes from his own dualistic conception of human nature, a conception greatly influenced by the thinking of the anthropological writer **Robert Ardrey**. In "The Enemy Within," for example, Shatner says, "I recognized that the essential human being is that composite of the animal and the intellect. One cannot function without the other. I tried to portray the animal, going so far beyond the bounds of behavior without the control of the intellect— and the weakness and opaqueness of the intellect without the blood and color of the animal."

Ego

Shatner has long had to deal with accusations from the media and the public that he is a rampant egomaniac. Many of these charges originated with his fellow **Star Trek** TV cast members. "Bill's the epitome of the star in many negative ways," **Walter Koenig** (Ensign Pavel Chekov on the TV series) once remarked. "He's totally preoccupied with himself and his career and his work on the show." In addition, Shatner's personal pest, **James Doohan**, has repeatedly made reference to the actor's "big, fat head." But as is the case with his **toupee**, Shatner exists in a state of deep denial about the widespread perception that he is full of himself. "I don't understand that," he once told an interviewer. "I'm not even aware of it, quite frankly."

> *"I don't know what ego means. It takes a certain amount of chutzpah to think that writing something on paper will interest you or standing in front of a camera will entertain you, so if that's ego, I have one."*
> —SHATNER in a 1995 online forum, responding to a *Star Trek* fan who accused him of having "an ego bigger than Texas."

Ellison, Harlan (B. 1934)

This diminutive science fiction writer, essayist, and self-promoting crank has had a running feud with Shatner (let alone Gene Roddenberry) for decades. In 1966, Ellison penned the classic **Star Trek** episode "The City on the Edge of Forever" (April 6, 1967), accepted numerous awards for it, then spent the ensuing thirty years complaining about the changes made to his TV script. This ridiculous controversy culminated in the 1996 vanity publication *Harlan Ellison's The City on the Edge of Forever*, which reprinted several drafts of the **Star Trek** teleplay—for anyone who still cared—and had room left over for a characteristically windy forty-six-page Ellison essay on the topic. In it, Ellison relates his version of a story about Shatner visiting his Hollywood home and reading the "City" script in 1966. Accusations of **line counting** on Shatner's part are the least of Ellison's insinuations. Not surprisingly, Shatner gives a markedly different account of their meeting in his 1993

Ten Embarrassing Moments William Shatner Would Probably Like to Forget

1. As a boy, getting his ass kicked by a farmer (see **Ass-kicking**)

2. As an adult, getting his ass kicked by punks (see **Fights**)

3. Being sued by lover Eva Marie Friedrick...and, a month later, being sued by lover Vira Montes (see **Palimony**)

4. Eating fruit salad at Woolworth's lunch counter twice a day (see **Fruit Salad**)

5. Falling asleep at the premiere of *Star Trek: The Motion Picture* (see **Star Trek: The Motion Picture**)

6. Freezing up on live television (see **Live Television**)

7. His idiosyncratic vocal performance of Elton John's "Rocket Man" (see **"Rocket Man"**)

8. Koko the Gorilla getting too friendly (see **Koko the Gorilla**)

9. Landing backside-down on a cactus (see **Motorcycles**)

10. Wearing a toupee (see **Toupee**) (also see **Leonard Nimoy** for *Life* magazine incident)

memoir *Star Trek Memories*. What may have started as a clash of two colossal egos has become exacerbated by Ellison's gleeful willingness to savage Shatner in print.

Evaluating Shatner's performance in *Star Trek: The Motion Picture* (1979), Ellison typically pulled out all the stops, accusing the actor of being "stuffy when he isn't being arch and coy; hamming and mugging when he isn't being lachrymose; playing Kirk as if he actually thinks he *is* Kirk, overbearing and pompous."

While it's hard to challenge that assessment on its merits, one can't be surprised by Shatner's wounded reaction. "Harlan Ellison is a surly young man," he has said, "who has spent years saying awful things about me, while

Shatner could be taking mental aim at James Doohan, Harlan Ellison, or any one of his many critics in this staged publicity still from the 1960s. [photo courtesy of The Everett Collection]

I find him admirable. In fact, 'City on the Edge of Forever' is my favorite of the original *Star Trek* series because of the fact that it is a beautiful love story, well told."

Despite all his bitterness toward the show's producers and its main star, Ellison was instrumental in keeping the sci-fi program from being smothered in its cradle by network executives. When NBC began rumbling about possibly canceling *Star Trek* during its debut TV season (1966–67), Ellison initiated a letter-writing campaign to save the show. He mailed out 5,000 letters to writers and sci-fi fans encouraging them, in turn, to write the network and its affiliates to voice their displeasure. The results exceeded expectations, as NBC found itself bombarded with over 100,000 letters. In the end, it decided to renew *Star Trek* for a second, and eventually a third, season. Ironically, Ellison, however, never wrote for the program again. The cantankerous author now appears regularly as a commentator on cable TV's Sci-Fi Network. He is the author of numerous award-winning short stories, including "I Have No Mouth and I Must Scream" (1967), "Jeffty Is Five" (1977), and "'Repent, Harlequin!' Said the Ticktockman" (1965).

> *"I don't agree with his adjectives. They're a little strong, but then, so is Harlan Ellison. He's little and he's strong."*
> —SHATNER, on Harlan Ellison's criticism of one of his performances

Explosive Generation, The

RATING: U U

This woefully low-budget, black-and-white 1961 movie has Shatner as a high school teacher who is suspended for teaching his students about...sex education. As progressive educator Peter Gifford, Shatner draws the ire of the conservative PTA when he assigns his class to write a paper about their sex lives. The students protest his suspension. The all-weird cast includes Ed Platt (the agency leader from TV's *Get Smart*, 1965–70), Stafford Repp (the police chief from TV's *Batman*, 1966–68), and a young Beau Bridges. Frequent *Gilligan's Island* (1964–67) player Vito Scotti plays a janitor. Commented *Variety*, "Canadian actor William Shatner...has a pleasant screen personality and brings a moving power of oratory to his speech about students protesting all over the world." The actor returned to the "ripped from the headlines" theme later that same year with the racial strife drama ***The Intruder.***

Family of Strangers, A

RATING: U U U

Directed by Sheldon Larry, this 1993 CBS-TV movie stars Shatner as the adoptive father of a young woman facing life-threatening brain surgery. When on-screen daughter Melissa Gilbert, a name made famous by TV's *Little House on the Prairie* (1974–83), demands her medical history, a dithering Shatner is forced to admit he is not her biological papa. The well-intentioned movie was based on a novel, *Jody* (1976), by Jerry Hulse.

Fans

Shatner has long had a love-hate relationship with his fans, that vast army of devoted souls who people the science fiction conventions of this land. "It's a fandom I don't know who else has," Shatner once observed. While the names **Leonard Nimoy, DeForest Kelley, George Takei, Walter Koenig,** and **James Doohan** immediately spring to mind in answer to Shatner's puzzlement, he is right that there is a special regard reserved for the once-and-future Captain James T. Kirk. "I may be becoming an institution without my even knowing it," he mused a few decades ago. "There's a touching quality—there's something touching about the way people look to me."

Unlock the Internet's Potential

The geniuses who run the various Shatner-related Web sites (see appendix) have used their technological expertise (and their copious free time) to provide Shatner fans with a number of digital gewgaws that make our tiresome trudge through this vale of tears slightly more palatable. Behold, five of the finest:

- **Shatner Shirt Swatches** (http://www.iwaynet.net/~grumblis/shatpics.html) allows you to save some of Shatner's wilder shirt patterns as background wallpaper in Windows 95.

- Those with Java-enabled browsers will have a ball playing **Shatneroids** (http://www.tardis.ed.ac.uk/~aardvark/java/Shatneroids/Shatneroids.html) a variation on the arcade chestnut Asteroids featuring Shatner's disembodied head.

- A grimacing **Shatner Clock** keeps time in both conventional and military format at (http://www.tardis.ed.ac.uk/~lard/java/sclock/index.html).

- Check the status of Shatner's ego with the **William Shatner Egometer** (http://www.tp.net/tp/users/lewser/Egometer.htm). Hmm, why does it seem fixed at the same high level all the time?

- And you disgruntled former members of the *Star Trek* cast (and I know you're reading this) can get your frustrations out with **Punch Captain Kirk** (http://www.well.com/user/vanya/kirk.html) a feature that allows you to batter the girdle off the old boy to your heart's content.

Shatner has not always found such extreme public adulation so poignant. "Those fans are like greyhounds racing to see who can get the rabbit," he groused of his followers in the late 1960s. "They only want to touch you or maybe get a souvenir, but if it gets out of control and reaches a flash point—well! They start pushing and grabbing, and then it becomes hysteria." Asked by *Playboy* in 1989 to provide the "early warning sign of a Trekkie," Shatner replied: "It's the wild-eyed look, the hands lifted above the ears and the shambling walk that breaks into a run as they approach me."

Shatner exacted the ultimate revenge on his fans with a December 20, 1986, appearance on NBC-TV's *Saturday Night Live*. The guest-hosting gig drew the ire of fandom for a brief sketch in which Shatner standing at a podium speaking to convention attendees poked fun at the Trekker phenomenon and its multitudinous fans, who seemingly have no life outside their fandom. It could even be said that the better the shape of Shatner's career outside the orbit of *Star Trek*, the worse he has treated his *Star Trek* fans. After all, when you are in need, you can't really urge your audience to get a life and then expect them to plunk down $20 for a ticket to one of your self-indulgent **one-man shows**, now can you?

> *"I take karate lessons and walk around with mace. They can be very violent people if you challenge their belief system."*
> —SHATNER, on how he deals with his overzealous Trekkies

Fatherhood

Shatner is the father of three daughters, **Leslie Shatner, Lisabeth Shatner**, and **Melanie Shatner** (see entries for each), all by his first wife, **Gloria Rand**.

During the divorce proceedings with Rand in 1969, Shatner ruminated about his failings as a father. "It bothers me that for years I haven't been able to give Leslie, Lisabeth, and Melanie the kind of time most fathers can give their children. I often think about it, and I often feel guilty. A large percentage of fathers of my age are at the peak of their vitality and earning power, and the demands on their time at this moment in their lives

Shatner found domestic bliss for a time with Gloria Rand and their three daughters—Leslie, Lisabeth, and Melanie. [photo courtesy of The Everett Collection]

are the greatest. It's unfortunate that at this precise time, children need their father the most. And yet, that's the way it is."

Favored Nations Clause

A clause was added to the Paramount Pictures contracts of Shatner and **Leonard Nimoy** that mandated to each actor the same salary and benefits won by the other. Shatner used the favored nations clause in his studio pact to secure the directorial reins on 1989's *Star Trek V: The Final Frontier* (Nimoy had already directed *Star Trek III* of 1984 and *Star Trek IV* of 1986). Nimoy held out for pay raises that brought his salary up to par with Shatner's. "You owe me a lot of money," Shatner once told Nimoy. However, because **directing** was always one of Shatner's artistic goals, "he's more than paid me back."

Fights

As a child, Shatner got into his share of scraps with other youngsters.

"I recall them as always being one-sided—there was always a multitude of them—two or three. And I remember the fights used to be where two or three kids would jump me and I'd be fighting them off and a group would gather around and be chanting, you know 'fight, fight, get him, get him' against me, for the attackers. But I also have a recollection of being rather good, and not really ever getting badly beaten up and doing more harm than getting harmed. In fact, there came a time when they stopped jumping me, because it was a problem for them." Shatner earned the nickname **"Toughy"** for his willingness to duke it out despite the odds.

Yet for all his macho bluster, Shatner has claimed he hasn't been involved in a fight since childhood. "The only way I could possibly get into a fight would be in my self-defense or self-defense [sic] of somebody I love," he has said. Nevertheless he came close to a scrape on a number of occasions. During his years on *Star Trek* he was constantly confronted by tough guys who wanted a piece of TV's famous Captain Kirk. Invariably these encounters occurred in bars. Luckily, one of Shatner's drinking buddies, *Star Trek* bit player David L. Ross, was an ex-Marine. He stepped in several times to help defuse a potentially ugly situation.

It is when Shatner is left alone without adult supervision that he gets into the most trouble. One such incident occurred during a theatrical production early in Shatner's acting career. A scene called for one of his supporting players to appear drunk. Some time after opening night, the actor began to hit Shatner on the shoulder during the scene—although this action wasn't called for in the play. Eventually, these blows became painful, and Shatner asked the man to stop. When the actor refused, Shatner complained to the director, then the producer, even to Actors Equity, but no one was able to help. Finally, Shatner took matters into his own

Former footballer Shatner clowns around with Tournament of Roses President Michael E. Ward after being named Grand Marshal of the 1994 Rose Bowl Parade. [photo courtesy of AP Worldwide Photos]

hands. One night, during the scene, after the man had clobbered him yet again, Shatner struck back, sending his fellow thespian reeling to the stage. When the curtain came down ending the first act, the actor attacked Shatner, cuffing an elderly prop man in the head before the other performers broke up the scuffle. The next day, the enraged actor continued his assault in Shatner's dressing room before the performance. Shatner picks up the story from there:

"Suddenly the veneer of civilization left me, and I saw in my mind's eye—me, going toward him like an animal—like a cat, really, my thumbs toward his eyes, and my teeth towards his jugular... I was an animal, and I was going to kill him. And when I look back on it, I *could* have killed him, if I had done what I had envisioned in that split second of seeing what I was going to do." Luckily for Shatner, and the man's family, the producer was able to separate the two antagonists. But the experience was revelatory for Shatner. "I realized there that I could have killed somebody," he explained. "It is within me to kill somebody, and by that primitive means of biting through the jugular vein."

Shatner's bloodlust had cooled somewhat by the late 1960s, when his next close call came at a miniature race car track where he had gone with his children. As he related to *TV Guide* in December of 1989: "Some eighteen-year-olds, verging on being hoodlums, kept banging into us [in our 'car'] and I was trying to avoid them. Finally, everybody stopped and one of those young punks came at me and I was so angry, I picked him up, held him above my head and flung him to the ground. Then his friends came at me and I realized that there was a line between fiction and non-fiction that I had crossed and that when four muscular young kids come at you, you're gonna have the crap beat out of you. So I said, 'Please don't hit me.' I was so embarrassed. I'd wanted to act brave in front of my kids." There ensued an **ass-kicking** to rival the one Shatner received from a Canadian farmer during his days at summer camp. "All three came at me and began to pound on me. Blood was spurting all over. One of them kept yelling: 'Don't get your blood all over me!' Captain Kirk was all over the floor."

Shatner's reluctance to scrap with his fellow alpha males can be ascribed to one reason—economics. An actor simply cannot afford to have his beautiful face undergo disfigurement. "A broken face, a broken hand, a toe, a scratch—I mean, I can't deal with those things. Do you know, if I get a scratch on my face, the way I work I'd be out for what? Three, four weeks. A broken nose—forget it—six months....All you need is one karate blow to the neck and it's all over....A kick in the balls—I mean, you could *die*. And I as an actor can't afford to be put out of business that way."

First Love

Shatner's first love was a college sweetheart whose name he has never revealed. They dated all through their years (1948–52) at **McGill University**, where Shatner was studying business. However, when he expressed his desire to become an actor, the girl—whom Shatner describes as "much more practical than I"—decided to marry a businessman and move to New York.

First Men in the Moon

This one-hour radio-style dramatization was performed live by an all-*Star Trek* cast on November 2, 1997. Shatner joined original series crewmate **Leonard Nimoy**, Dwight Schultz (Lt. Reginald "Greg" Endicott) of *Star Trek: The Next Generation* (1987–94), John DeLancie (Q) of both *Star Trek: The Next Generation* and *Star Trek: Voyager* (1995–), and Ethan Phillips (Neelix) of *Star Trek: Voyager* for a read-through of the pioneering 1901 H.G. Wells classic on cable's Sci-Fi Channel and its Internet Web site, the Dominion. Shatner's appearance was kept a secret from the public until he stepped onstage to great applause at the Museum of Television & Radio in Beverly Hills.

The Shatnerific Trivia Challenge

PART ONE: *STAR TREK*
(THE TV SERIES AND THE FEATURE MOVIES)

1. What was the original name of the Starship *Enterprise*?

2. You've just received a phaser for Christmas. You should familiarize yourself with those two settings—what are they?

3. Every Trekkie remembers that Jeffrey Hunter was replaced as the original Captain Kirk, but the show's first pilot also featured two actors who held on to their roles. Can you name them?

4. Who was producer Gene Roddenberry's first choice to play Spock in the 1966 TV series?

5. The TV show's second pilot featured an actor who, just two years later, appeared in one of the great sci-fi classics of the big screen. Who is he?

6. How fast can the *Enterprise* go when it really needs to m-o-o-o-v-e!?

7. Though viewers rarely saw more than the eight principal actors, how many crew members were actually on board the Starship *Enterprise*?

8. Scotty can't beam you up if your _____ isn't turned on.

9. Hold on to your lunch: How long does it take for the *Enterprise* to go from standing still to light speed?

10. Which two *Star Trek* TV series regulars are from Canada?

11. Who supplied the voice of the *Enterprise*'s talking computer?

12. "Khan! Khan! Khan!" Captain Kirk keeps screaming. Doesn't anyone remember the man's full name?

13. A question for more educated Trekkies: The namesake of an *Enterprise* cast member wrote a classic play called *The Three Sisters*. Name him.

14. If you were real friendly with Sulu, you would know that his first name is _____.

15. And Scotty's mother called him _____. And McCoy's first name is _____.

16. Which crew member is named after a Roman emperor?

17. If they sent out announcement cards in the twenty-third century, one might have read: "Sarek and Amanda announce the birth of a son, named_____."

18. The Enterprise was not the first starship to reach the edge of the galaxy. Who got there first?

19. You can spot a Romulan starship a mile off. By what descriptive name is it known?

20. The final episode of the Star Trek TV series gave Shatner his greatest acting challenge on the TV show. What did he portray?

Answers on page 279

Flying

"Flying my own plane has become a passion with me," Shatner once said. "There is something not only thrilling about it but exhilarating to the utmost degree. When in the air, I feel that the plane and I are one. Yes, flying is the skill of the twenty-first century; driving and sailboating, of the twentieth."

Shatner learned to fly in the 1960s, the apex of his daredevil period. Reportedly, he flew solo in a Cessna 150 after only eight hours of training. The experience terrified him, but managed to arouse all his macho sense of adventure. "I had to fight fear, but I conquered it," Shatner boasted. "Every aviator has to do that, especially while practicing stalls." Shatner likened the experience to his first attempt to ride a horse, when he "was dreadfully afraid that I'd fall off and that the animal would fall on me."

For the People

This hour-long crime drama, Shatner's first television series, ran for thirteen weeks on CBS-TV from January 31 to May 9, 1965. Shatner played David Koster, a headstrong New York City assistant district attorney who is always butting heads with his superiors (much like his counterparts in TV shows of the late 1990s, such as *Law & Order*, *The Practice*, *Ally McBeal*, and *Michael Hayes*). "I like to stamp on any toes that get in my way," Shatner told the *New York Post*, speaking in the Koster persona. "I do a regular Spanish Flamenco heel dance on the toes of anybody who crosses my way." It costarred Howard Da Silva (his boss), Lonny Chapman (his police detective helper), and Jessica Walter (his wife).

Shatner had high hopes for this show. "If I'm successful, the series will be," he predicted. "But there's something more immediate about it. The people I'm working with, feel fondly toward, will be employed if it is.... I hope any optimism they may have felt will be justified." Sadly, it was not. *For the People* earned plaudits from critics but had the misfortune to share a time slot with the NBC network hit *Bonanza*. As a consequence, it lost out in the ratings and was canceled.

Foundation: The Psychohistorians

Shatner was nominated for a Grammy Award for his reading of **Isaac Asimov's** classic science fiction novel *Foundation* (1942) in 1976 for Caedmon Records. Set in deep space thousands of years in the future in the closing centuries of a vast Galactic Empire modeled, most obviously, on the rise and fall of the Roman Empire, *Foundation* and its follow-up companion novels chronicle the evolution of a colony full of brilliant humanoids over several hundred years of psychohistory.

4419 Girouard Street

Address of Shatner's childhood home in Montreal, Quebec, Canada.

Friedrick, Eva Marie (B. 1960s)

Personal assistant who filed a $2 million **palimony** suit against Shatner in 1989. The former model joined Shatner's staff in 1986, ironically on the recommendation of his then-wife **Marcy Lafferty**. The two quickly became lovers. The relationship reportedly soured after Friedrick was injured in a car accident in October of 1988.

Fruit Salad

Shatner detests fruit salad, a dislike dating back to his **starvation years** as a young actor in Ontario, Canada. In those days, when he was earning a scant $31 a week at the **Canadian National Repertory Theatre** in Ottawa and spending most of that salary on rent, Shatner would eat the twenty-seven-cent fruit salad at Woolworth's as often as he could, sometimes twice a day.

Future

Once a self-proclaimed futurist, Shatner has in recent years embraced a more pessimistic view of mankind's ultimate prospects. This shift is

SO SAYETH SHATNER

ON MANKIND'S PROSPECTS:

"The future is eternally fascinating because it hasn't happened yet."

reflected in his 1990s **TekWar** book and television series, which depicts a future where powerful cartels use advanced technology to control society. "The world hasn't really changed," Shatner mused in 1996. "We're more likely to destroy ourselves than we ever were. We're a technological world, and we're blind to the terrible toll that technology is exacting all around us." Shatner even proposed modifying the mission he once promulgated on TV's **Star Trek** in the 1960s: "To cautiously go where everyone has gone before?"

William Shatner, Prophet or Blowhard?

Soothsaying is hardly an exact science. Even the most prescient seer is just blowing smoke (or merely guessing) ninety-nine percent of the time. William Shatner is no exception. He has used his access to the media to issue periodic forecasts on the state of mankind and technology. Here are a few of his prognostications:

> *"We are headed for a computerized and automated civilization."*
> —SHATNER, in 1967

> *"By the year 2540, we'll have a device that will disintegrate the atoms of a human being. These atoms will be sprayed through millions or billions of miles to some planet and then reassembled, just the way our TV signals are today."*
> —SHATNER, in 1967

> *"Human beings always act as they have. That hasn't changed since Shakespeare's day, so certainly it won't have changed by the 23rd Century."*
> —SHATNER, in 1989

> *"There is every reason to believe we will be in a catastrophic situation [fifty years from now]. Our population will increase by billions—to the point where the planet can't take the load. We can only hope that mankind will steer a different course than we are now."*
> —SHATNER, in 1994

> *"In defiling our planet, we have given ourselves a life term, and the electric chair is slowly coming our way.... It won't happen suddenly; we're all going to expire in a rather ugly way unless we do something about it."*
> —SHATNER, in 1994

Go Ask Alice

RATING: U U

The ninety-minute 1973 ABC-TV network movie aired a scant eleven days after Shatner's previous telefilm, **Incident on a Dark Street**. In this one he is the father of a teenage girl who gets hooked on hard drugs and suffers a bad LSD trip. Based on the real-life diary of a teenager, the film also stars Jamie Smith-Jackson as Alice, Ruth Roman as a psychiatrist, and Andy Griffith as a priest. (Shatner played a similar role in the 1988 telefilm **Broken Angel**.) *Go Ask Alice* was the first of two TV movies Shatner made in tandem with Andy Griffith. The second was **Pray for the Wildcats** (1974).

God

Shatner has long harbored a profound metaphysical streak. He has tried to bring these concerns to bear in his work, from early films like **Incubus** (1965), in which evil forces tempt a saintly man, to the quest for God that serves as the centerpiece of **Star Trek V: The Final Frontier** (1989). Even Shatner's 1968 LP album **The Transformed Man** addresses the ultimate questions of human experience. Its title track, with words by Frank Devonport, concerns a man who breaks free from the mundane concerns of everyday life in hopes of reaching "the eternal now." After much struggle, in which he must wait "for the hand of faith to lift the darkness," he finds his vision cleared and is able to attain his goal. Or, as Shatner powerfully bellows to the accompaniment of strings and a soaring choir, "I had touched the face of God!"

After the death of his father, Joseph Shatner, in 1967, Shatner began speaking out more in public about his spiritual orientation. His quotes, while often contradictory, show a man struggling—much as the "transformed man" struggled—to solve the basic riddles of existence.

> *"I'm a Jew. But I do not believe in your God...I do know that we are all afraid of dying...we are all afraid of loneliness. Those are universal truths. Are you scared? I'm scared...I love you...I need you."*
>
> —SHATNER, to the National Conference of
> Christians and Jews convention in 1968

"I want to know, for example, if a medium can communicate with a spirit. It'd be proof that something exists out there. It would be like believing in God. How comforting to know that if you say your prayers and behave you'll be rewarded in the end."
—SHATNER, in *TV Guide*, June 1968

Golden Boy

The 1937 Group Theatre play by Clifford Odets was a favorite of the teenaged Shatner. The drama concerns a moody Italian-American youth who longs to be a violinist, but instead settles for a more lucrative career as a prize fighter. Shatner has said that he empathized with the young man's dilemma, having himself had to choose between football and acting at **West Hill High School**. In fact, he has described filing past his jock buddies on the way to a play rehearsal as "tantamount to carrying your violin case while passing the school. Because the jocks at high school would say: 'Whaddya mean going to a play? What are you, weird or something?'"

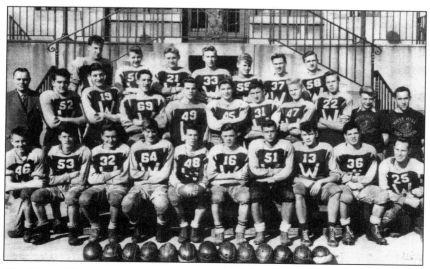

The West Hills High School football team. Shatner is #45, middle row center. [photo courtesy of Seth Poppel]

Goulart, Ron (B. 1933)

The science fiction and mystery writer served as consultant to Shatner on his recent *Tek* book series. The prolific Goulart is the author of more than sixty novels of his own, including *After Things Fell Apart* (1970), *Even the Butler Was Poor* (1990), and *Now He Thinks He's Dead* (1992). But he eschews the term "ghostwriter" when discussing his role on the *Tek* literary project. "I'm just an adviser," he told *Entertainment Weekly*. "I just give Shatner my opinion from time to time. I help with timing and tone and other technical things." "Goulart doesn't actually edit me," Shatner contends, dismissing the consensus opinion of the science fiction community that the relationship is something like that of a ventriloquist and his dummy. "He just sort of suggests things and does some rewriting. He's a great help, and I've tried to give him as much credit as possible—short of putting his name on the covers."

> *"Whatever Bill told you, I'll go along with that."*
> —RON GOULART, when asked to define his role
> as a consultant on Shatner's *Tek* novels

Great Bird of the Galaxy, The

The epithet given to Gene Roddenberry (creator of *Star Trek*) by Herbert Solow, the executive in charge of production of the TV series, and then taken up by Roddenberry's fans worldwide. The appellation itself came from a line in the *Star Trek* episode "The Man Trap" spoken by Sulu. As said by this sci-fi series character, it was meant as sort of a humorous blessing. One day Solow called Roddenberry "The Great Bird of the Galaxy" and it stuck. The rest is history. Solow also once jokingly referred to Roddenberry as "The Great Blotter of the Galaxy." Solow was referring to Roddenberry's monomania about his creation, in which he absorbed ideas and concepts for it from various writers and then called them his own without any apparent credit given to the original source.

Gritz, Bo (B. 1938)

Reportedly, this soldier of fortune was paid $10,000 by Shatner in the early 1980s as part of a development deal with Paramount Pictures. Gritz may have used this money to finance an illegal mission to rescue American POWs trapped in Laos. See **Operation Lazarus.**

Guthrie, Tyrone (1900–1971)

This renowned English theatrical director founded the **Stratford Shakespeare Festival** (in Ontario, Canada), and subsequently took Shatner under his wing. According to Shatner, Guthrie told him he "would be a great actor in the tradition of [Sir Laurence] Olivier." In 1956, Shatner was awarded the Tyrone Guthrie Award as the Festival's then most promising actor. He used the $750 prize to pay for his move to New York, where he embarked on a career in theater and television.

Heroes

As a boy, Shatner's heroes were cowboy and space opera idols like Buck Rogers, Tom Mix, and the Lone Ranger. He would often pretend he was Buck Rogers flying through the galaxies and sometimes other children would join him. "We played a lot on rooftops, especially in winter," Shatner recalled in 1967. "We dared each other to jump into space and land on a snow drift."

As he grew older, Shatner began to look to real-life heroes such as soldiers, **policemen**, and firefighters. "As we get older, we see that our idealistic heroes are human beings whose failings and sorrows are the same as ours," he declared. "What I find admirable today is the person who sacrifices himself for an ideal."

High Chair Controversy

A conflict emerged on the set of Paramount TV's *Star Trek* in 1967 over the folding chairs provided to the cast. The so-called Big Three—Shatner, *Leonard Nimoy*, and **DeForest Kelley**—all had towering canvas seats with special receptacles for their scripts and personal effects. The supporting cast members, whom Shatner later labeled the **seven dwarfs**, had noticeably shorter furniture. However, resentment over the chair situation did not reach a fever pitch until **Walter Koenig** joined the cast in the fall of 1967. The popularity of his Ensign Pavel Chekov character emboldened Koenig to demand a chair as high as the three established

The Curious Case of T. W. Hooker

T. J. Hooker may have been based on the real-life exploits of Thomas Warren Hooker, a decorated L.A.P.D. cop. Although the show's producers always denied the connection (perhaps to avoid compensating T. W. Hooker for borrowing his life story) there are a number of strong similarities between the fictitious *gendarme* and his real-life counterpart. Come to think of it, there are similarities to both men and Shatner as well. Clip and save this handy chart for future reference!

T. W. Hooker	T. J. Hooker	William Shatner
Born in Los Angeles	Policed Los Angeles	Lives in Los Angeles
Joined police force in 1960	Joined ABC lineup in 1982	Joined SAG in 1952
Divorced in early 1970s	Divorced before pilot aired	Divorced in 1969 and 1994
Partner shot and killed	Partner shot and killed	Partner Nimoy died in *Enterprise* radiation chamber
Once rushed into a burning apartment building to lead occupants to safety	Often rushed into the path of speeding cars to catch criminal suspects	Once posed with firehose on the scene of a soundstage fire on set of *Star Trek III*

stars. He jealously guarded his new perk, but his lofty position was short-lived. The other cast members all demanded high chairs as well, and soon the entire *Enterprise* crew was breathing the same rarefied air as the Big Three. Ironically, a third-season *Star Trek* episode, "The Cloud Minders" (February 28, 1969), concerned a rebellion by worker drones who toil in underground mines against an elite class of overlords who dwell in an ethereal cloud city. A veiled commentary on the high chair controversy, perhaps? See **Phone Controversy**.

Hollywood Walk of Fame

Shatner received his star on the Hollywood Walk of Fame, the 1,762[nd] one issued, on May 19, 1983. **Leonard Nimoy** joined him for the ceremony. For those visiting Hollywood, Shatner's cement marker is located outside the legendary Mann's Chinese Theatre between the stars of German-born movie director William Dieterle (1893–1972) and comedian/singer Danny Thomas (1914–1991) of TV's *Make Room for Daddy* (1953–65).

> *"I think any guy who controls space as well as he does deserves some space on the sidewalk."*
>
> —LEONARD NIMOY, at ceremonies honoring Shatner's enshrinement on the Hollywood Walk of Fame.

Horror at 37,000 Feet, The

RATING:

Shatner has carved a nice niche for himself playing passengers aboard haunted airliners. Previously a hysterical passenger aboard a jet being sabotaged by a gremlin in the similarly-titled *Twilight Zone* episode "Nightmare at 20,000 Feet" (October 11, 1963), Shatner ups his altitude for this ninety-minute 1973 TV movie starring Chuck Connors, Buddy Ebsen, France Nuyen, Roy Thinnes, Paul Winfield, and Tammy Grimes. The hackneyed plot concerns a jumbo jet and especially those passengers in first class, which is being haunted by ghosts because of a druid stone in the baggage hold. Shatner plays passenger Paul Kovalik in this drama directed by David Lowell Rich. Look fast for Russell Johnson (as Jim Hawley), the beloved Professor from TV's *Gilligan's Island* (1964–67).

The leading light of Canadian drama poses over his star on the Hollywood Walk of Fame in 1983. [photo courtesy of AP Worldwide Photos]

Six Degrees of *Star Trek*

France Nuyen (Annalik in *The Horror at 37,000 Feet*) sparred with Shatner in the third-season *Star Trek* episode "Elaan of Troyius" (December 20, 1968). Paul Winfield (Dr. Enkalla) went on to play Captain Terrell, a casualty of the Ceti Eel, in ***Star Trek II: The Wrath of Khan*** (1982).

Horseradish

This ancient herb is one of Shatner's favorite condiments. He ate horseradish for the first time as a small child during a Jewish holiday celebration in Montreal. Having subsisted on baby food up till then, Shatner saw ingesting the pungently spicy root as a rite of passage.

"I was given a small portion of the red, mushy substance but took too much on my fork. My eyes welled with tears, my face flushed, my nose ran, my ears burned. It was the Queen's Coronation, Fourth of July, and Simchas Torah, all rolled into one."

Horseradish is one of the five bitter herbs of the Passover festival, and is usually grated, added in sauces, or used as a condiment for fish or meat.

"If you eat enough horseradish, nothing matters in the world, except the explosion in the center of your head."
    —SHATNER, on the palliative effects of horseradish, in 1975

Horses

Shatner is a dedicated breeder of quarter horses, with ranches in the bluegrass country of Kentucky and California's Simi Valley (northwest of Los Angeles). In 1983 and 1985, he rode his own mounts along a three-mile stretch of Sunset and Hollywood Boulevards as part of the annual Christmas Lane Parade, held on the Sunday after Thanksgiving. In recent years, he has enjoyed his most notable success with American Saddlebreds, the high-stepping, five-gaited mounts, ownership of which Shatner likens to a religious experience. Frequently, Shatner appears in charity fundraisers at the Equestrian Center in Burbank, California, some 15 miles north of downtown Los Angeles.

Shatner caught the saddlebred bug after visiting a stable while on location for an episode of his TV series **T. J. Hooker** (1982–87). "It was one of those enchanted moments," Shatner told the *New York Times* of this encounter. "I fell in love from across a crowded room, a crowded barn, really." He subsequently purchased the world champion stallion Sultan's Great Day to stand as stud at his **Belle Reve** farm in Versailles, Kentucky. His horse **Kentucky Dream** won the National Horse Show in 1986.

"These horses are an esthetic delight, and the pleasure they give the eye is

Dedicated horseman Shatner rode one of his mounts in the 1994 Tournament of Roses Parade. [photo courtesy of AP Worldwide Photos]

magnified by the motion they have," he told the press in November of 1986. "I took one look and just fell in love."

Shatner first learned to ride in 1963 while filming the failed TV pilot **Alexander the Great**. In the beginning, he was terrified the animal would rear up and fall on top of him. However, he quickly overcame his fears. By the close of the shooting, Glen Randall, cowboy movie star Gene Autry's own trainer, was telling Shatner, "You have more natural ability as a horseman than anyone I've ever worked with." By his own admission, however, Shatner did not do much more than "hack around" on horses until the mid-1980s. "The more time I spend doing this, the more I profoundly know that I don't know how to ride horses," he admitted once to the media. It was only until he trained for championship horse shows that his skills as an equestrian improved. By 1990, spectators at the National Horse Show were cheering for him as he snagged a blue ribbon in the Saddlebred Five-Gaited class, on a mount named Time Machine.

Shatner has spoken at length about his passion for riding. "The beauty of the horse, the feeling of two entities joining. The athleticism, the competition, the excitement of a galloping horse and the art that is needed to control and yet be free." He often compares horses to women. "A pretty girl is certainly comparable to a good horse," he informed an interviewer in 1996. That same year, he told a convention audience in Atlanta about another part of horse rearing that appeals to him. "I love to birth the babies," he said. "I love to take the babies out of the mother's womb."

Beyond the sensual aspects of horsemanship, Shatner has recognized the sport's utility in serving his favorite causes. Over the years, he has given time and money to Ahead with Horses, a therapeutic group that uses horseback riding to rehabilitate disabled children. In 1991, he started the Hollywood Charitable Horse Show, which has annually raised close to $50,000 for various children's charities. The show combines quarter horse competition with Western style barbecue and celebrity contests and raffles—including one in which Shatner auctions himself off for dances to the highest bidder.

Like many a horseman, Shatner has had his share of riding accidents. On the set of his 1975 TV series **The Barbary Coast**, he suffered a broken ankle when a horse stepped on his foot. Then, in 1993, his mount was startled by a golf cart and reared unexpectedly, collapsing on top of him. Shatner suffered torn ligaments and had to be rushed to the hospital for treatment. At the time, the leg injury seemed the least of his problems. "It wasn't like my television show **Rescue 911** [1989–92]," he said afterwards. "It was much messier. This guy, the EMT leaning over me, was sweating and perspiring and dripping on me."

In a case of art imitating life, Shatner as Captain Kirk rides horses extensively in the feature film **Star Trek: Generations** (1994). To relieve the chafing on his legs, the Canadian wore **panty hose** all through the filming.

> *"Being around this breed of horse is just like show business, only better."*
> —SHATNER, on the charms of the American Saddlebred

Hound of the Baskervilles, The   RATING: Ʊ

This ninety-minute 1972 ABC-TV movie is based on Sir Arthur Conan Doyle's famous (and frequently filmed) detective novel (1902). In this version Stewart Granger plays Sherlock Holmes, with Bernard Fox as Dr. Watson. Shatner has third billing as villainous George Stapleton, whose "abrupt and limp demise" was lamented by the reviewer for *Variety*. Abrupt and limp are two words no man ever wants to hear. The telefeature served as the pilot for a proposed detective anthology series that was never consummated.

Houses

The type of home an actor owns is often a barometer of his status in show business.Thus, the chronology of Shatner domiciles tells a tale of a career marked by dramatic ups and downs.

In May of 1957, Shatner signed his first Hollywood movie contract, a two-year deal with MGM worth $100,000. With a young wife, **Gloria Rand**, and plans for a family, he naturally looked to purchase his first residence, now that he was based in Los Angeles instead of New York City. The couple initially considered a palatial Hollywood spread with a pool, a barbecue pit, and a glass-enclosed living room. However, Shatner's agent convinced them this was not a good idea. "Don't mortgage yourself to Hollywood," the young actor was told. The Shatners ended up taking a one-bedroom apartment instead.

It proved to be good advice, as Shatner soon found himself bitten by the Broadway bug. With no movies upcoming under his MGM pact, he and Gloria returned to Manhattan in 1958, where Shatner was slated to open in *The World of Suzie Wong* that October. In June of 1959, the couple finally bought their first house, a fifty-year-old, eight-room Victorian country home in the idyllic community of Hastings-on-Hudson, about twelve miles north of Manhattan on the Hudson River. To avoid the cost of hiring laborers, they painted the place themselves.

When he landed the role of **Captain Kirk** on *Star Trek*, Shatner had to move back to the west coast. The financial security of being the star of a network TV series no doubt influenced his choice, as he and Gloria opted for a home in the upscale Cheviot Hills section of Los Angeles, west of Beverly Hills and south of Century City.

One of Shatner's most interesting dwellings was the one that cost him the least. In 1969, following his divorce from **Gloria Rand**, Shatner scraped together enough money to make a down payment on a small home in Los Angeles. This was at the low point of Shatner's career, during his **lost years** when work was scarce, and he found himself with only $300 left over for furniture. It was enough—barely. Shatner scoured downtown L.A. for used and irregular pieces, such as a bed with a torn mattress that had come out of a damaged crate. Then, to economize even further, he simply used the crates as tables. Fortunately, he did not have to live in the house for long, or use the makeshift furniture much. He spent most of those years on the road pursuing work, and moved out of the house soon after marrying **Marcy Lafferty** in October 1973 in Brentwood, California.

The newlyweds soon moved into a two-bedroom ranch in Los Angeles' Hillcrest section in northern Glendale. It was an upgrade, if for nothing else than it had real furniture, but it also boasted a swimming pool. When Shatner's fortunes took an upswing in the 1980s, he and Marcy moved into a lavish mountaintop residence in Studio City in the San Fernando Valley. An oceanfront cottage in Malibu provided them with a cozy getaway spot as well.

While Shatner has been lucky with his own domiciles, he found his credibility tested when he tried to peddle homes to others. In 1997, he provided narration for a marketing video touting Lennar Realty Corporation's voice-operated Home of the Future. "If you're not living in Lennar's Home of the Future, you're living in the past," Shatner intones on the video, which promises prospective buyers a high-tech domicile complete with an electronic butler to respond to their every whim. Unfortunately, reality fell far short of fantasy, as ABC-TV's *Good Morning America* reported in January, 1998. Homeowners found the Home of the Future full of bugs that made everyday living an irritating, even dangerous, process. "Our dog would bark, it would make long-distance calls," one dissatisfied customer reported. "Stereos would blast in the middle of the night...it's like living with a poltergeist." The electronic butlers repeatedly ignored their masters' commands, or carried out the wrong commands. Promises of lower utility bills and a life free of inconvenience proved unrealized. "We thought we were buying the Jetsons, instead we got the Flintstones," groused one unlucky homeowner, who had put down nearly $200,000 for the high-tech money pit. "All they saw was a demo, and they saw William Shatner's video," explained *GMA* consumer correspondent Janice Lieberman, who cautioned against buying futuristic products sight unseen. The aggrieved homeowners filed a $5 million class action lawsuit against the Florida-based Lennar Corporation.

Hunter, Jeffrey (1925-1969)

This handsome actor was replaced by Shatner in the role of the commander of the Starship *Enterprise* on TV's **Star Trek** (1966–69). A Twentieth Century-Fox contract star in the 1950s (*Fourteen Hours*, 1951, *White Feather*, 1955, *The Searchers*, 1956, *No Down Payment*, 1957, etc.), Hunter made his screen name playing Jesus Christ in *King of Kings* (1961). Hunter was hired to be Captain Christopher Pike in the initial *Trek* pilot, "The Cage," shot in 1964. However, he soured on the idea of shooting a second pilot on the advice of his wife, who thought series television was definitely beneath him. **Star Trek** creator **Gene Roddenberry** briefly considered Jack Lord as his replacement (he later played Detective Steve McGarrett on TV's *Hawaii Five-O*, 1968–80), but finally settled on Shatner. The network, which found Hunter's style too wooden anyway, was pleased with the substitution. Footage of Hunter as Pike was later excised from "The Cage" and used as flashback material in the classic two-part *Star Trek* episode "The Menagerie" (November 17 and 24, 1966).

"He's dead, Captain January"

In making the transition from Hunter to Shatner, *Star Trek*'s TV producers also had to come up with a new name for their starship commander. Here is a list of the ones they considered, before settling on Kirk:

Boone	Hannibal	Patrick
Christopher	Hudson	Raintree
Drake	January	Richard
Flagg	Neville	Thorpe
Hamilton	North	Timber

IDIC Medal

The medallion designed by *Star Trek* creator **Gene Roddenberry** is offered for sale through his marketing company, Lincoln Enterprises. IDIC stands for "Infinite Diversity in Infinite Combinations." There were several different versions of the pendant put on the market at various times. One of the more common ones is a two-inch diameter medallion in twenty-two-karat goldplate and Florentine silver with a gemstone setting. A variety of earrings, keychains, and charms bearing the IDIC insignia have also been made available.

In 1968, Roddenberry wrote a scene in the *Trek* episode "Is There in Truth No Beauty?" (October 18, 1968) in which Captain Kirk presents one of the medallions to an *Enterprise* crewmember. However, Shatner refused to take part, claiming it demeaned the show to have its characters functioning as shills for the executive producer's products. In the end, Leonard Nimoy agreed to perform the scene instead. A few years later, Shatner chose to become a shill for a less benign product, **Promise margarine**, in a series of famous television commercials with his second wife **Marcy Lafferty**.

Impulse

See **Want a Ride, Little Girl?**

In Alien Hands

The second novel in Shatner's **Quest for Tomorrow** science-fiction series, this 1997 follow-up to **Delta Search** finds youthful Jim Endicott on the run from warring bands of intergalactic mercenaries. The character and place names—Korkal, Hunzza, Thargos, Brostach—sound like items on a Moroccan restaurant menu. Nevertheless, *Kirkus Reviews* labeled the book "agreeably inventive, well plotted, interestingly peopled, deftly paced and controlled: a quantum leap ahead for Shatner, following the abysmal **Man o'War**."

Incident on a Dark Street   RATING: U L

This two-hour 1973 television movie, made by Twentieth Century-Fox TV, features Shatner in a small role. It was the pilot for an abortive series about the inner workings of a U.S. Attorney's office. The telefeature also stars James Olson and David Canary. The plot concerns the murder of a low-level hood who is about to testify against an organized crime syndicate. In his role as Deaver Wallace, a U. S. Justice Department official investigating the situation, Shatner proves he is no Sherlock Holmes-type gumshoe.

Incubus   RATING:

This 1965 feature film, set in the mythical land of Nomen Tuum, has Shatner playing a decent man beset by evil demons. In his final pre-**Star Trek** theatrical feature, Shatner speaks dialogue written entirely in Esperanto, an international language developed in 1887.English subtitles aid those who opted for French as their foreign language in high school. The director, Leslie Stevens (1924–1998), creator of the classic sci-fi television series **The Outer Limits** (1963–65), as well as such other well-known TV series as *McCloud* (1970–77), which starred Dennis Weaver, and *It Takes a Thief* (1968–70), which headlined Robert Wagner, put up his own money to start the unusual movie project. Stevens hoped that, once started, he could win studio backing as he went along. One day in 1965, filmmaker Stevens brought an incomplete version of the movie to the Desilu Studios, in an attempt to convince *Star Trek*'s producers to provide the money to allow him to finish filming. An incredulous Herbert Solow, executive in charge of production, looked on as his newly-hired *Enterprise* captain walked through his paces parroting incomprehensible gibberish. When the lights finally came up, Stevens was quick to fill the void of silence, reminding the assembled executives that millions of people worldwide spoke Esperanto. Yes, Solow conceded, "there are 300 in Chicago, 100 in Spokane, 400 in London, 17 in Bakersfield—but not enough in any one city to even partially fill any one theater more than any one night." Needless to say, *Incubus* was completed without Desilu backing. It premiered in the U.S. to great hoopla at the 1966 San Francisco Film Festival, but has remained largely unseen.

> *"Why would* anyone *make a feature film in Esperanto?"*
> —Television executive HERBERT F. SOLOW,
> on SHATNER's movie *Incubus*

Indict and Convict   RATING: U U

On January 6, 1974, a mere three weeks after Shatner's previous TV movie, *Pioneer Woman*, the ABC-TV network aired his next offering. It was a courtroom drama starring George Grizzard, Eli Wallach, and Harry Guardino. Shatner appears as Sam Belden, a deputy district attorney working on a murder case. Eli "Mr. Freeze" Wallach plays a flamboyant defense lawyer. For nostalgic value, Myrna Loy plays the judge. Critics found little to like outside of courtroom verisimilitude.

Six Degrees of *Star Trek*
Arlene Martel (Ann Lansing) played T'Pring, Spock's betrothed, in the classic *Star Trek* Episode "Amok Time" (September 15, 1967).

Interracial kiss

Shatner and Nichelle Nichols shared network television's first interracial kiss on November 22, 1968. In the *Star Trek* episode "Plato's

Stepchildren," Kirk and his crew come under the dominion of the Platonians, a community of intergalactic faux Greeks with telekinetic power. In one hilarious scene after another, they force the **Star Trek** regulars—not to mention dwarf actor Michael Dunn—to perform degrading acts of musical comedy for their amusement. The torture session ends with Nurse Chapel (Majel Barrett) and Lieutenant Uhura (Nichelle Nichols) being compelled to lock lips with Spock and Kirk, respectively.

Not surprisingly, given the nature of network politics, the scene did not come off easily. The original script called for Spock to kiss Uhura, but Shatner protested—vehemently, according to some accounts. "If anybody's going to get to kiss Uhura, it's going to be me—I mean, Captain Kirk," he railed. Typically, Shatner took credit for the whole concept.

"I thought that it would be a good idea that Kirk, who was—who liked a lot of women—would be attracted to an obviously attractive woman, but also would hide it under the professional exterior of doing his job."

To inoculate themselves against a feared racist backlash, **Star Trek**'s writers made it crystal clear that both parties were being forced against their wills to kiss each other. They even filmed the TV series scene two ways—once with Kirk refusing to give in to the Platonians, power, and once with him succumbing. However, Shatner played the non-kissing version of the scene with deliberately crossed eyes and such a comically tortured delivery that the footage could not be used. Eventually, blooper reels surfaced with this take, as well as a loop of Shatner and **Nichelle Nichols** kissing over and over again.

"We did try some variations," Shatner said later. "There could have been a whole different story, if anybody had wanted to emphasize an interracial love story. But in fact, that wouldn't have made the point as effectively. Kirk and Uhura wouldn't even think of a kiss or a love story as interracial. That would be the *last* thing they would think about. If we did any good with that kiss or anything we did on **Star Trek**, it was to push in the direction of not having to think about that."

In the end, NBC's jitters proved unfounded. "Plato's Stepchildren" inspired an unprecedented flood of positive fan mail. The network received all of one complaining letter about the scene, from a self-described opponent of race-mixing from the South. However, even he conceded that "any time a red-blooded American boy like Captain Kirk gets a beautiful dame in his arms that looks like Uhura, he ain't gonna fight it."

Intruder, The   RATING: U U U

This black-and-white feature film is one of two socially relevant melo-dramas Shatner made in 1961 (the other is *The Explosive Generation*). Based on Charles Beaumont's 1959 novel, the plot has Shatner as villain-ous Adam Cramer, a racist rabble rouser who encourages the white citizens of a small southern town to terrorize blacks in response to the threats of integration. Later, he frames a young black man for rape but is undone by his own sexual appetites.

Shatner gives a lusty, impassioned performance in this Roger Corman-directed opus, which was shot inexpensively on location in Charleston, Missouri. Townsfolk reportedly did not take kindly to the film's depiction of them as race-baiting cracker trash. They refused to allow the crew to shoot in certain locations and repeatedly intimidated the cast. At one point, the state militia had to be called in to safeguard the production.

Nevertheless, Shatner gave his all to a movie whose message he clearly believed in, for a salary reported to be about $200 above his actual expenses. He was rewarded with a Best Actor Award at the 1962 International Peace Festival. The *Los Angeles Times* called *The Intruder* "the boldest, most realistic depiction of racial injustice ever shown in American films." Unfortunately, the movie's controversial subject matter scared away many potential distributors. Later, in the mid-1960s, it played under more sensational titles like *I Hate Your Guts!* and *Shame*, sometimes on a double bill with *Poor White Trash* (1957). Look fast for veteran fantasists Charles Beaumont, William Nolan, George Clayton Johnson, and Ocee Ritch (all of whom wrote for *The Twilight Zone*, 1959, 1962–65, 1986–87) in small roles.

Six Degrees of *Star Trek*

Playing the part of Phil West is George Clayton Johnson, a science fiction author who went on to write the first-season *Star Trek* episode "The Man Trap" (September 8, 1966).

It Didn't Have to Happen: Drinking and Driving

This gory 1994 educational documentary is narrated by Shatner. The nineteen-minute video features graphic recreations of fatal traffic accidents to hammer home its message about the inadvisability of drinking *and* driving. Shatner, at his stentorian best, also presents statistics and information on the scope of the problem.

Judgment at Nuremberg   RATING: U U U U

The 1961 roadshow black-and-white film about the Nuremberg war crimes trials features Shatner as part of an all-star ensemble. He plays Captain Byers, a military lawyer who assists the presiding judge (Spencer Tracy). Shatner has often retold a story about the day he complimented veteran actor Tracy on his ability to memorize pages and pages of dialogue. Tracy, who was sixty at the time, took the remark as a sarcastic comment about his age and refused to talk to Shatner for the duration of shooting.

Burt Lancaster, Maximilian Schell, Richard Widmark, Judy Garland, Marlene Dietrich, and Montgomery Clift also appeared in the prestige Stanley Kramer production. Werner ("I'm not a Nazi but I play one on TV") Klemperer (the son of famed German classical conductor Otto Klemperer) and a facially reconstructed Montgomery Clift add some levity to the grim proceedings. *Judgment at Nuremberg* won Academy Awards for Best Actor (Schell) and Best Adapted Screenplay and was nominated for nine others. Abby Mann based his 190-minute scenario on his April 16, 1959 teleplay for CBS-TV's *Playhouse 90*.

Junior Justice Connection Project

This California organization is designed to shepherd youthful offenders away from the juvenile justice system. Shatner donated considerable time and money to the project in the 1980s.

"JJCP takes kids that are not hardcore cases but are in trouble for one reason or another, and keeps them out of the arms of the law," Shatner told the *New York Daily News* in 1985. Professionals working with the JJCP range from physicians who remove insignia tattoos from former gang members to caregivers willing to provide halfway houses for juveniles coming from troubled families.

ON KARATE:

"How marvelous to be able to use your hands in such a manner that you can defend yourself and not be afraid of being hit in the face or being killed by some idiot in the streets."

Karate

The Asian art of self-defense teaches its users how to disable an attacker by using crippling hard, fast kicks and punches. Shatner first began to study karate in 1966 under the tutelage of Hollywood screenwriter and black belt expert Terry Bleecker, who was impressed with the work habits of his star pupil. "His discipline as an actor and his gift for total recall make him a prime student of karate," Bleecker remarked.

Despite such high praise, Shatner has always downplayed his skill at self-defense. "I want to be very clear about the karate," he said in 1979. "I'm not good at all . . . my ability in karate has been greatly exaggerated." By whom it had been exaggerated Shatner did not make clear, but he was positive he would like to become a karate expert, if only he could find the time. To be good at karate, he conceded, "requires a fanaticism which I just don't have the time to do [sic]."

For a while, anyway, Shatner's interest in karate *did* border on the fanatical. In the mid-1970s he became fascinated by martial arts movies, convinced that by studying them he could make his own onscreen fight scenes more believable. He drove his second wife **Marcy Lafferty** to distraction by dragging her to see the low-budget Hong Kong movie fightfests.

Kelley, DeForest (B. 1920)

This veteran American character actor plays the gruff but lovable Dr. Leonard "Bones" McCoy in the *Star Trek* television and film series. A fixture in Hollywood westerns (*Gunfight*, 1957, *Warlock*, 1959, *Johnny Reno*, 1966, etc.) since the late 1940s, Kelley at first seemed an odd choice to replace, first, John Hoyt, then, Paul Fix as the Starship *Enterprise's* intergalactic medicine man. However, **Gene Roddenberry's** casting hunch paid off. "Dee," as he was known around the set, brought a wry irascibility to the McCoy character that perfectly complemented the hot and cold styles of his coleads. That lukewarm water approach extended behind the scenes as well. "Kelley was very savvy in the ways of Hollywood," explained *Star Trek* bit player David L. Ross. "He went way back...Kelley had experienced the ups and downs of the business and banked his money. He was very careful and always gracious. He never took sides with either Shatner or [Leonard] Nimoy."

My Career's Dead, Jim

It sure seems like Shatner's *Star Trek* costars do a lot of yakking about his ego, doesn't it? Well, like your mom always said, consider the source. The supporting players haven't exactly built stellar careers in the ensuing decades, which may explain why they enjoy taking hacks at their more successful counterpart. Here are the lowlights of the post-Trek careers of some of Shatner's most vocal critics:

- James Doohan (lasted one season on the Saturday morning sci-fi embarrassment *Jason of Star Command*, 1979)

- Walter Koenig (starred in the execrable sci-fi bomb *Moontrap*, 1989) (However, he alone has been successfully transplanted for occasional appearances on another sci-fi series, *Babylon Five*, 1994–)

- Nichelle Nichols (released unlistenable album *Uhura Sings*, 1986)

- George Takei (helped design Los Angeles' abortive subway system, 1990s)

- Grace Lee Whitney (alleged drug and alcohol haze, 1968–1975)

Kentucky Dream

This saddlebred horse is owned by Shatner, and is the winner of the 1986 National Horse Show. Kentucky Dream was originally named Sinatra, but Shatner suggested a name change. "Kentucky Dream is just such a nice name," he told the *New York Times* in 1986. "It was an executive decision of mine, though I know everybody still calls him Sinatra behind my back." Shatner himself rode Kentucky Dream around the ring at Madison Square Garden in Manhattan the night he won the prestigious national prize. As is his preference, the actor wore traditional English-style riding apparel, including a bowler hat.

Khambatta, Persis (1950–1998)

Born in India, this beautiful actress/model played Lieutenant Ilia, the bald-headed Deltan navigator, in ***Star Trek: The Motion Picture*** (1979). The exotic-looking former Miss India got to keep her shaved pate (as originally designed for the part) in the film despite the objections of Paramount Pictures, the same folks who had found Spock's pointed ears "Satanic" in the late 1960s. While Shatner reportedly flirted with her mercilessly during production, he once called Khambatta a "stunningly bad actress," and gleefully retold a story about her needing nineteen takes to speak the single line, "No," Khambatta's Hollywood career sputtered thereafter. Her other credits include *Megaforce* (1982) and *Warrior of the Lost World* (1984). She died in August of 1998 from a heart attack.

Kidd, Nerine (B. 1959)

Shatner's third wife wed him in a ceremony at the Winterbourne Mansion in Pasadena, California, on November 15, 1997. A statuesque ex-model, Kidd is thirty years younger and several inches taller than the 5'8" Shatner. The couple met in 1993 while Shatner was still married to **Marcy Lafferty**. Their courtship included romantic trips to Europe and several canceled wedding ceremonies, reportedly because of Shatner's unwillingness to tie the matrimonial knot without a prenuptial agreement. (He was fleeced for a reported $26 million in his previous divorce case.) Over the course of 1997, however, Kidd wore down Shatner's resistance on this point and the two set a mid-November date at one of southern California's poshest mansions.

More than one hundred guests turned out for the affair, including **Leonard Nimoy**, who served as best man. Actors Kevin Pollack and Greg **"Jake Cardigan"** Evigan were also in attendance. A pouring rain forced the celebrants underneath an immense white tent, decorated in a fairy tale motif. There Judge Jack Tanner performed the ceremony, with wedding vows composed by the couple. The bride wore a sleeveless ivory satin gown, while Shatner donned a black tuxedo. The five-course menu included caviar, prawns, stuffed mushrooms, Lobster Newburg, and Dom Perignon champagne. Shatner refused to accept gifts, urging his guests to give the money to charitable causes instead. He did not place any such limitation on himself, however, as he presented his ecstatic bride with a gorgeous Tennessee walking horse as a token of his fealty. The freshly-minted couple cut into the three-tiered white wedding cake, then cut it up on the dance floor to the soulful strains of Leroy and the Do Got Band. Leaving their guests to revel without them, Shatner and Kidd then climbed into his black Mercedes and headed off to his estate in the Hollywood hills for the first stop on their honeymoon.

> *"She is my fountain of youth. Our age difference isn't a problem at all. Her love energizes me."*
>
> —SHATNER, about his third wife Nerine Kidd

Kidnapping of the President, The   RATING: ∪∪⟮

The 1980 feature film, based on Charles Templeton's novel (1975) is directed by George Mendeluk, and stars Shatner as intrepid Secret Service agent Jerry O'Connor. When President Hal Holbrook is snatched by Third World terrorists in Toronto, Shatner *must* find a way to rescue him from their armored car hideaway. Van Johnson appears as the vice president. A gruesome opening sequence featuring dismemberment in an Argentine jungle seems to bear no relation to the rest of the film. Electronic music was provided by someone—or something—called Nash the Slash. This R-rated thriller, which boasted a cameo by famed film star Ava Gardner (from the Golden Age of Hollywood), didn't last long in theaters and was quickly shunted to TV.

King

This is Captain Kirk's designation in Paramount's twenty-fifth anniversary *Star Trek* chess set in 1991. Dubbed "the chess set that transcends time and space," the novelty game board pits the *Enterprise* crew against a dream team of Klingons, Romulans, and assorted anti-Federation villains. "The battlefield is outer space," declared an ad which appeared in major magazines. The pieces were solid pewter. Kirk's opposing king is "Space Seed" ubermensch Khan Noonian Singh.

Those passionate fans who ordered the chess set were billed by the piece at $29.50 per month, for a total of thirty-two pieces, which comes to $944. The chessboard was thrown in for free. What a deal!

Kingdom of the Spiders   RATING: U U U

One of Shatner's finest cinematic accomplishments, this 1977 horror film was directed by John Cardos. It depicts the gruesome consequence of indiscriminate pesticide use, as ten thousand hungry tarantulas descend on an Arizona town when their food supply is destroyed by spraying.

A bewildered Shatner wonders what happened to his film career as he sleepwalks through Kingdom of the Spiders *(1977). [photo courtesy of The Everett Collection]*

As intrepid veterinarian "Rack" Hansen, Shatner must battle an army of voracious tarantulas in Kingdom of the Spiders *(1977). [photo courtesy of Photofest]*

Shatner's World of Pain

Does Shatner ever get the impression his directors don't like him? It wouldn't be surprising, considering how much agony they've put his characters through. Here are just some of the tribulations Shatner has had to endure on screen.

- Burned at the stake by angry Puritans (*The Devil's Rain*)
- Riddled with bullets during police ambush (*Big Bad Mama*)
- Crucified by Ernest Borgnine (*The Devil's Rain*)
- Overrun by voracious tarantulas (*Kingdom of the Spiders*)
- Melted in Satanic rainstorm (*The Devil's Rain*)
- Kicked off a catwalk by Malcolm McDowell (*Star Trek: Generations*)

Shatner plays Rack Hansen, a veterinarian who investigates the phenomenon. In 1989, he signed a deal to direct and star in a sequel, but after the
failure of *Star Trek V* (1989) the new spiders project never materialized.
His second wife, **Marcy Lafferty**, appears here under the name Marcy
Rafferty. This film is not to be confused with the inferior and Shatnerless
insect horror movie *Empire of the Ants*, also released in 1977.

Kirk, Captain James Tiberius

This role has proved to be Shatner's most indelible show business portrayal. He has said repeatedly that he modeled the commander of the
U.S.S. *Enterprise* after himself. "I utilize aspects I know about myself in
portraying Kirk," he once said, "and sometimes I discover things about
myself through Kirk." Kirk's middle name, Tiberius, was deliberately
chosen by Gene Roddenberry, *Star Trek*'s creator, to be the same as the
Roman Emperor Tiberius, who reigned from 14 to 37 A.D. Roddenberry
used this middle name before for one of his hero characters, William
Tiberius Rice, in the 1963–64 TV series, *The Lieutenant*.

In 1968, during his second season on *Star Trek*, Shatner discussed
the many similarities between himself and his creation. "I have a quick-
ness to anger," he said. "I am alternately cursed and blessed with this
quality which Kirk has also. I strive mightily to control it, as does
he.... Kirk has to control his feelings being in charge of 435 people. I,
too, have found that I have to disguise my emotions involving my private life on the set."

At first, Shatner did not realize the impact his portrayal had on a
generation of couch potatoes. Over the course of the 1970s, however, he
began to notice the strange reverence with which he was held by those
who grew up with *Star Trek*. One time late in the decade Shatner saw a
young woman wearing a Captain Kirk tee-shirt. "It's a bizarre feeling,"
Shatner joked, "to see your face on somebody's chest. Jiggling."

By the time he made *Star Trek II: The Wrath of Khan* in 1982,
Shatner was completely at ease with his big-screen alter ego. "When I
shave my sideburns to a point the first time I feel as if I'm drawing my
sword from its scabbard," he said shortly after the sequel's release.

Unlike Leonard Nimoy, who once titled an autobiography *I Am Not
Spock* (1975), Shatner wisely has never run away from his *Star Trek* char-

acter. "No matter how I felt about playing Kirk in the past, it was impossible not to feel sad," he said on the occasion of his on-camera death in the 1994 feature *Star Trek: Generations*. "So much fuss has been made over *Star Trek* and Kirk over the years that it felt funny to realize I'd never be playing him again."

In 1994, Shatner offered perhaps his most succinct epitaph for the intrepid starship commander. "Captain Kirk lived pretty much the way I wanted him to live. He was a distillation of all that I would like to be: heroic and romantic, forceful in battle and gentle in love, wise and profound. The ideal soldier/philosopher."

Shatner vs. Kirk: The Tale of the Tape

	SHATNER	KIRK
Birthdate	March 22, 1931	March 26, 2229
Sign	Aries	Aries
Place of Birth	Montreal, Quebec, Canada	Iowa
Citizenship	Canadian	Terran
Occupation	Actor/director/writer/producer	Starship captain
Height	5'9" (wears lifts)	6'
Weight	varies	159 lbs.
Hair	fake	light brown
Eyes	brown	hazel

Koenig, Walter (B. 1936)

This personable actor/writer played the part of Ensign Pavel Chekov on seasons two (1967–68) and three (1968–69) of TV's *Star Trek*. Koenig (pronounced KAY-nig) was a largely unknown quantity when **Gene Roddenberry** plucked him out of obscurity in 1967. Koenig was cast on the basis of his resemblance to diminutive Monkee Davy Jones. He was then asked to adopt a Russian accent to give the *Enterprise* crew more of an international flavor. Equipped with a moppish Beatle wig, he was positioned to appeal to the emerging youth audience.

The other cast members were initially upset at the newcomer's popularity, but eventually accepted him as part of the **Star Trek** family. Even Shatner was kind to Koenig, who in his early days on the show rarely followed his costars' lead in bashing the star. "He's a gentleman and a gentle man," Koenig once said of Shatner. "He tells very cool jokes and keeps everyone relaxed during the tensions of the day. It was Bill who helped me to develop the character of Chekov."

By the time of **Star Trek II: The Wrath of Kahn** movie (1982), however, Koenig had felt the full sting of Shatner's efforts to hog screen time and dominate the on-camera action. "Bill has a very strong sense of his value to **Star Trek**," Koenig told *Starlog* magazine, in what seemed like a calculated understatement, "and he explores and exploits it to its zenith. He will do whatever he can to make the picture better in terms of his performance. On the one hand, that's meritorious, but on the other hand, it may be at the sacrifice of the other performers." But like his fellow **seven dwarfs**, Koenig was loath to put his money where his mouth was. "At some juncture it was our responsibility to stand up [to Shatner]," he told *TV Guide* in 1998. "The fear was that we'd have our legs chopped off and find ourselves unemployed. But we never tested that." On the set of **Star Trek: Generations** in 1994, Koenig summed up his relationship with his "kyep-tin" this way: "He's not my pal, and there's no love lost between us. But he's not a monster." Not exactly a ringing endorsement.

Since the **Star Trek** movies, Koenig has resurfaced in another sci-fi television series, the syndicated *Babylon 5* (1994–98), in which he had the recurring part of a mind-reading officer in Earth's "Psi Corp" Intelligence Service.

Koko the Gorilla (B. 1971)

This world-famous mountain gorilla learned sign language from her keepers. Ever the daredevil, and always keen for publicity, Shatner got the chance to share a cage with the enormous ape—and nearly paid the ultimate price. "I got scared. The only thing I could think of was to say to Koko 'I love you, Koko.' Because I knew that if I said 'I love you' then I would start to feel 'I love you.' It's a simple actor's trick." Looking deep into Koko's eyes, Shatner began repeating this amorous mantra to the fearsome simian, whose body language seemed gradually to soften. Then, he told an interviewer, "she put her hand out…and grabbed me by the balls!" Koko has so far kept mum about the encounter.

Lafferty, Marcy (B. 1946)

Shatner's second wife married him in 1973, and divorced him in 1994. The daughter of television producer Perry Lafferty and radio performer Mary Frances Carden, Lafferty studied ballet in New York but abandoned the art when her family moved to Los Angeles. She graduated *cum laude* from the University of Southern California. Following a failed early marriage, she pursued an acting career.

Lafferty first met Shatner on the set of **The Andersonville Trial** TV movie in 1970, where she was working as director George C. Scott's assistant. "I was down on my luck," Lafferty remembered, "and George wanted a female—it was an all-male cast—to run lines with the actors. And Bill was the only one who wanted to turn lines with me because his part was bigger than Hamlet. And I fell in lust with him." At first, this lust went unrequited. Lafferty spent weeks ogling Shatner while he ran his lines, but had trouble grabbing his attention. "Then one day he started looking a little more," she explained. Or as Shatner put it, "I gave her my 'look.' And I reached out and kissed her." Various reports have Lafferty's knees buckling under the pressure of his

Shatner and second wife Marcy Lafferty arrive in London for the British premiere of Star Trek: The Motion Picture *(1979). [photo courtesy of AP Worldwide Photos]*

smoldering manhood. Two weeks after filming completed, Shatner called to ask her out on a date. At the time she had never seen a single *Star Trek* episode. The relationship quickly turned sexual. At first, Shatner resisted commitment. "Bill had just been through a terrible divorce and a folded series," she recalled later. "He didn't want to get involved." But the leggy, dark-haired beauty wore down his resistance. Shatner surprised Lafferty by proposing to her in July of 1973. They were married on October 20. At twenty-seven years old, she was fifteen years his junior.

The marriage ceremony was marked by a curious incident. "I heard a sob coming from someplace," Shatner reported. "I turned around—'who is that sobbing?' And it was *me. I* was sobbing." Whether Shatner was envisioning the enormity of the eventual divorce settlement of this failed marriage is unknown.

Lafferty supported Shatner through the most difficult period of his personal and professional life, the so-called **lost years**. While the period was difficult, Lafferty never gave up on her man. "I didn't stay because I knew I'd get the brass ring if I stayed," she said. "I stayed because I loved him—and it was just more good than not good."

Elsewhere Lafferty described her role in the marriage: "I make his life run as smoothly as possible, so he is free as an artist." Unfortunately, Shatner used that freedom to green light big screen stinkers like *Big Bad Mama* (1974) and *The Devil's Rain* (1975). The former featured three notorious **nude scenes** with Angie Dickinson, which Marcy claimed not to be bothered by at the time.

Marcy's tune began to change, however, when Shatner's real-life love affairs became increasingly public. Two **palimony** suits were filed against him in the early 1990s, by one-time personal assistant **Eva Marie Friedrick** and Mexican actress **Vira Montes**. Both lawsuits were settled out of court, but the sting of infidelity hit Marcy hard. She acceded to Shatner's requests for reconciliation at first, but when he began seeing future third wife **Nerine Kidd** in 1993, the marriage was over.

"Life took us apart and it was time to move on," was how Lafferty assessed their marital breakup. "We both share the highest regard for one another and our loved ones." In fact, Lafferty had such high regard for Shatner that she socked it to him in the subsequent divorce settlement to the tune of $8 million. Though bitter over this financial misadventure, Shatner took much of the blame for the marriage's failure.

> "She is essentially good, whereas I am not. Her essence is good, but I can be evil."
>
> —SHATNER, on second wife Marcy Lafferty

> "I think he is one of the greatest actors."
>
> —MARCY LAFFERTY, presumably on Shatner's ability as a stage, television, and movie performer

Land of No Return, The

RATING:

This low-budget 1978 disaster movie, directed by Kent Bateman, features Shatner and singer Mel Tormé. The "Velvet Fog" actually has a bigger role than Shatner, which gives you some idea of how Shatner's career was going at this point. The story concerns a circus plane that crash-lands in a snowbound wilderness in Utah. As Curt Benell, Shatner must battle captive animals unleashed by the crash and, then, rescue the plane crash survivors. Also known as *Snowman* and *Challenge to Survive*, *The Land of No Return* was filmed in 1975 and lay on the shelf marinating for three years before its unremarkable release.

Law of War, The

As a follow-up to **Man o' War** (1996), this second entry (1998) in Shatner's War book series again focuses on twenty-second century diplomat Benton Hawkes, who is now attempting to arrange a peace agreement between his homeland (Earth) and warring factions on Mars. When the bargaining sessions collapse, a harassed Hawkes must flee his enemies, who include unfriendly forces from both Earth and Mars. *Publishers Weekly* enthused: "One can hardly quarrel with Shatner's spritely pacing or abundant and well-handled action scenes..." The publication also wondered of the prolific author/actor: "Wherever does he find the time?"

Line Counting

The practice of counting up one's lines of dialogue in a script is usually used to compare one's total to the number of lines given to other actors in the project. Reportedly, Shatner was a notorious line counter on the set of TV's *Star Trek*. He was principally concerned that costar **Leonard Nimoy** should not receive more lines than he did. In his 1996 account of the tortured birth of his 1966 teleplay "The City on the Edge of Forever" (April 6, 1967), **Harlan Ellison** talks about Shatner line counting the script in his Hollywood home, then lobbying for rewrites when he discovered Spock had more lines than Kirk. (A corollary anecdote about Shatner's **toupee** falling off upon his arrival at Ellison's house has been relegated only for *Star Trek* convention audiences.)

Shatner's efforts to maximize his own screen time on the teleseries often affected the other cast members. For example, in her 1994 memoir *Beyond Uhura*, **Nichelle Nichols** (Lieutenant Uhura) explained how Shatner interrupted shooting of a scene in which her character had a significant part. "Later, when I scanned the revised script, my lines had been cut to 'I have Starfleet Command, sir,' before he and Spock took over." Nichols reports being furious over the incident, but it wasn't the first time she was a victim of Shatner's power plays. Even the performers' attempts to improvise fell under the star's domineering purview. As **George Takei** (Lieutenant Sulu) has explained, "Even if I tried to ad lib an entirely appropriate 'Aye, sir' to a command, he would nix it, claiming it would take away from the rhythm of the scene. This despite the fact that some of us had precious little to do in many of the scripts. Bill seemed totally immune to the sensitivities or the efforts of those he worked with."

Shatner claims to have remained oblivious to these complaints for many, many years. "I've always felt that the cast had a typical actor's sense of competition," he remarked to biographers in 1979. "We weren't saints, and we had actor's needs. But it was a good, healthy sense of competition, mostly focused on doing a good job, mostly good for the show."

Shatner's dialogue counting antics continued on the set of the first *Star Trek* movie in 1979. He even refused to feed lines off-camera to the other actors as they were being filmed for their closeups. "Bill was the reminder to me that coming back to *Star Trek* also meant coming back to nettlesome irritation," Takei observed in his autobiography *To the Stars!* (1994).

Liquor

An avowed teetotaler, Shatner nonetheless served as his fellow actors' official taster during his days as a struggling performer in Ontario, Canada. The actors were so poor they tried to make their own spirits, which Shatner then sampled for their degree of potency. "When I keeled over from the mixture, they knew it was ready for imbibing," Shatner, the drink-tester, recalled years later.

Literacy

Shatner saw his 1997 sci-fi novel **Delta Search** as a valiant effort to stem the tide of illiteracy, especially among teenagers. "My hope is that once people get started reading the book, they won't put it down," he told reporters in a conference call to promote the book. "I have been speaking to experts in the field of literacy, and they've found that the best way of hooking someone into reading is finding something that interests them." He went on to tell the story of an overweight teenage girl who refused to attend school. Every few hours, her mother, at work and feeling guilty about her daughter's plight, would have food delivered to the house. Naturally, this only resulted in the youngster becoming more bloated and listless.

"They were able to reach her by giving her a nutrition book," Shatner explained, "and the nutrition book became her Bible. She lost weight and learned to read and went to college and became a nutritionist."

Little Women   RATING: U U ᑌ

This lavish four-hour 1978 NBC-TV movie retold the Louisa May Alcott classic (1868) about three loving sisters growing up in the shadow of the Civil War. Shatner is on hand, accent and all, as Professor Frederick Bhaer, the husband of Jo March (Susan Dey), the central female character of the narrative. Dorothy McGuire, Greer Garson, Robert Young, Meredith Baxter Birney, Ann Dusenberry, and Eve Plumb—Jan Brady of TV's *The Brady Bunch* (1969–74)—also star. In the short-lived *Little Women* TV series (1979) that followed, David Ackroyd assumed

Shatner's role. For the definitive version of Alcott's classic, check out the 1933 film, starring Katharine Hepburn, Joan Bennett, Frances Dee, Jean Parker, Edna May Oliver, and Douglass Montgomery, with Paul Lukas as Professor Bhaer.

Six Degrees of *Star Trek*

William Schallert (Reverend March in the 1978 *Little Women* TV movie) played Nilz Barris in the *Star Trek* episode "The Trouble with Tribbles" (December 29, 1967). John DeLancie (Frank Vaughn in that same 1978 TV movie) went on to play the mischievous Q Entity on *Star Trek: The Next Generation* (1987–94), and on *Star Trek: Voyager* (1995–).

Live Television

Shatner enjoyed some of his finest moments as an actor in live performances during television's "Golden Age" in New York City. Among his memorable portrayals were the leader of a lynch mob in the *Playhouse 90* production **"A Town Has Turned to Dust"** (CBS-TV, June 19, 1958)

A smiling Shatner basks in the glow of early Hollywood success. [photo courtesy of Archive Photos]

and a virtuous western lawman in the *The U.S. Steel Hour* playlet "Old Marshals Never Die" (CBS-TV, August 13, 1958). "Live television is exciting, a true art form," Shatner once observed. "You are performing for an audience, an audience of one, the director."

There are many pitfalls to live television that keep an actor up at night worrying. Among these is the fear that he will freeze up under the hot lights and the enormity of the proceedings. This happened to Shatner *once*, during the performance of the CBS-TV *Studio One* two-part live drama "No Deadly Medicine" with Lee J. Cobb on December 9 and 12, 1957. Shatner was nonchalantly crossing the stage when, suddenly, it hit him: "My mind went, my God, there are 30 million people watching me walk," Shatner admitted to *Playboy* in 1989. For a brief moment, he found he could not move his limbs and had lost control of all motor functions. "I was asking 30 million people to suspend disbelief and assume that I was this person walking across the room." He quickly recovered and went on with the show.

There is one actor's nightmare to which Shatner has never fallen prey: forgetting his lines on live TV. He credits this to his uncanny ability to memorize dialogue. "I suppose I'm a quick study," he has said. "I think memorizing lines is a matter of confidence."

To illustrate this point, Shatner told a story about Bert Lahr (1895–1967), the comedic actor best known for his portrayal of the Cowardly Lion in *The Wizard of Oz* (1939). Shatner worked with Lahr on the live TV production of Jean Baptiste Moliere's classic *The School for Wives* in 1956. "He came to the first rehearsal with all his lines memorized, while the rest of us had barely cracked the book. But as rehearsals went on he began forgetting lines and by the last rehearsal he had to carry the script around with him. He had just choked up about the show."

Locklear, Heather (B. 1961)

Curvaceous blonde who played pert Officer Stacy Sheridan from 1982 to 1986 on Shatner's police drama series *T. J. Hooker* (ABC, later CBS). "The ultimate pinup," Shatner once dubbed the very sexy leading lady. He was similarly unequivocal in listing the actress's principal attributes. "Her skin, eyes, teeth, all exude health. She's the criterion by which the clean, sexy, athletic California blonde is measured." Unfortunately, Locklear did not hold Shatner in nearly so high esteem. "I think it's chauvinistic," she declared of the macho cop series after *People* magazine named it one of the ten Worst Shows for Women in 1984. "But that's probably because William Shatner's on it." Locklear admitted to feeling intimidated by her world-famous costar, whose monopoly on derring-do left little for her character *to* do. "When it's your show, you can't be wrong," said Locklear. "You wouldn't see Captain Kirk—I mean T. J. Hooker—doing something wrong. It kind of frustrates me, because I'm always wrong. He's supposed to be a hero, and heroes can't do anything wrong. Right? I always had at least one line, but I was so nervous I couldn't always get it out. I would get really nervous when Bill Shatner would talk to me."

At the same time she was filming *T. J. Hooker*, Locklear was playing the vixen Sammy Jo Dean on the hit TV nighttime drama *Dynasty* (1981–89). That series role helped make her an international sex symbol—something Shatner says he could see coming all along. "Heather never had any sense that she was beautiful," he noted in 1995. "She had no sense of her appeal. I think she knows she's desired by America now, though." Locklear is currently living out Shatner's prophecy as the beautiful calculating Amanda Woodward on FOX-TV's *Melrose Place* (1993–).

Los Angeles Pet Memorial Park

This celebrity pet cemetery (5608 Old Scandia Lane, Calabasas, CA 91302, telephone: 818-591-7037) is where Shatner had his beloved Doberman pinscher, China, laid to rest in 1988. "The Beauty Girl" is the inscription on the grave marker, which bears the likeness of the seven-year-old canine. Shatner had the dog buried in a secluded spot behind some shrubbery because, as he put it, "China always liked to spread out under the shade of a tree." Soon after China's interment, overzealous *Star Trek* fans began descending on the park looking for the last resting place of Captain Kirk's best friend. Officials at the renowned pet cemetery to the stars did not aid them in their search. China's neighbors in eternal slumber include Tori Spelling's pet poodle, Angel; Tony Orlando's beloved Yorkshire terrier, Bambi; and the ashes of game show host Bob Barker's family of cats.

Lost Years

Commonly accepted term for the period (1969–79) of Shatner's show business career between the cancellation of *Star Trek* and the premiere of *Star Trek: The Motion Picture* (1979). The bad decade was characterized by a steep personal and professional decline marked by insipid movie assignments, broken relationships, and erratic personal behavior. Catalysts for this descent include the death in 1967 of the actor's father, **Joseph Shatner**, the end of the TV *Star Trek*, and the dissolution of his marriage to **Gloria Rand**, both in 1969. Lowlights of this dark time include Shatner's nude love scenes with Angie Dickinson in *Big Bad Mama* (1974), his role as a perverted psycho killer in *Want a Ride, Little Girl* (1972), and his bizarre performance of Elton John's song **"Rocket Man"** at the 1978 Science Fiction Film Awards.

The worst part of the lost years seems to have been the stretch from 1969 to 1973, spanning the demise of his first marriage until his second wedding day. "There's a five-year period that I really don't remember," he says of this dead zone. "I'd meet people and have no recollection of their faces. There are women I knew and had abiding relationships with, who I have completely forgotten."

During this dismal span, the Los Angeles-based Shatner lived out of a camper shell hooked up to the back of a beat-up pickup truck. During summer months, when TV work was scarce, he hit the open road to seek out and explore strange new worlds of regional theater. Once, when he was parked outside a friend's house in Millburn, New Jersey, a small boy knocked on the door of his camper and asked for a tour of his "spaceship."

SO SAYETH SHATNER

ON HIS LOW-INCOME LOST YEARS:

"Somehow, I can't help but feel like the victim of some grand cosmic plan whose sole purpose is to kick the shit out of me."

Shatner obliged, showing the tyke such high-tech features as the transporter module (shower stall) and the control panel (stove range top).

What might have passed for romantic slumming at an earlier age was a living nightmare for the fortysomething Shatner. His meager income was quickly gobbled up by taxes, agents' fees, and alimony. At one point, he found he lacked the funds to cash a check for fifteen dollars. "I'd travel—two or three jobs in one day, if I could—just to make some money to get...[everything] together again. I became frantic, obsessed." By the end of the 1970s, he was reduced to appearing on TV game shows like *Tattletales*, *Celebrity Bowling*, and ***The $10,000 Pyramid*** to supplement the paltry $40 in annual residuals he then received for his ***Star Trek*** series work in the 1960s.

Ironically, it was Paramount Pictures, which steadfastly declared ***Star Trek*** as a loss despite its enormous popularity in reruns, that returned Shatner to national consciousness. The 1979 release ***Star Trek: The Motion Picture***, while an artistic disaster, resuscitated Shatner's moribund career and allowed him to give up much of the low caliber acting work that had sustained him during his long, lean period.

"I was insane the way an animal is insane, because I had lost my family, I'd lost everything, and I was scrambling, clawing to get everything back and put it together again."
—SHATNER, on his state of mind during the lost years

Man o' War

The first in Shatner's proposed series of science fiction books featuring dyspeptic diplomat Benton Hawkes, this novel was published in 1996. Borrowing elements from such revered sources as Ray Bradbury and Robert Heinlein, Shatner spins the tale of a human-settled Mars beset by labor squabbles and political machinations. The protagonist, a cranky middle-aged dog lover, seems like a stand-in for Shatner himself. *Kirkus Reviews* was not impressed: "Shatner will have to do better than stock situations, hackneyed plotting, and such ludicrous Trekkisms as spaceships with built-in gravity and instantaneous communications between Mars and Earth." Despite these objections, in early 1998, the Showtime cable network was developing a TV series based on the novel. The second book of the series, ***The Law of War***, was released in June of 1998.

Marriage

Shatner has been married three times: to **Gloria Rand** (née Rosenberg) from 1956 to 1969; to **Marcy Lafferty** from 1973 to 1994; and to current wife **Nerine Kidd** as of November 15, 1997. Each of his first two unions ended in divorce, with alleged charges of constructive abandonment and chronic philandering hurled Shatner's way. Nevertheless, he has remained committed to the idea of a permanent, monogamous relationship.

Addressing a **Star Trek** convention audience in Great Britain, Shatner could have been speaking of any of his marriages when he said: "A husband and wife live in a balance between humor and anger, ease and dis-ease. As with any relationship, there can be more positive or more negative elements. In my marriage there is tension, anger, and dissatisfaction."

Shatner and first wife Gloria Rand shared twelve happy years—but the thirteenth was unlucky. They divorced in 1969. [photo courtesy of The Everett Collection]

I Married Shatner!

Shatner's on-screen marriages have been every bit as unstable as his real-life relationships. In fact, divorce lawyers could have a field day with some of the problems that have bedeviled Shatner as a TV movie husband. Here are some of the more egregious examples of marital dysfunction:

Wife	Movie	Possible Cause for Divorce Action
Patty Duke Astin	*The Babysitter*	Daughter tormented by psycho sitter
Susan Blakely	*Broken Angel*	Daughter joins hedonist cult
Julie Adams	*Go Ask Alice*	Daughter gets hooked on LSD at unchaperoned party
Michelle Phillips	*Secrets of a Married Man*	Cheats on wife with succession of sleazy prostitutes

Matzo Kneidlach

These are traditional Passover dumplings, a recipe for which Shatner graciously submitted for *The Celebrity Kosher Cookbook* (New York: Parker, 1975). Apparently inspired by his grandmother's "tightly packed, indestructible and delicious kneidel," the recipe requires two separated eggs, three tablespoons of chicken fat, a half a cup of hot water, a quarter cup of matzo meal, salt, and two quarts of boiling broth or hot water. The egg yolks are beaten with the chicken fat until well blended and thick, and then poured over the hot water (or hot broth) and then well heated. The matzo meal with salt added next is folded into the egg whites and the resultant concoction chilled for about thirty minutes. Then the mix is shaped into small balls, dropped (gently) into the two quarts of boiling broth (or salted water) and covered. The heat is reduced and everything gets cooked gently for about twenty-five minutes. Shatner insists that the recipe should make about eighteen dumplings. A perfect must-have item for any picnic!

> *"To prevent rising beyond your station, [my grandmother] put a kneidel in your stomach. It made it very difficult to rise at all."*
> —SHATNER, on the effect of his grandmother's dumplings

McGill University

This is Shatner's alma mater. Founded in 1821, McGill is the oldest university in Montreal. Located on two campuses (the downtown campus and MacDonald campus), McGill today has over 30,000 enrolled students. For many decades, it has been a leader among Canadian universities in graduate studies and research. Shatner attended McGill's College of Commerce, majoring in business (not the long-rumored **dentistry**) from 1948 to 1952.

Shatner's years at McGill differed little from the typical collegian's experience. "I did very badly at the university. I never attended classes. I took notes from other people's notes, went to exams and barely passed exams." Despite his abysmal student record, the university saw fit in 1995 to rename the Student Union the **Shatner Building** in his honor.

Shatner did excel at one thing—acting. He put in long days on campus in pursuit of what was becoming his overriding passion. He wrote, produced, and directed college musicals, including his magnum opus, *The Red, White, and Blue Review* (1952), which received media coverage across Canada. In those days before the widespread availability of television, Shatner also served as president of the university's **radio** club, experience he used to land paying gigs acting on radio in Montreal.

Meaning of Life

Mr. Shatner explains it all:

"I've been preoccupied of late with the meaning of life and our existence," he expounded in 1967. "I've been thinking about the destruction of religious ideals that gave our lives larger meaning. Maybe the problem which faces many of us today is that we have no cause to live, or die, for. We all need some personal purpose, some goal, even if it's just learning to paint by numbers. I've tried to find challenges in my own life. My work is a daily challenge. I challenge myself with new skills, like motorcycling or tennis. The big challenge is to become a success as an actor."

Montes, Vira (B. 1959)

Mexican actress who filed a $6 million **palimony** suit against Shatner following a six-year love affair. Shatner met Montes (best known for playing Esperanza in the 1992 feature *American Me*) in 1984 when she appeared on an episode of his TV series *T. J. Hooker* (1982–86). He quickly began courting the raven-haired, twenty-five-year-old beauty, employing an unusual, but effective "mating" ritual, his customary tactic of rubbing his body up against hers during filming (a technique he used to less effect with costar **Heather Locklear**). A reported series of lunch and dinner dates followed, though Shatner was married at the time to **Marcy Lafferty**. Before long, Shatner and Montes were allegedly enjoying a torrid romance.

"I cannot believe what a fantastic lover he is," Montes once said of Shatner. "He makes me feel like no other man has made me feel. He is like no other man in my life, and nobody has ever had that effect on me. No one has ever handled me like Bill."

By the close of the decade, however, Vira was hands-off; the relationship had soured and was headed for litigation.

> *"We were in close quarters a lot, and strangely, Bill just kept bumping into me. He especially kept making sure our chests kept rubbing together. I was very attracted to him, and who wouldn't be?"*
> —VIRA MONTES, explaining how Shatner won her heart on the set of *T. J. Hooker*.

Motorcycles

Cycling in the southern California desert became a way to blow off steam for Shatner during his years (1966–69) on TV's ***Star Trek***. "He would go off on weekends and come back bruised and slashed," series costar Leonard Nimoy remembered. "He was forever running into tree branches and bramble bushes and God knows what else." When asked what had happened, an animated Shatner would report on his latest life-threatening wipe-out.

Shatner's boon companion on many of these outings was ***Star Trek*** bit player David L. Ross, a Kato Kaelin-like pal who happened to excel at many dangerous activities. "He was really a man's man," Ross said of his friend, "the kind of guy who does the macho thing for the pleasure of it—not to tell *Variety* all the time: 'Look what I did.'" Ross was present

Not-so-easy rider Shatner became famous for taking spills on his hog in the 1960s.
[photo courtesy of The Everett Collection]

for Shatner's first **scuba diving** excursion, and for one of his more embarrassing motorcycle moments. The two men were out riding in the desert one time with actor Gary Lockwood, who played glowing-eyed villain Gary Mitchell in the second **Star Trek** pilot, "Where No Man Has Gone Before" (September 22, 1966), when Shatner wiped out and landed backside-down on a cactus. It was embarrassing enough that his two friends had to pull the thorns from his bare rump, including one so big it had to be removed with pliers, but also, at just that moment, a couple of female hikers wandered on the scene. The incident caused the bleeding Shatner much consternation on his long walk back to town.

> *"William Shatner was much more macho than Steve McQueen ever was, but it was never publicized."*
> —DAVID L. ROSS, Shatner's motorcycling companion

Mountain Playhouse

This Montreal summer stock theatre (in Quebec, Canada) gave Shatner his first job out of college. He began working there in 1952 as the theatre's business manager, but quickly proved incompetent in that position. With little training in management and supervision, Shatner repeatedly mislaid receipts and lost tickets while incessantly lobbying for auditions with the theatre company. Eventually, the owners acquiesced, providing Shatner with his first break as an actor. He later relied on a professional reference from the Mountain Playhouse to secure a place with the **Canadian National Repertory Theatre**.

MTV Music Awards

Shatner has appeared twice on the annual music video awards program created by the cable TV network. In 1992, playing off the camp value of his hideous 1968 LP rock album *The Transformed Man*, Shatner performed, accompanied by xylophone and bongo drum, recitations of the lyrics of the songs nominated for an award. Shatner's overwrought take on "I Want to Sex You Up" was a surreal highlight. In 1996, he returned to the annual award show in a parody of the Brad Pitt thriller *Seven* (1995), playing three characters, including **Captain James T. Kirk**.

Mysteries of the Gods   RATING: U U

This static documentary (1977) is directed by Charles Romaine and narrated by Shatner. It examines the possibility of extraterrestrial visitations in Earth's distant past. Loosely based on the writings of Erich von Daniken, the film relies on interviews with scientists, UFOlogists, and clairvoyants to assess the "alien astronaut" theory of human religions, which purports to explain mankind's most sacred yearnings as the detritus of a close encounter between cavemen and spacemen way back in mankind's prehistory. Shatner himself subscribed to this crackpot theory at the time. The general level of the film's credibility is indicated by the presence of tele-psychic Jeanne Dixon among the interviewees.

Helping Shatner coordinate scientific interviews for the film was **Jesco von Puttkamer**, the NASA official who also served as a technical adviser on *Star Trek: The Motion Picture* (1979). In fact, Shatner prepared for *Mysteries of the Gods* while filming *Star Trek: The Motion Picture* and performing his **one-man show** *Star Traveler*. It was a truly brutal schedule. Explained von Puttkamer, "He learned the lines in three days, *while* we made the film. And he would joke, laugh, carry on a serious conversation, plan how to handle the interviews of scientists for the film—all at the same time."

Shatner tried to break the tension during what must have been a grueling period for him professionally by resorting to his old *Star Trek* standby—**practical jokes**. Von Puttkamer tells of one time when Shatner was interviewing him on camera about extraterrestrial life: "You have to be very tight, you know, for the interview, for the closeups—very close together—nose to nose. We had been working on it and I was not used to it. I was a little stiff or something. He wanted to loosen me up. All of a sudden Bill leaned forward and *he kissed me!*" The ensuing hysterics helped both men get through the scene more easily. Just goes to show that kissing will do it every time.

National Lampoon's Loaded Weapon I   RATING: U L

This painfully unfunny 1993 PG-13-rated feature film is a lame spoof of the *Lethal Weapon* action series (1987, 1989, 1992) that starred Mel Gibson and Danny Glover. Shatner plays deranged military man General Mortars. That name alone gives a strong clue to the prevailing level of humor in this screen farce. Emilio Estevez and Samuel L. Jackson are the unfortunate leads. **James Doohan** of *Star Trek* fame has a cameo as an espresso machine repairman. "William Shatner is allowed to ham it up disturbingly," wrote Lawrence Cohn in *Daily Variety*. Perhaps the reviewer was thinking of the scene in which Shatner sticks his face into an aquarium and pulls out a fish with his teeth.

Six Degrees of *Star Trek*

Whoopi Goldberg (Sergeant York in this poor excuse of a film) played Guinan, the clairvoyant barmaid, on *Star Trek: The Next Generation* (1988–94) and in the 1994 theatrical feature *Star Trek: Generations*.

Is There in Truth No Booty?

Shatner's own sexual appetites have been well-documented. But what of Captain Kirk's? He spread his space seed far and wide in the course of the *Enterprise*'s three-year televised mission. From the following list of twelve names, choose the episode characters Kirk had sex with—or we can reasonably assume he had sex with on screen, given the censorship constraints of the day. A few obvious red herrings have been thrown in to root out the poseurs among you.

A. Dr. Carolyn Palamas ("Who Mourns for Adonais?" 9/22/67)

B. Shana ("The Gamesters of Triskelion," 1/5/68)

C. Deela ("Wink of an Eye," 11/29/68)

D. Comdr. Matthew Decker ("The Doomsday Machine," 10/20/67)

E. Areel Shaw ("Court-Martial," 2/2/67)

F. Miranda Jones ("Is There in Truth No Beauty?" 10/18/68)

G. Reena ("Requiem for Methuselah," 2/14/69)

H. Roberta Lincoln ("Assignment: Earth," 3/29/68)

I. Hengist ("Wolf in the Fold," 12/22/67)

J. Gem the Empath ("The Empath," 12/6/68)

K. Balok ("The Corbomite Maneuver," 11/10/66)

L. Edith Keeler ("The City on the Edge of Forever," 4/6/67)

Answers on page 280

Newman, Paul (B. 1925)

This blue-eyed and guilelessly charming stage, TV, and film actor from Ohio has had a success that Shatner has often used as a measuring stick for his own multi-media career. Shatner lost out to Newman for the prize role of Brick in the 1958 MGM film version of Tennessee Williams' ***Cat on a Hot Tin Roof***, the start of a trend in which Shatner found himself shut out of movie projects in favor of more marketable actors (see *The World of Suzie Wong*). "As a star I was one step down from Paul Newman," Shatner told *TV Guide* in 1968, "a good actor, but not popular enough to bring in big audiences." Ironically, the two men worked together on the 1964 bomb *The Outrage*, a reworking of the 1950 Japanese classic film and its 1959 Broadway adaptation.

Nichols, Nichelle (B. 1933)

Leggy, beguiling African-American actress who played Lt. Nyota Uhura in the *Star Trek* TV and film series. An accomplished singer and dancer before her days on television, she brought to *Star Trek* a versatility that was not always fully utilized by the show's creators, or acknowledged by her costars. Nichols' most memorable contribution to *Star Trek* was one she shared with Shatner, providing television's first **interracial kiss** in the episode "Plato's Stepchildren" on November 22, 1968.

Born just outside Chicago, Nichols wrote a ballet for a musical suite by Duke Ellington at the age of sixteen. She later moved to New York, where she performed at the famed Blue Angel and the Playboy Club. In the early 1950s, she toured the United States, Canada, and Europe as a vocalist with the Duke Ellington and Lionel Hampton bands. Back on the West Coast, she appeared in such stage productions as *Roar of the Grease Paint, Smell of the Crowd*; *For My People*; and was acclaimed for her performance in James Baldwin's *Blues for Mr. Charlie*.

Nichols' debuted on television in a 1963 episode of *The Lieutenant* opposite Don Marshall, at a time when there were too few black faces on TV. The producer of that show, **Gene Roddenberry**, remembered her when he cast the role of Uhura three years later. She served as an important role model for many African-American women (including the future Whoopi Goldberg, who would later follow Nichols' trail to Roddenberry's universe as Guinan, the telepathic barmaid, on *Star Trek: The Next Generation* in 1988). However, the thankless part Nichols was given by *Star Trek*'s writers (check how many episodes her dialogue consists solely of the line, "Hailing frequencies open, sir") began to take its toll. At the end of the first season, Nichols seriously considered leaving the show, but was persuaded to stay on by no less a personage than Martin Luther King Jr., who feared the loss of such a prominent role model.

Over the years, Nichols' relationship with Shatner has occasionally been strained. In her 1994 memoir *Beyond Uhura*, she accused him of cutting her lines and general boorishness on the **Star Trek** set. In addition, the two were embroiled in a minor media controversy when Shatner used off-the-record discussions and out-of-context quotations as grist for his own book **Star Trek Memories** (1993).

Nichols has not been as unrelentingly critical of Shatner as, say, **Jimmy Doohan**, and she actually has some nice things to say about him. Principal among them is an anecdote about Shatner saving her from injury when she collapsed on the set of an early **Star Trek** episode as a result of a dizzy spell. "I remember seeing everyone on the bridge in slow motion as they turned toward me, then Bill Shatner looking at the director, then back at me, and then Captain Kirk leaping across the bridge toward me, screaming, 'Uhura!' then catching me in his arms with my head just inches from hitting the floor.... His behavior that day was totally in character with the Bill I would come to know and love during the first year of the series: warm, open, fun."

Her tell-all autobiography, *Beyond Uhura*, contains many anecdotes about their complicated relationship. Beyond the **Star Trek** TV series and subsequent big-screen **Star Trek** features, Nichols' screen work has been minor: *Truck Turner* (1974), *The Supernaturals* (1984), etc. She also hosted *Inside Space*, the science magazine on the Sci-Fi cable channel in 1992.

Nickname

According to David Alexander in his 1994 book, *Star Trek Creator, the Authorized Biography of Gene Roddenberry*, "Shatner...had a healthy opinion of himself, his talents, his place on the show, and his future in Hollywood. The crew quickly came up with a nickname—'Shat,' and it wasn't an affectionate shortening of his name."

Nimoy, Leonard (B. 1931)

This cerebral, saturnine actor has won an enormous cult following worldwide with his portrayal of Science Officer Spock on **Star Trek** (1966–69). The son of Ukrainian Jews who fled Europe during the Russian Revolution, Nimoy grew up in Boston idolizing actors Lon

Shatner and Nimoy don black tie for a public appearance in the 1980s. [photo courtesy of Archive Photos]

Chaney and Paul Muni. His early screen credits included the Grade Z science fiction turkey *Zombies of the Stratosphere* in 1952. He built a reputation playing Indians in low-budget westerns before joining the Starship *Enterprise* crew in 1966. In the years since TV's **Star Trek**, Nimoy has become an accomplished director, with the third and fourth **Trek** features and the comedy hit *Three Men and a Baby* (1987) to his credit. In 1998, he returned to the sci-fi genre as an actor in an expansive television production of Aldous Huxley's *Brave New World*.

Shatner and Nimoy first met while filming an episode of television's *The Man from U.N.C.L.E.*, "The Project Strigas Affair" (November 24, 1964). Previously, Nimoy's performance on TV's *The Lieutenant* (February 29, 1964) caught the attention of **Star Trek**'s brash young creator and producer, Gene Roddenberry, who subsequently cast him in the sci-fi series' first pilot as Mr. Spock. When the Starship *Enterprise*'s first captain, actor Jeffrey Hunter, bowed out on the advice of his wife, Shatner and Nimoy were aligned for a pairing that would change the face of television science fiction.

Nimoy remembers his first impressions of Shatner as being "[e]xtremely professional, extremely talented, extremely energetic, extremely communicative....I was very pleased because he had a very fine reputation as an actor and I felt that was a healthy sign about the possibilities [for the series]."

Despite their mutual respect, the two actors occasionally clashed on the series shot at the Desilu Studio in Hollywood. "We were extremely energetic and extremely aggressive about expressing our ideas and sometimes there was a conflict," Nimoy has said. Reportedly, Shatner resented the sacks of mail from adoring fans and feature coverage from the media that Nimoy received once his Spock character caught on with viewers. One day, that envy exploded into anger. A *Life* magazine camera crew had set up around Nimoy's makeup chair to photograph every step of the star's pointed-ear application process. Unluckily, Shatner was in the next chair having his hairpiece applied. "The top of his head was a lot of skin and a few little odd tufts of hair," coplayer **Jimmy Doohan** later recalled. "The mirrors on the makeup room walls were arranged so that we could all see the laying on of his rug." A simmering Shatner, dismayed that the secret of his **toupee** were being revealed to a national magazine audience, leapt from his chair, demanding that all future makeup sessions be held in his trailer.

"Bill Shatner's problem," scriptwriter Norman Spinrad (author of the **Star Trek** episode "The Doomsday Machine," October 20, 1967, and later a well-known sci-fi novelist) once observed, "was that he wasn't given as interesting a character to play as Nimoy was." Eventually, both men were dueling each other for lines, screen time, and character development on the series. The writers' attempts to mollify both actors' egos proved awkward and insufficient. The conflict reached its nadir midway through the first season (1966–67), when a despondent **Gene Roddenberry** turned to science fiction wise man **Isaac Asimov** for advice. The famed sci-fi author suggested that Roddenberry accentuate the closeness of the relationship between these two lead characters, thus making their byplay less argumentative and more believable. In the end, the show's costars settled into an uneasy truce. They even negotiated their contracts in concert with one another, including a **favored nations clause** ensured no benefit enjoyed by one would be denied to the other.

This practice carried on through the *Star Trek* movie series, and was used to secure directorial privileges for Shatner on *Star Trek V: The Final Frontier* (1989).

On a personal level, Shatner and Nimoy have little in common, outside of a shared love of fried egg sandwiches on rye bread. "I try to be diplomatic, but Leonard tends to be more forthright," says Shatner. "He's a very passionate guy," observes the taciturn Nimoy. "He plunges into stuff. . . . I like to tease him: 'Bill, why don't you do something with your life?'" In 1992, the two men took their Alphonse and Gaston act on the road for a series of joint appearances to commemorate *Star Trek*'s twenty-fifth anniversary. The eleven-city **Twenty-Five Year Mission Tour** played to sellout houses across America.

For all their differences, Shatner and Nimoy do share one dubious achievement. Both men recorded albums in the late 1960s that in more lucid decades became kitsch classics. Shatner's effort, *The Transformed Man*, is more ambitious. However, for sheer tone-deaf caterwauling, Nimoy's *The Way I Feel* (Dot Records, 1968)—containing renditions of "Proud Mary" and "If I Had a Hammer"—stands alone in the pantheon of self-deluded celebrity LPs. Nimoy is also the author of several books of poetry and prose, including *Warmed by Love* (1983), *I Am Not Spock* (1975), and the 1995 memoir *I Am Spock*.

> *"If his version of "Lucy in the Sky with Diamonds" is as good as mine, he should burn it."*
>
> —LEONARD NIMOY, on Shatner's singing career

911 Calls

Among Shatner's many quirks are two especially strange tendencies: a propensity to get involved in bizarre **traffic incidents** and to make calls to the dedicated emergency assistance line 911. While most people can go a lifetime without stumbling upon a life-threatening emergency, Shatner has done so on three documented occasions:

"I was doing theater in Philadelphia," he told *TV Guide* in 1989, "and one night, when the show was over, I was driving through the inner city, and I saw a man on top of something and the flash of a knife. Up ahead was a phone booth. I leapt out, dialed 911, then jumped back in my car, intending to help. It was a one-way street and, because we're all so regimented, instead of backing up, I drove around the block. I made three right turns. By the time I got back to the scene, there were two cop cars and they had the guy collared. He'd been trying to rape somebody and was holding a knife on her."

On another occasion, Shatner was walking on the beach in front of his Malibu, California, home when he came upon a pair of swimmers on the verge of drowning. He leapt into the sea to keep one of the bathers afloat while the other ran for 911 assistance.

Finally, in one incident that combined both his favorite hobbies, Shatner was witness to a serious traffic accident and immediately used his car phone to dial 911. His only difficulty came in convincing the ambulance dispatcher he really *was* William Shatner and not merely a prank caller.

In 1993, Shatner—by then having hosted the reality-based television series **Rescue 911** (1989-92) and a national spokesperson for safety—was himself the object of the attentions of an EMT (Emergency Medical Technician) when he was thrown from his startled horse, which then fell on top of him, at a charity equestrian show. "It wasn't like my television show," reported Shatner afterwards. "It was much messier." For more details, see **horses**.

> "It's a tragic thing to call 911 without it being serious."
> —SHATNER, in the *New York Post*, 1989

North Beach and Rawhide   RATING: U U

This two-hour CBS-TV movie (shown in two installments on November 12 and 13, 1985) stars Shatner as Rawhide McGregor, a Father Flanagan-type figure who operates a correctional ranch for wayward urban boys. Tate Donovan plays North Beach, a teen troublemaker whom Rawhide endeavors to rehabilitate. Chris Penn and Leo Penn—Sean's younger brother and actor/director dad respectively—and Ron O'Neal (the star of several black exploitation features such as 1972's *Superfly*) round out the adequate cast.

Shatner was not the original choice for Rawhide, the one-time convict turned do-gooder. However, when journeyman actor Frederic Forrest bowed out at the last minute, the ex-Captain Kirk leapt at the chance to act alongside so many beautiful horses. "We filmed in northern Los Angeles," Shatner told the *New York Daily News*. "It was a rare experience galloping across the land and sharing a unique experience with my horse, so unfettered and away from everybody. I love to ride!"

Nude Scenes

Shatner has done a number of scenes undressed over the course of his acting career. When he played Tom, a swinging tennis instructor, in the play *Remote Asylum* in 1971, he had to simulate sex with Anne Francis live on stage. "I had to reach an orgasm at the Ahmanson Theatre in Los Angeles, in front of 2,200 people, every night for six weeks. That was tough. Because how much do you reveal? Are you a screamer or aren't you?"

There was no such trepidation when it came to Shatner's most famous movie nude scenes, opposite Angie Dickinson in the 1974 "B" feature **Big Bad Mama**. "Angie is beautiful. She is luscious, sensuous, intelligent," Shatner enthused to *Playboy* in 1989. The pair appeared naked on three separate occasions in the low-budget action yarn. Dickinson, who at the time was a national sex symbol for her role as TV's *Police Woman* (1974–78),

A vigorous Star Trek-*era Shatner during the time when he eagerly took his shirt off for the camera. [photo courtesy of The Everett Collection]*

quickly overcame her fears of being filmed in the buff with the esteemed Captain Kirk. "Angie started the movie about two weeks before I did," Shatner reported. "When I came in, the first scene, of course, was the nude scene. So I got my body make-up on and wore my shorts under a kimono on the set. Angie was already there, in her dressing gown on the bed. I awkwardly took off my slippers and stepped out of my shorts and kept my robe clutched around me. That's when I noticed that her robe had spilled open a little and she wasn't wearing *any* shorts." Shatner's pubic hair is briefly visible in one of the scenes, photos from which were later published in adult men's magazines.

Thereafter, time was not kind to either performer. Dickinson employed a body double for her nude scenes in the 1987 sequel *Big Bad Mama II*, while Shatner had bloated so much by 1991 that he demanded that technicians airbrush his gargantuan behind in *Star Trek VI: The Undiscovered Country*. See **butt tightening**.

One-Man Shows

Shatner mounted a series of one-man stage performances in the 1970s under a variety of titles. Common elements of the performances included live readings from great literature, laser light shows, and a space travel theme. Occasionally, Shatner incorporated into the proceedings some of his own prose and poetry. He described one such ambitious early production as "a history of the imagination and how it's been limited by various forces like religion and science."

The early one-man shows were popular on college campuses and helped alert Shatner to the mushrooming phenomenon of **Star Trek** fandom. By the end of the 1970s, thanks largely to the interest generated by the as-yet-unreleased *Star Trek: The Motion Picture* (1979), Shatner's stage "evenings" had developed into multimillion dollar coliseum productions featuring the latest in laser-concert technology.

The 1976 national tour of *An Evening with William Shatner* featured recitations from the works of Shakespeare, Bertolt Brecht, Edmund Rostand, and H. G. Wells. It played at forty-five college campuses to audiences totaling more than 100,000 people! In 1978, Shatner took to the stage again with *Symphony of the Stars: Music from the Galaxies and Beyond*, this time with musical accompaniment from local philharmonic orchestras. In 1977, he reworked the material from this trek and performed it under the title *Star Traveler*. An album compiling material from Shatner's one-man shows was released in 1978 under the title **William Shatner: Live.**

Shatner was surprised by the level of comfort he felt performing in such a demanding acting setting. To his delight, he found he could apply his one-man show experience to ensemble acting as well. "I used to learn lines and leave them half-unlearned so that I could react," he said in 1978, "developing the role as I came onto the scene. But because I've had to learn in terms of monologues with no response, I've come to deal with concepts. In other words, I try to think of what the concept must be and how I can best effect it. So now I'm kind of amplifying my vision from what used to be learning a scene by words to kind of a larger picture."

So Sayeth Shatner

ON HIS ONE-MAN SHOWS:

"If I can do this show—if the audience lets me do my material—I can go even further than that. I take them on a trip. I do an extraordinary thing, if they'll let me do it."

Operation Lazarus

A code name for a covert military operation into Laos led by American soldiers in 1983, the sortie was partially funded by Shatner. This unsuccessful mission to rescue American prisoners-of-war caused an international incident and resulted in the deaths of three Laotian guerrillas. The tangled web of intrigue began, of all places, on the set of *T. J. Hooker* (1982–86), Shatner's ABC-TV police drama. There he met Bo Gritz, a self-promoting former Green Beret and itinerant mercenary. Shatner reportedly became fascinated by Gritz's life story and paid him $10,000 to develop a TV movie about himself for Paramount Pictures. "What he was going to do with the money was none of my business," Shatner said after the cause célèbre became public.

What Gritz did was to violate the U.S. Neutrality Act. Using an additional $35,000 from other sources, including funds from actor/director Clint Eastwood, he assembled a high-tech strike force and invaded Laos in Southeast Asia through neighboring Thailand. Hoping to free American servicemen who, he was convinced, were being held in a cave near the Mekong Delta, Gritz instead found himself ambushed and charged with illegal entry and arms possession. Bankrolling such an illegal operation could have earned Shatner a three-year jail term. However, he repeatedly denied all knowledge of Gritz's activities and was never charged with wrongdoing.

Outer Limits, The

In one of his final television performances prior to signing on as Captain Kirk in *Star Trek* (1966–69), Shatner played a beleaguered astronaut on the September 26, 1964 installment of this ABC-TV science fiction anthology series (1963–65). In thirty minutes, "Cold Hands, Warm Heart" spins the tale of Col. Jeff Barton, a space traveler who returns from a mission to Venus only to find himself mutating into a creature with scaly forearms, webbed fingers, and a low body temperature. The slow-moving script is not among the series' finest, but Shatner's intense portrayal makes the episode somewhat entertaining.

Six Degrees of *Star Trek*

Malachi Throne, later Commodore Mendez in "The Menagerie" (November 17 and 24, 1966), plays a doctor here; extra Larry Montaigne would go on to play Decius in "Balance of Terror" (December 15, 1966) and Stonn in "Amok Time" (September 15, 1967).

Outrage, The   RATING: U U L

This 1964 black-and-white MGM drama is directed by Martin Ritt. It features Shatner and **Paul Newman** in an allegorical tale dealing with "what is truth." Originally titled *Judgment in the Sun*, it's an ill-conceived western remake of the Akira Kurosawa classic *Rashomon* (1951, and winner of an Oscar as Best Foreign Language Picture). Shatner is cast as a timid, disillusioned clergyman. The *New York Times* found Shatner's supporting performance "callow and unsure." The badly-miscast Newman is even worse as a boisterous, drunken Mexican bandit. Laurence Harvey, Claire Bloom, and Edward G. Robinson round out the unlucky cast. The screen version was by Fay and Michael Kanin, who had written a 1959 Broadway adaptation of *Rashomon*, which featured Rod Steiger, Claire Bloom, Akim Tamiroff, Oscar Homolka, and Noel Willman (in the role Shatner handled on screen).

Six Degrees of *Star Trek*

Paul Fix, who plays an Indian here, went on to play Dr. Mark Piper in the second *Star Trek* pilot "Where No Man Has Gone Before" (September 22, 1966).

Owen Marshall, Counselor at Law   RATING: ∪ ∪

A 1971 ABC-TV movie made by Universal Television, it stars Arthur Hill in the title role, with Vera Miles, Shatner, Dana Wynters, and Tim Matheson in support. The two-hour picture was directed by Buzz Kulik. Dubbed "*Marcus Welby* with torts" by *Variety*, the film served as the pilot for a successful, critically well-liked, one-hour weekly ABC-TV series of the same name (1971–74). (To avoid confusion with the series, the TV movie was retitled *A Pattern of Morality* for future airings.) The plot for the made-for-television picture involves a hippie (Bruce Davison) falsely accused of murdering a well-to-do housewife. Shatner plays Dave Blankenship, the district attorney who prosecutes the case and comes up in court against the efficient Owen Marshall. Shatner played another prosecutor the previous year in the TV movie *The Andersonville Trial* (1970).

Palimony

Shatner has been the subject of two multimillion-dollar palimony suits by former lovers, both with whom he reportedly carried on affairs during his marriage (1973–94) to actress **Marcy Lafferty**. The first suit, filed in December of 1989 by his one-time personal assistant, **Eva Marie Friedrick**, sought $2 million in compensation based on alleged promises of jobs and acting roles Shatner had made to her while, reportedly, they were romancing. Friedrick claimed that Shatner dismissed her and disavowed their close relationship following her injury in an October 1988 car accident. "I was fired when he got tired of me," an incensed Friedrick later confided to a friend. While she was recovering from her injuries, Shatner reportedly had all of her personal belongings taken out of his Paramount studio trailer and left on its roof for her to retrieve.

A second palimony suit, filed in January 1990 by Mexican actress **Vira Montes**, sought a total of $6 million in damages from Shatner. The twenty-eight-year-old Montes, whom Shatner met and romanced on the set of his ABC-TV series *T. J. Hooker* in 1984, claimed she was suddenly rejected by the actor after an alleged six-year affair. During the purported relationship, Montes routinely had to pretend to be Shatner's niece while she accompanied him on such jaunts as ski weekends in Canada. Shatner even purchased a house for the aspiring starlet in the San Fernando Valley, near Los Angeles. For six years, Montes claimed, Shatner had been "materializing in her bed and then beaming back up to his wife."

Both palimony suits were settled out of court in 1992 for sums not disclosed to the public. In 1994, Marcy Lafferty filed for divorce, ending her twenty-year marriage to Shatner.

Panty hose

Shatner wore panty hose on the set of *Star Trek: Generations* (1994) and encouraged costar **Patrick Stewart** to do the same. The tight leggings helped ease the chafing caused by spending long days of filming on horseback. Ever the sensualist, Shatner prefers sheer panty hose, with a seam in the middle, for their aesthetic qualities.

SO SAYETH SHATNER

ON THE PLEASURES OF WEARING PANTY HOSE:

"It's a rather pleasant feeling, akin to scratching yourself all the time."

People, The
RATING: U U U

This ninety-minute TV movie (1972) was directed by John Korty, and starred Shatner, Kim Darby, Dan O'Herlihy, and Diane Varsi. Francis Ford Coppola served as executive producer for this ABC offering, which is based on the sci-fi novel *Pilgrimage: The Book of the People* (1961) by Zenna Henderson. The supernatural story concerns a community where parents and their children possess superhuman powers. Shatner is Dr. Curtis, the town physician. Carmine Coppola, the great director's father and an Oscar winner that year for *The Godfather* (1972), provided the score for this thriller. The telefeature boasts such special effects as children seemingly flying over houses and trees and was shot on location in Nicasio, California, located some thirty-five miles north of San Francisco.

Six Degrees of *Star Trek*
Kim Darby (Melodyne Amerson) previously worked with Shatner in the *Star Trek* episode "Miri" (October 27, 1966).

Perilous Voyage
RATING:

This 1976 NBC-TV movie, directed by William A. Goldman, was originally filmed in 1968. It features Shatner as a passenger on a hijacked cruise liner. As Steve Monroe, a high-living playboy, Shatner gets to act drunk for the first half of the hastily assembled picture, which also stars actor veterans Michael Parks, Lee Grant, Frank Silvera, Victor Jory, and Charles McGraw. The plot involves the takeover of the luxury ship by South American revolutionaries. The lackluster film remained in steerage for eight years before a reluctant NBC finally aired it on July 29, 1976. Its original title was *The Revolution of Antonio DeLeon.* Viva la revolution!

Tired of deep space, Shatner embarked on an undersea adventure in the TV movie Perilous Voyage *(1968). [photo courtesy of Photofest]*

Pettyjohn, Angelique (1943–1992)

This buxom actress played Shahna, Kirk's "drill thrall" in the memorable *Star Trek* episode "The Gamesters of Triskelion" (January 5, 1968). The pair shared a torrid love scene on screen, and for years had been romantically linked off camera by the *Trek* fandom rumor mill. However, Shatner apparently had trouble picking her out from among the many genetic oddities he seduced on camera during the series' three-year (1966–69) network TV run. "Was she the big-busted girl with the hair?" he queried *Playboy* in 1989. "I remember her." Pettyjohn—who also acted under the name Heaven St. John—later screen-tested for the role of Nova in the 1968 feature *Planet of the Apes*, coming perilously close to experiencing the rare privilege of costarring with both Shatner and Charlton Heston in the same lifetime.

Phone Controversy

Like the **high chair controversy**, the phone controversy was a "my perk is bigger than your perk" battle that broke out on the set of the *Star Trek* TV series. The competitive situation developed after episode directors complained about the amount of time Shatner spent monopolizing the one and only sound stage telephone. It wasn't entirely his fault; after all, he was in almost every scene, and needed some nearby place to conduct his personal business during working hours. A second phone soon was installed on the set, but Shatner soon found it convenient to keep this line open for his incoming calls. When series executive producer/creator **Gene Roddenberry** issued an edict banning *all* personal calls from the set, an enraged Shatner demanded that a phone be put in his dressing room. At that point, Herb Solow, the executive in charge of production for both Desilu Studios and Paramount, exploded.

"No!" Solow commanded. "If Bill Shatner gets a phone, then Leonard [Nimoy] wants a phone, De[Forest Kelley] wants a phone, Nichelle [Nichols] wants a phone, Jimmy [Doohan] wants a phone, George [Takei] wants a phone, Walter [Koenig] wants a phone, and Majel [Barrett] probably wants a phone." Solow went on to speculate about how the Shatner phone demand might impact other current Desilu TV series productions, such as *Mannix* and *Mission: Impossible*.

"The only Desilu actor on the lot who ever had a dressing room phone is Lucille Ball. And she owns the place!" In the end, Shatner abandoned his campaign for a dressing-room phone. However, he stopped speaking to Gene Roddenberry and continued to use the stage phones to everyone's consternation.

Shatner's avid use of telephones continued in the ensuing decades, through his promiscuous use of **911 calls**. In the 1990s, he endeavored to make dialing easier for others through his hawking of **pre-paid phone cards**.

Pioneer Woman   RATING: U U

Joanna Pettet plays the comely trailblazer in this 1973 ABC-TV movie set in the Wyoming Territory of 1867. Shatner is John Sergeant, Pettet's husband, who brings his family into the frontier country but is killed (off camera) soon thereafter. The film represented ABC's attempt to tap into the sensitive frontier atmosphere exhibited by the CBS-TV hit, *The Waltons* (1972–81). Shatner's on-camera daughter is played by Helen Hunt, later the star of TV's *Mad About You* (1992–) and an Oscar winner for 1997's *As Good As It Gets*. Filmed on location in Alberta, Manitoba, Canada, this was Shatner's fourth and final TV movie of 1973, his most prolific year in that medium.

Also, this was the fifth and last TV movie featuring Shatner to be helmed by respected director Buzz Kulik.

Policemen

Shatner has long been fascinated by policemen. He has played them on numerous occasions such as TV's ***T. J. Hooker*** (1982–86), narrated their exploits on the reality drama TV series ***Rescue 911*** (1989–92), and even invented the cop of the future in **Jake Cardigan**, the gumshoe hero of his 1990's ***TekWar*** book series. Shatner has even likened his most famous creation, **Captain James T. Kirk**, to an intergalactic *gendarme*.

Shatner's regard for cops may be reflected in his own high-energy, risk-taking lifestyle. "I think they're adrenaline junkies," he has said of society's "new centurions." "Very macho. I think a policeman has an overabundance of testosterone." His impressions then tend to drift off into a litany of "me Tarzan" ramblings of the kind inspired by his reading of anthropological theorist **Robert Ardrey**. "They're the hunters," Shatner observed. "You know, bop the prey on the head and drag it home for you to eat."

Practical Jokes

Shatner was and is an inveterate prankster. As a child, he loved to show up unexpectedly at his sisters' birthday parties, turn off the lights, and tell ghost stories. On Halloween, he had two standard tricks. In the first, he put a coin at the end of a string and left it on a person's doorstep. After ringing the bell, he waited in the bushes for the poor pigeon to emerge. When the person bent down to pick up the coin, Shatner pulled the string, luring his quarry away from the door. An accomplice would then dump a bucket of water on top of the unsuspecting homeowner. In another, less creative gag, Shatner would simply shoot pellets of red paint at his victim, causing them to think they, indeed, had been shot.

Shatner's passion for practical jokes continued on the set of TV's *Star Trek*. Perhaps his most famous prank involved costar **Leonard Nimoy**'s red bicycle. The contemplative actor had acquired the bike to pedal back and forth to the Desilu studio commissary during breaks in shooting. Before long, Shatner became obsessed with it, bent on taking it, hiding it, suspending it from the ceiling, doing whatever he could to keep it out of Nimoy's hands. At one point, Shatner had the vehicle hidden in his trailer, with Morgan, one of his legion of Doberman dogs standing guard over it. An exasperated Nimoy eventually had to lock the bike in his Buick to keep it away from his costar. Even at that, Shatner simply had Mr. Spock's car towed away. Nimoy quickly realized his only recourse was to sink to Shatner's boyish level. So, one day, he put a bucket containing Shatner's body makeup into a refrigerator. When the ice cold concoction was then slathered all over the bare skin of the unsuspecting Shatner, Captain Kirk howled in consternation.

Pray for the Wildcats   RATING: U U

This 1974 ABC-TV two-hour movie offers Shatner as Warren Summerfield, one of three advertising executives who are challenged by no-nonsense businessman Andy Griffith to accompany him on a wild motorcycle ride through the Mexican Baja. Marjoe Gortner and Robert Reed play the other two ad men. To no one's surprise, the trip takes a deadly turn. Also in the cast are Angie Dickinson (Shatner's costar in the same year's **Big Bad Mama**) and Lorraine Gary (of the *Jaws* film series). They play, respectively, Reed's and Shatner's on-screen spouses.

Pre-paid phone cards

Shatner has twice lent his services to companies promoting collectible telephone calling cards, first for struggling long-distance challenger MCI, then for telecommunications behemoth AT&T.

In December of 1994, Shatner and fellow **Star Trek** captain **Patrick Stewart** (of *Star Trek: The Next Generation*, 1987–94) teamed up for a series of live conference calls with 12,000 fans. Well-heeled Trekkers forked over $100 for a phone card bearing the commanders' likenesses, while a lucky few were selected at random to lob soft questions at the actors, who were handsomely paid for their brief efforts.

In 1998, Shatner joined with AT&T to promote a line of pre-paid phone cards featuring **Star Trek** characters. Captain Kirk himself appears on the first of the four collectible phone cards, with favorites from the other *Trek* TV series on the remaining three. "After more than 30 years of four TV series and eight movies, **Star Trek** has become an institution," Shatner remarked at a press conference in New York to introduce the cards. "I'm excited about teaming up with another great American institution like AT&T to offer fans a colorful collectible item that's also very practical." With the issuance of these cards, AT&T became the official prepaid card provider for **Star Trek**.

Priceline

This airline ticket purchasing service currently (1998) has Shatner as a celebrity spokesperson. Priceline (http://www.priceline.com) allows travelers to name their own price for airline tickets. The carriers then locate a flight and time that matches the customer's specified price. "This could be *big*!" Shatner intoned in radio ads for the service, a sound byte that will no doubt be sampled out of context in countless ribald permutations for years and years to come.

Book Another Flight, Shatner's on the Plane

Next time you're traveling, check the seat next to you for a burly sixty-something man with a curiously full head of hair. It could be Shatner, and that spells danger for your flight/cruise/train ride. Because on screen, wherever Shatner goes, disaster follows, as this handy chart indicates.

Opus	Shatner Role	Disaster
Twilight Zone: "Nightmare at 20,000 Feet"	Jittery airline passenger	Gremlin on wing causes near-fatal crash
Horror at 37,000 Feet	Jittery airline passenger	Ghosts in cargo hold attack passengers
Perilous Voyage	Drunken cruise ship passenger	Ship is hijacked by South American revolutionaries
Disaster on the Coastliner	Con man on board high-speed train	Demented engineer sets train on collision course

Amazingly, in two other TV movies, *Sole Survivor* and *The Crash of Flight 401*, Shatner is hired to investigate the cause of airplane crashes. Hmmm, maybe they should have checked the flight manifest for his name.

Prisoner of Zenda, Inc.   RATING: U L

This 1996 television film is loosely based on the classic adventure novel *The Prisoner of Zenda* (1894) by Anthony Hope, with more than a passing nod to Mark Twain's *The Prince and the Pauper* (1882). In this updated version Shatner plays Michael Gatewick, an evil executive seeking control of a computer firm. He kidnaps his own nephew and replaces him with a perfect lookalike, a visiting high school baseball champ. The impostor goes along with the scheme because Shatner has promised his father a job. Later released to video under the title *Double Play*, the fanciful 107-minute movie took a pasting from critics, though Shatner was credited with providing camp value to the project. "The plump Shatner mesmerizes," observed a reviewer for *Entertainment Weekly*, adding that his bushy false mustache made him look like Teddy Roosevelt. "Too bad the only double he has is a chin."

Producing

Repeatedly frustrated in his ability to play meaningful parts in quality screen projects, ambitious Shatner has at times tried to produce his own work. In the mid-1960s he formed Lemli Productions (named after his daughters Leslie, Melanie, and Lisabeth) in hopes of attracting socially relevant screenplays in which he could star. However, while he had no trouble locating screenwriters willing to sell him their moldering scripts, Shatner found himself stonewalled by the major studios when he requested money to bankroll such productions.

During the **Star Trek** TV years of the late 1960s, Shatner used his popularity to attract attention to a number of pet projects including *Where I Stand: The Record of a Reckless Man*, the life story of newspaper mogul Hank Greenspun, and *The Twisted Night*, a screenplay by veteran fantasist Jerry Sohl. Shatner even tried to get a green light for a script about the Vietnam War, but was told by studio executives the subject was box-office poison.

"Half the job of producing a picture is getting the property and its ingredients," Shatner once observed. "From then on, it's a matter of coagulating the elements." The victim of the monetary equivalent of a blood clot, Shatner eventually threw up his hands and quit the producing business entirely. It was only after he returned to prominence as a result of the successful **Star Trek** film series in the 1980s that he found himself able to coagulate—er, produce—successfully. "There were three companies vying for **TekWar**," he said of the 1994 cable TV series based on his science fiction novels. "That had never happened [before]....I had spent a lifetime trying to get a project of my own going."

By the end of this decade, Shatner has become an international wheeler dealer, thanks to the overseas syndication market. He sold the rights to his **Quest for Tomorrow** novel series (1997 onward) to the British production company Cloud 9 in 1998, and plans to develop other TV shows with it as well. "The global side of the business is very attractive," Shatner enthused to the *Hollywood Reporter* in 1998. "To be able to syndicate worldwide and save the U.S. syndication market as a plum and still show a profit is an enormous step forward." For someone who couldn't cash a $15 check in the early 1970s, it certainly was!

> *"Major studios, which have again and again evinced their interest in young blood because the old blood is dying of old age, have made it almost impossible for young blood to get into that activity."*
> —SHATNER, on the plight of the independent film producer in Hollywood

Promise margarine

This oleaginous breakfast spread was pitched by Shatner and his then-wife, **Marcy Lafferty**, in a series of television commercials in the 1970s. In an interview for NBC-TV's *Today Show*, host Jane Pauley asked Shatner whether it was demeaning for Captain Kirk to be shilling butter substitutes. "For Captain Kirk, maybe, but for William Shatner it was perfectly feasible," replied the obviously irritated actor.

Protectors, The

Proposed title for the series that became ABC-TV's *T. J. Hooker* (1982–86).

Puberty

A unique specimen in all respects, Shatner not surprisingly claims to have had a most untypical puberty. "I never went through that off-put-ness, that adolescent, awkward puberty," he once told biographers. Shatner also claims he never suffered from acne, but had trouble attracting the opposite sex. "I never fulfilled that adolescent dream," he has said. A dream, one assumes, of the soil-the-sheets variety. "I think there must be inside me a sense of unworthiness—that brings me up short, many times—so that whatever physical attributes people think I have, I don't see."

I Heartily Endorse This [Product or Service]

In a 1980 *Today Show* appearance, Shatner tartly reprimanded hostess Jane Pauley for casting aspersions on his hawking of Promise margarine. Little did Pauley know that her interview guest was about to embark on a two-decade odyssey of televised shilling. Here are just a few of the products Shatner has done commercials for in recent years:

1980: Wishbone Salad Dressing
1981: Commodore Computers
1984: The Olympics
1986: Western Airlines
1987: U.S. Open Tennis Tournament
1988: Oldsmobile (with daughter Melanie)
1990: The Sierra Club
1991: Guide Dogs for the Blind
1993: MCI Friends and Family (with *Star Trek* costars)
1993: PSA (Public Service Announcement) promoting AIDS Awareness
1994: Tournament of Roses Parade on KTLA-TV in Los Angeles
1994: The Winter Olympics
1998: AT&T
1998: Priceline

Quest for Tomorrow

This series of novels has been penned by Shatner with the assistance of writer Bill Quick. The *Quest for Tomorrow* books, beginning with 1997's *Delta Search*, chronicle the adventures of teenager Jim Endicott, who carries in his DNA the secret of transforming the human race into a powerful organic supercomputer.

In 1998, Shatner struck a deal with Great Britain's Cloud 9 production group to develop the novels for television. Cloud 9 agreed to make a two-hour feature film that would introduce a new syndicated series for the small screen. Cloud 9 planned to produce the show in English, then dub it into other languages for sale in the lucrative international market. Shatner promised to devote all of his talents to the new project. "I will produce and direct and if need be will act in a small capacity," he told the *Hollywood Reporter*. Shatner became involved with Cloud 9 while working on another syndicated project, **William Shatner's A Twist in the Tale**.

Racial stereotypes

Like many actors who gained their professional start in the 1950s, Shatner has played his share of racial caricatures. His gallery of offensive portrayals includes a full-blooded Comanche in the 1968 Spanish-lensed feature **White Comanche** and a **Burmese sailor** in a notorious episode of *The Naked City* (*"Without Stick or Sword"*—March 28, 1962). However, unlike many performers who outgrew the slanted eyes and pidgin English approach by the mid-1960s, Shatner's heavy-handed manner of portraying ethnic characters continued even into the politically correct 1990s. It is especially apparent in his reading of an abridged book-on-tape version of his 1991 novel **TekLords**. Keith DeCandido, in his review of the tape in *Library Journal*, said, "Shatner's range of voices is limited: his female voices are unconvincing, his rendering of Japanese characters border on the offensive, he uses a third-rate Speedy Gonzalez voice for Cardigan's partner, Sid Gomez. This abridgement ... is actively awful."

> *"I love to see the variations in people and things. I love the variations in skin tone and characteristics, and the slant of the eye and the color of the skin. Diversity is the magic of the world."*
> —SHATNER, on the manifold variety of humanity

Radio

Shatner has done occasional parts on radio over the years. In fact, one of his first regular acting gigs was with the Montreal Radio Fairytale Theatre, for which he started performing at the tender age of ten in 1941. For three years, Shatner acted out the roles of such famous fairy tale heroes as Prince Charming for broadcast by the Canadian Broadcasting Corporation (CBC).

During his college days (1948–52) at **McGill University**, Shatner worked as a radio announcer for the CBC. He not only gained valuable experience, but also earned enough to pay for his college books and fees.

In November of 1997, Shatner made a return to radio when he played the part of the Martian king in a televised live reading in Los Angeles of H. G. Wells' *First Men in the Moon*, featuring an all–*Star Trek* cast.

Ralke, Don (B. CIRCA 1930S)

Born in Battle Creek, Michigan, this prolific composer, arranger, and record producer arranged and produced Shatner's 1968 album *The Transformed Man*. Known for working with celebrity singers, Ralke was a veteran of the Hollywood studio system with a twenty-five-year background in films, television, and pop recordings. He convinced Shatner to eschew singing in favor of talking song lyrics over a musical background, much like Rex Harrison did on stage for his role in the musical *My Fair Lady* (1956–1964). Ralke's other golden throat credits include *Ringo* (1964), the lone album from Lorne Greene, patriarch Ben Cartwright on TV's beloved series *Bonanza* (1959–72).

Rand, Gloria (B. 1932)

Shatner's first wife, a Canadian actress, was born Gloria Rosenberg. The couple were married from 1956 until 1969 and produced three daughters: **Leslie Carol** in 1958, **Lisabeth Mary** in 1961, and **Melanie Ann** in 1964.

Shatner met Rand in January 1956 while he was appearing on Broadway in *Tamburlaine the Great*. At the time, Rand was struggling to find work as an actress. Smitten with the pretty blonde, Shatner arranged for her to join him in Toronto on the set of *Dreams*, a CBC television drama he had written and in which he was starring. Romance blossomed, and they were married on August 12, 1956. The newlyweds honeymooned in Scotland, where Shatner was appearing in the Edinburgh Festival's production of Shakespeare's *Henry V.*

Curiously, while Rand went out of her way to accompany her new husband wherever his budding career took him, he did not return the favor. Late in 1956, Rand secured a featured role as the Player Queen in the **Stratford** (Ontario, Canada) **Shakespeare Festival** production of

Shatner shares a happy moment on his hog with wife Gloria Rand and daughters Leslie, Lisabeth, and Melanie. [photo courtesy of Archive Photos]

Hamlet. However, she gave up what may have been her big break when Shatner chose to move to New York to pursue TV and stage roles. "I'm the breadwinner," Shatner later reasoned about such matters. "And it's just perforce that [my wife] must come with me if I go on location."

By 1967, however, Shatner did not want the company. He flew to Spain without his family and spent three months filming the cheesy western **White Comanche**. Gloria never forgave him and they separated shortly after his return to the United States. Several attempts at reconciliation failed, and they split for good in March of 1969. In the divorce proceeding, Rand cited Shatner for keeping irregular hours and spending too much time away from home. In the ensuing divorce settlement, she received their home, alimony, child support, and half of their other assets. The breakup hit Shatner hard. "Working as I did," he admitted to *TV Guide*, "not a day off in three years, I never realized how dependent I was on my wife and children. It brought on a whole new sense of aloneness."

Rehearsal Table

This command center was established by Shatner for emergency rewrites and script conferences on the set of TV's **Star Trek**. Located outside his dressing room, the Rehearsal Table was more often than not the cemetery where the lines of supporting cast members were laid to rest. "Every time you would hear 'Cut. Print,' you'd have these guys under Bill's command rushing over to the table to work on the next scene," recalls episode director Joe Pevney. Shatner used these conferences to maximize his own dialogue at the expense of the rest of the cast. It got to be such an infringement on the director's function that Pevney refused to work on the show. "When you're doing television in five or six days," Pevney complained, "there's no time for this constant rehearsal—with pencils in hand making changes.... It destroys the disciplinary control of the director."

Rescue 911

This reality-based rescue program on CBS-TV was hosted by Shatner from 1989 to 1992. *Rescue 911* featured actual recordings of emergency phone calls and film of real-life police, paramedics, and rescue workers in hectic action. The hour-long information show premiered as a series of specials in April of 1989 and quickly caught on with viewers. It began its weekly outings on September 5, 1989. Two years later, it was airing in forty-five countries and had inspired—heaven help us—numerous international imitations.

Shatner claims he was attracted to the concept because of its potential for drama. "It has two things going for it," he told the *New York Post* in 1989. "It rips your head off with excitement. You hear the real telephone call, see the news footage and watch the harrowing things that are happening in front of you. And it serves a purpose by showing what a 911 call does. It's useful information." Shatner's own propensity for making **911 calls**—and bragging to the media about it—may have something to do with this interesting career choice as well.

Shatner prepared for his portentous voice-over narration by visiting a real-life 911 dispatch center. "I am fascinated by the whole machinery of civilization taking care of itself," he told the *Washington Post* in 1991.

"I've learned how it all works, from the time somebody in dire need calls up. **Policemen** in their hours of boredom and their moments of terror, or firemen and doctors for that matter, intrigue me."

"*Rescue 911* is something I'm extremely proud of," Shatner has acknowledged. He claims the show has helped save over three hundred lives since it debuted. Certainly it saved its host's television career in the 1990s. As a result of *Rescue 911*'s success, Shatner has become something of an itinerant spokesperson for safety and first aid. His face has appeared on the cover of the National

Shatner mans the barricades as America's guardian of public safety on Rescue 911 *(1989-92). [photo courtesy of The Everett Collection]*

Safety Council's *First Aid Handbook*, and he has hosted such reality-based videotapes as **Ultimate Survivors** (1991) and **It Didn't Have To Happen: Drinking and Driving** (1994).

> "*Rescue 911 is to me the best show on television. It makes me laugh and cry more than any other show on the air.*"
> —SHATNER, on his reality television program *Rescue 911*

Return, The

This 1997 **Star Trek** novel, written by Shatner, once again features a resurrected Captain James T. Kirk. This time it's a coalition of Borg and Romulan forces who bring the deceased spacefarer back from the beyond in a cynical plot to destroy *Enterprise* Captain Jean-Luc Picard. Spock, McCoy, Data, and Riker also appear in the fast-paced novel, which like **Avenger** blends the fictional universes of the original *Star Trek* (1966–69) and its syndicated TV follow-up, *Star Trek: The Next Generation* (1987–94).

Riel

This late 1970s Canadian Broadcasting Corporation television feature tells the tale of Louis Riel (played by Raymond Cloutier), the half-French, half-Indian Canadian nineteenth-century rebel leader. The lumbering historical drama, directed by George Bloomfield, follows Riel through his battles against the Canadian federal government, which finally resulted in 1873 in the creation of the province of Manitoba. Christopher Plummer (as Canada's first prime minister), Arthur Hill, and Leslie Nielsen were featured. Shatner had the supporting role of the Canadian army officer who tracks down Riel. Variety rated the effort as "half-baked, clogged with an abundance of declamatory speeches, passed off as normal conversation," and complained that it was "sloppy technically." Shown in two ninety-minute segments on the CBC in May 1979, the project, begun in 1975, was later edited into a 150-minute video cassette version.

Six Degrees of *Star Trek*

Christopher Plummer went on to play Chang, the Shakespeare-quoting Klingon, in *Star Trek VI: The Undiscovered Country* (1991).

Rock Music

Shatner has long been enamored with rock stars. "The rock world today is where it's happening," he once advised an interviewer. "Rock is expanding the horizons of our ability to entertain. Rock stars are dynamites of creativity and energy, and we have nothing but to learn from them." Apparently, what Shatner chiefly wished to learn was how such unattractive, uncouth guys could get so many hot-looking chicks. "A hit record gets you club dates and fairs," he marveled. At various points in his long career, he has tried to reinvent himself as a rock 'n' roll performer in order to tap into this wellspring of loving. It all began in 1968, when Shatner released his concept album **The Transformed Man**. A weird mixture of dramatic monologues and spoken-word renditions of pop songs, it could only tenuously be deemed a rock record. In 1976, Shatner tried again with a series of **one-man shows** on college campuses. Borrowing from such super groups as Led Zeppelin and Pink Floyd, he employed synthesizers and a complex laser light show as accompaniment to his rants about space travel. Veteran rocker Mark Goldenberg, a member of the Al Stewart Group, played guitar at some of Shatner's performances. A 1977 double album from Lemli Records, ***William Shatner Live!***, replete with gatefold cover and rock star glam shots, commemorated the events on vinyl.

"Rocket Man"

The Elton John hit song (1972) performed by Shatner at the Annual Science Fiction Film Awards. Shatner served as emcee for the event, which was televised live in Los Angeles on January 21, 1978, on KTLA and syndicated stations. The surreal performance defies description and *must* be seen to be believed! Anyway, here is one man's attempt at synopsis:

After an introduction by Elton John's lyricist Bernie Taupin, a pensive, tuxedoed Shatner appears, seated on a stool, clutching a cigarette in the European manner. Slowly, he begins to speak the song's lyrics. Before long, a wailing synthesizer joins him, its otherworldly tones adding to the prevailing mood of alienation. After the first chorus, the brooding "Shatner One" is joined, via video trickery, by his alter ego, a clear-eyed, puffed-chest version full of false bravado. About halfway through the number, these two are joined by yet a third (!) incarnation: a shimmying, presumably inebriated figure with his tie and cummerbund undone. Shatner, playing each of the three characters with a gravity that would be admirable if it weren't so hilarious, never quite crosses the line between reciting and singing. The performance is marked by the actor's trademark staccato delivery, inexplicable pauses, and idiosyncratic line readings ("I'm a rocket, man" he intones at one point; at another he's a "rock-*it* man.")

Word of mouth has made this amazing clip legendary. Bootleg copies of the hard-to-find performance have been circulating among

Shatner aficionados for decades. Elfin alternative rocker **Beck** even aped the "three Shatner" motif in the music video for his 1996 song "Where It's At." Shatner himself seems to acknowledge his musical camp value (and that of his 1968 album ***The Transformed Man***) by spoofing his musical persona at the 1992 **MTV Music Awards.**

> *"He couldn't sing. He was smoking, so he would talk the lyrics between puffs. It was horrible and hilarious at the same time."*
> —Actress Susan Tyrell, on Shatner's
> performance of "Rocket Man"

Hey Mr. Shatner, Play a Song for Me

Can't get enough of Shatner the singer? Locating "Rocket Man" is only the first step on your path to building a Shatner musical collection. Here are three other gems no well-dressed Shatner fan should be without:

In the *Star Trek* episode "Plato's Stepchildren," at the behest of their telekinetic captors, Kirk and Spock perform a rousing duet called "I'm Tweedledee, he's Tweedledum." The lyrics convey but a taste of the hilarity as the singers verbalize abnout their happy-go-lucky adventures in the worlds of outer space.

In the 1975 CBS variety special *Mitzi and a Hundred Guys,* Shatner joins host Mitzi Gaynor and a twenty-five-man chorus that includes Leonard Nimoy, Tom Bosley, and Monty Hall. Unfortunately for his fans, Shatner's voice is submerged beneath the general din.

The 1985 all-star ABC-TV cabaret *Night of 100 Stars II* once again finds Shatner high-stepping and belting as part of a kickline of celebrities. In the rousing finale, the stars release 100 helium balloons, hoping their careers won't imitate the balloons disappearing into the air above them.

Roddenberry, Gene (1921–1991)

The bluff, burly *Star Trek* creator cast Shatner in his most famous role, as James Tiberius Kirk, commander of the Starship *Enterprise*. When Gene Roddenberry launched what he called "*Wagon Train* to the stars" on September 8, 1966, he could not foresee the cultural phenomenon he was creating. By the time of Roddenberry's death in 1991 *Star Trek* had spawned five feature films, a second successful television series, well over a hundred books, and nearly half a billion dollars in merchandising sales. Roddenberry, known as **"The Great Bird of the Galaxy"** among his coterie of admirers, once said that he created *Star Trek* because he thought "science fiction hadn't been done well on television." However, he did not take on that genre until relatively late in his life.

Eugene Wesley Roddenberry was born in El Paso, Texas, on August 19, 1921. Soon after his birth, his parents moved to Los Angeles, where his father joined the police department. Always interested in flight and exploration, Roddenberry served as a B-17 pilot during World War II and was awarded the Distinguished Flying Cross. Later he worked as a commercial pilot for Pan Am. He began writing for television in the 1950s, and in 1963 sold his first TV series, *The Lieutenant*, to NBC. There he worked with two of his future *Star Trek* actors, **Leonard Nimoy** and **Nichelle Nichols**.

When *The Lieutenant* flopped after only twenty-nine episodes, Roddenberry began pitching his next show, an action/adventure set in outer space he likened to the western TV drama *Wagon Train* (1957–65). After much cajoling, NBC green-lighted a pilot episode, written by Roddenberry, called "The Cage," in 1965. **Leonard Nimoy** and Majel Barrett, Roddenberry's future wife, were brought in as part of the supporting cast.

Shatner was not Roddenberry's first choice for the lead role. He originally cast **Jeffrey Hunter** as Captain Christopher Pike, but Hunter bolted after filming the first pilot. Jack Lord and Lloyd Bridges were also briefly considered to take over the part, before Shatner was brought in to play Captain **James Tiberius Kirk** in a second pilot, "Where No Man Has Gone Before."

Roddenberry's first impressions of his new star were less than favorable, even though his acting credits were impressive. "He came in and said, 'I have a few comments about the script' and I thought 'Oh no,'"

Roddenberry told *TV Guide* in 1966. **"The great bird"** soon learned to give in to most of Shatner's suggested changes for the sake of harmony on the set.

A control freak who prided himself on dominating every aspect of *Star Trek*'s production, Roddenberry soon came to chafe at the input of his two main stars. "[Shatner and Nimoy] live that show so intently that by now they're convinced they created the whole thing," he carped. There were long stretches during filming when Roddenberry and Shatner simply did not speak to one another.

In his 1993 memoir *Star Trek Memories*, Shatner claimed to have regretted the "cool working relationship" he had with Roddenberry over the years. "There was never anything said," Shatner explained. "It's just that working with somebody for years, you'd think that there'd be more warmth in the relationship and there never was."

The years immediately after *Star Trek*'s cancellation were professionally trying ones for Roddenberry. Without his signature TV series, he seemed at a loss for good ideas. He launched three abortive sci-fi TV pilots in rapid succession: *Genesis II* for CBS in 1973; *Planet Earth* for ABC in 1974; *The Questor Tapes* for NBC in 1974. A fourth, *Spectre*, bombed for NBC in 1977. Desperate to relaunch **Star Trek** in some form, Roddenberry even produced the execrable **Star Trek animated series** for NBC from 1973 to 1975. Only the phenomenal success of George Lucas' big-screen sci-fi adventure *Star Wars* (1977) allowed Roddenberry to realize his dream of a **Star Trek** movie in 1979. However, the finished product, **Star Trek: The Motion Picture**, was a tedious bore for most viewers. Roddenberry's windy, derivative script was considered the chief culprit.

Roddenberry remained involved with **Star Trek**, in a diminished capacity, through each of the subsequent five feature films. "I invented the term 'executive story consultant,'" he boasted to *Variety*, "and set the rules: that they have to show me everything they do...from the first lines [through] all the rewrites and the dailies." But the sad truth was that Roddenberry's advice was paid very little heed by studio executives after the debacle of **Star Trek: The Motion Picture** (1979). Often his objections to story elements in the various features went completely ignored. By the late 1980s he was searching for something meaningful to do. He returned to the small screen, where his talents were best suited.

In the fall of 1987, Roddenberry created a new television series, *Star Trek: The Next Generation*. Set seventy-eight years after the final **Star Trek** episode, the new syndicated show introduced an entirely new set of characters, including a new Starship *Enterprise* commander—chrome-domed, tea-drinking Frenchman Jean-Luc Picard, played by veteran British actor **Patrick Stewart.**

In the early days of that new series, Roddenberry took an active part in the development of the characters and story lines. However, he was slowed by a series of debilitating strokes and other maladies. His health deteriorated dramatically in the years leading up to his death. He was seen less and less often on the *Next Generation* set, usually in a wheelchair. He died of a heart attack on October 24, 1991, in Santa Monica, California.

In a critical summation in his 1994 Roddenberry biography, Joel Engel states, "Roddenberry's real accomplishments were constructing **Star Trek**'s parameters, selling the series, seeking quality writers, and often recognizing brilliance when he saw it. He also insisted on a multiracial, multiethnic supporting cast.... Those accomplishments alone entitle him to the lion's share of credit for **Star Trek**."

In 1994, Shatner joined Stewart and the rest of the *Next Generation* crew in the feature **Star Trek: Generations**. While it met with a mixed critical reception, the film represented a harmonious blending of the two fictional universes of which Roddenberry would no doubt have heartily approved.

Rosenberg, Gloria

See **Gloria Rand.**

Sakata, Harold (1926–1982)

This burly, intimidating Japanese wrestler turned to acting in the 1960s. Best known for his portrayal of Oddjob, James Bond's hulking nemesis, in *Goldfinger* (1964), Sakata appeared with Shatner in the low-caliber feature film **Want a Ride, Little Girl?** (1972). Shatner has on numerous occasions retold a story about saving Sakata's life during filming of a scene in that trashy movie in which the strongman was nearly asphyxiated. The sequence called for Shatner, playing a psychotic killer, to pummel Sakata while the Asian actor hung from a clothesline. Unfortunately, the cord got twisted around Sakata's thick neck, strangling him, until a quick-thinking Shatner used a knife to cut him free. The unleashed weight of Sakata's 250-pound frame yanked the line around Shatner's finger, fracturing it. Filming continued on the exploitation drama, which is considered one of the lowest of low points in Shatner's **lost years**.

Sakata's acting career included such (economy) films as *The Wrestler* (1975), *Jaws of Death* (1976), *Kill Factor* (1978), *Goin' Coconuts* (1978), etc. He was a regular on such TV series as George Kennedy's *Sarge* (1971–72) and the short-lived sitcom *Highcliffe Manor* (1979), starring Shelley Fabares.

Saturday Night Live

Shatner hosted the December 20, 1986, edition of the popular satirical comedy NBC-TV show (1975–), with musical guest Lone Justice. The highlight of the program was a sketch set at a ***Star Trek*** convention, in which Shatner lambasted the loyal Spock-eared throngs with his withering admonition to "get a life." The nasty skit became notorious in the world of science fiction fandom and Shatner was regularly heckled during subsequent convention appearances. In other sketches, Shatner sent up ***T. J. Hooker*** (1982–86), his cop TV series, and essayed the part of a pompous actor. Not exactly a stretch. . . .

Scuba Diving

Shatner first learned the art of scuba diving in the late 1960s. After training for weeks in a Los Angeles swimming pool with ***Star Trek*** bit player David L. Ross, his frequent **motorcycling** companion, a fortified and brave Shatner, crowding onto age forty, was finally ready to take to the ocean. Joining him on his first attempt were Ross and rangy actor Christopher George. After encountering difficulty getting air for Shatner's tank (he was not yet a certified diver), the group reached the shore, which was beset by a fearsome storm. The sea was angry that day, and Shatner had to fight the fierce currents to keep away from jagged rocks that threatened to cut him to ribbons. He survived this bruising baptism with only a few nicks, however, and could cross another dangerous activity off his list of must things to do.

Secrets of a Married Man
RATING: **U**

This 1984 NBC-TV movie, directed by William A. Graham, presents Shatner as a middle-aged husband with a compulsive need for the company of prostitutes. As Chris Jordan, a beefy, bewigged Shatner rides up and down red-light streets gawking at available hookers in hot pants. Eventually he falls for a conniving call girl (Cybil Shepherd) who helps destroy his on-camera marriage to his no longer sympathetic spouse (Michelle Phillips). Working titles for this trashy TV venture, filmed in Vancouver, British Columbia, Canada, included *Trick Eyes* and *Portrait of a John.*

Cybill Shepherd tugs on Shatner's tie, and ruins his marriage, in the tawdry TV movie Secrets of a Married Man *(1984). [photo courtesy of Photofest]*

Seven Dwarfs

This term became Shatner's derisive epithet for the supporting members of the **Star Trek** TV series cast: **Jimmy Doohan**, **George Takei**, **Nichelle Nichols**, **Walter Koenig**, and **Majel Barrett** (though there are only five in actual number). All of them at one time or another fell victim to Shatner's penchant for trimming the dialogue lines given to his fellow performers. For obvious reasons, they kept their objections largely to themselves. "Other than **Leonard [Nimoy]**, Bill could have had any of them fired," bit player David L. Ross once remarked. Several of the *dwarfs* later used their published memoirs as a forum to punch back at their tyrannical leading man.

"From the beginning, Bill believed the credits—that there were three actors above the title and the rest of us below. The rest of us were not significant, not only as actors, but as people."
—WALTER KOENIG, on Shatner's attitude
toward the "Seven Dwarfs"

Sex

When it comes to *l'amour*, gallant Shatner admits to having no sexual inhibitions or taboos. Such frankness has led some observers to speculate about Shatner's sexual preferences. The testimony of Iggy Pop guitarist **Ron Asheton** has fueled persistent rumors that—at the very least—Shatner went through an alleged experimental phase in the 1970s. If that were true, of course, he would be no different from countless other celebrities including John Lennon, Mick Jagger, and Marv Albert.

Like many actors, Shatner sees a sexual component in his one-on-many relationship with his audiences. He has spoken candidly about "making love to a whole audience—making them my lover, and I theirs." Shatner's musings on sexuality have even extended outside the realm of terra firma. In a wide-ranging *Playboy* interview in 1989, he expounded on extraterrestrial erotic technique:

"First of all, you take off your boots. Then you have to find the erogenous zones.They differ on every alien. An alien erogenous zone can lead you down some strange paths—some of which I can tell you and some of which I can't. Let's just say that when you scratch your head, you may be fulfilling the sexual fantasies of some alien."

Still, Shatner has saved his best work for the fairer sex. "I'm so content being a man that I would miss the clanging of my balls," he told

SO SAYETH SHATNER

ON SEX:

"Anything done supremely well is an act of sex."

Playboy. His line of reputed conquests over the years reportedly has included performers Angie Dickinson, Joan Collins, and Yvette Mimieux. "If I'm Hollywood's number one love machine—in terms of quantity and quality—it certainly is a distinction," Shatner informed the *National Enquirer* in 1995.

Sex Education, Shatner Style:

Sigmund Freud was famous for reading a sexual subtext into our perception of everyday objects. But Herr Doktor may have met his match in Shatner, for whom a cigar is never just a cigar. Here is a partial list of things and activities that get Shatner's sap a-rising:

ARCHERY: "The arrow and the bow as you draw it taut, gathering the tension—your strength, your power pumped into it, behind the thrust, and then the release— like an ejaculation, thrusting the arrow forward to impale the target. The arrow arcs up and flies straight home and penetrates the center of the bull's eye."

FLYING: "You have this stick between your legs and you're turning, and the centrifugal force is forcing the blood down....I mean, it's all sexual."

HORSEBACK RIDING: "There's a real connection between love and riding a horse well. You've got to use your body, you've got to use your hands, you've got to make love to the horse, and she's a neat lady."

ROCK 'N' ROLL: "A real sexual thrill takes place hearing the hot beat of a rock number."

Horseman Shatner controls an unruly mount. [photo courtesy of The Everett Collection]

Sing a Song of Shatner

"Shatner" by The Wedding Present was not the first song to name-drop Canada's most famous human export. Many rockers have found Shatner grist for their lyrical mill. Here are some requests to phone in to your local deejay:

- Spizzenergi's 1979 single "Where's Captain Kirk" places the punk band on board the *Enterprise* with no commander.

- "Everyone's a Captain Kirk" wails Teutonic rocker Nena in the English-language version of her 1984 anti-nuclear hit "99 Red Balloons."

- Infantile comedian Adam Sandler's absurdly popular 1996 novelty tune "Chanukah Song" lists Shatner in its catalog of Jewish celebrities.

- "Oh, Canada," a 1997 track by the Denver-based ska combo Five Iron Frenzy, lists the many pleasures of the Great White North, including the fact "that William Shatner is a native citizen."

"Shatner"

This song has been recorded by British pop group, The Wedding Present. The oblique ode to the icon actor appears on the band's 1987 album *George Best*, joining other offbeat, frenetically played confections like "Everyone Thinks He Looks Daft" and "My Favourite Dress." The musical group, based in Leeds, England, recorded another self-described "William Shatner number" for its 1988 release *Tommy*. That song, "Felicity," was written by a Scottish musician named James Kirk.

Shatner, Anne (19??–19??)

Shatner's mother brought forth not only William but also two sisters, Joy (Shatner) Ruttenberg and Farla (Shatner) Cohen. A Montreal native, Anne Shatner graduated from college and taught diction before staying home to raise three children. While she did not take to the stage herself, she provided the early impetus for her son to become an actor. "It's genetic," reported Shatner's sister, Farla. "My mother was a bit of a clown. She never really pursued her acting in a professional way, but she had talent." "She dreamed that her son would be a star one day," added Shatner's close friend Hilliard Jason. Anne Shatner's other legacy to her only son includes, according to him, his sense of humor. "My mother is an amusing person," Shatner once remarked. "My mother is probably the source of the humor. I think she probably provided me the impetus of trying to be amusing." Among the manifestations of this birthright is Shatner's fondness for **practical jokes**, which he indulged in relentlessly on the set of *Star Trek*.

Shatner Building

The Student Union Building at McGill University in Montreal was renamed in 1995 to honor its most famous graduate. Dubbed The William Shatner University Centre, the five-story brick and poured concrete structure houses student activities and administrative offices, as well as a cafeteria. It is notable for a long staircase which winds up the center of the building. McGill officials estimate that 2,000 students navigate their way through Shatner Centre on a daily basis.

The decision to rename the building after Shatner was not without controversy. When asked why a living person received this honor the dean of McGill replied, "He's the only student to captain a starship within fifteen years of graduation." But Shatner's tribute came at the acclamation of the student body, not the administration, which demanded a donation from the actor in return for the renaming. Shatner refused to pay up, and as a result some McGill officials still refuse to recognize the new name.

In 1997, the Shatner Building came under fire from the Office for Students with Disabilities for being inaccessible to persons with physical impairments. An audit was conducted in which the Shatner edifice was cited for its high elevator keyholes, heavy bathroom doors, and lack of room numbers printed in Braille. As a result, explained disabilities activist Eleanor Girt in the *McGill Tribune*, "Students with disabilities are not using Shatner at all."

Shatner, Joseph (????–1967)

William Shatner's father was the son of Jewish immigrants who moved to Montreal in the early 1900s. Joseph and William Shatner shared a stormy relationship, often arguing over the younger man's choice of career. The elder Shatner headed Admiration Clothes, a successful clothing manufacturing company in Montreal. Joseph hoped his only son would follow him into the family business. When William decided to pursue a show business career instead, Joseph cut him off from all financial support.

"For five years I lived in cheap rooms and starved," Shatner *fils* told *People* magazine in 1982, "which didn't make my father happy. It's a terrifying decision for a parent to take away a child's support." Joseph Shatner asked his son to return home, but William refused. Joseph eventually gave up his dream of handing over the family business and hired a young assistant to take the place of his son.

Joseph Shatner died of a heart attack on a Florida golf course in 1967. Shatner received the news of the tragedy on the set of the ***Star Trek*** episode "The Devil in the Dark" (March 9, 1967). Overcome by grief, he nevertheless insisted on completing the day's shooting. An almost numb Shatner had trouble remembering his lines but managed to struggle through the scene in which Kirk directs his men to search for the deadly Horta. "We quit around five or six o'clock and I went home," Shatner said later. "And *everybody* was crying when we made that scene."

On the flight home to Montreal with his father's body, Shatner experienced an epiphany of his own spiritual desolation. "I remember banking over the city and looking out the window. But what I was really doing was looking into myself. What I saw was an empty pit—and it terrified me." The death of Joseph Shatner is widely believed to be a contributing factor in the long personal and professional descent known as William Shatner's **lost years.**

Shatner, Leslie Carol (B. 1958)

First daughter of Shatner and **Gloria Rand,** Leslie was born on August 13, 1958. A precocious child, she was teaching her parents a new way to tell time even in infancy. "Let's see if I can explain it," Shatner told interviewers in 1959. "She starts cutting a tooth. It hurts for a while. And then the tooth begins to show, and it doesn't hurt anymore. But then, a month or so has passed. After that, whenever we wait for a month to pass by, we look on it as the length of time it took Leslie to cut a tooth, not as thirty days, or four weeks."

A few years later, Papa Shatner educated his daughter in the workings of the Hollywood class system. "Daddy, are you a star?" Leslie asked her father in 1967, soon after he began work on TV's *Star Trek*. "No, I'm a working actor," Shatner replied.

A commercial artist, Leslie Shatner, in 1991, married Hollywood talent agent Adam Isaacs (who represents James Bond movie girl Famke Janssen, among others). The ceremony was held at the Shatner's home in Los Angeles. The couple have two sons, the first of what may be many mighty Shatner grandchildren.

Shatner, Lisabeth Mary (B. 1961)

The second daughter of Shatner and **Gloria Rand** was born on June 6, 1961. When she was only five, Lisabeth felt the sting of abandonment as Shatner left the house to begin work on TV's *Star Trek* in 1966. "I stood on the front porch, begging him not to go. He appeared only once or twice a week after that to see me and my sisters."

Despite the pain caused by her parents' divorce in 1969, Lisabeth later reconciled with her father. She pursued a modeling career in Los Angeles, but found success as a writer. With input from her father in 1989, she wrote *Captain's Log: William Shatner's Personal Account of the Making of* **Star Trek V**.

Shatner, Melanie Ann (B. 1964)

The third daughter of Shatner and **Gloria Rand** was born on August 4, 1964. Following in her father's footsteps, she has pursued an acting career, mainly in low-budget science fiction films.

"Do something else!" was her father's response when Melanie told him she was going into show business. "Acting in TV or movies may be financially rewarding, but isn't emotionally or artistically rewarding—except for some brief moments—and that isn't enough to sustain a person for a lifetime." However, Melanie found the lure of the bright lights too strong. She attended Beverly Hills High School, then majored in theater at the University of Colorado. She played the part of a yeoman in *Star Trek VI: The Undiscovered Country* (1991). Her other film credits include the features *The First Power* (1990), *Cthulhu Mansion* (1990), *Syngenor* (1990), *Bloodstone—Subspecies II* (1993), and *Bloodlust—Subspecies III* (1994); and the TV movies *Camp Cucamonga* (1990), *Unknown Origin* (1995), and *Their Second Chance* (1997). In 1988, she appeared in a series of Oldsmobile TV commercials with her dad that featured the tag line "This is not your father's Oldsmobile."

Melanie has also picked up her father's knack for business. She founded her own clothing company, Thou Art Jeans. "A friend and I had decorated some jeans," she told *Los Angeles* magazine. "We added different styles of patches—some plain and some dressy, such as black velvet with pearls. A shop in the Beverly Hills Center actually wanted to stock them so we decided to start a business. Before long, we had more orders than we could handle."

Asked to choose between fashion and films, Melanie Shatner is noncommittal. "I'd rather do film because you have more time to do things in between," she told interviewers in 1989. "But it really doesn't matter."

Shirtlessness

Early in his acting career, Shatner was never shy about removing his shirt on screen. Over time, it became one of his trademarks. The origins of his inclination to disrobe go back to his earliest days on television. "I was doing a scene in a judo costume," he explained, "and it was subtly agreed it would look better to leave the long outside coat off." From that moment on, Shatner knew his muscular figure was his meal ticket. He worked out with weights for a year prior to filming the TV series pilot *Alexander the Great* in 1963 "so I could take off my shirt and look like a hero."

"Part of what you're buying when you watch an actor perform is appearance," Shatner once explained. "People in Hollywood are expected to be beautiful. Viewers want to see a perfect specimen. They want you bigger than life."

Bigger than life is exactly what Shatner was during much of his time on TV's *Star Trek*, when he was bedeviled by a persistent and very visible **weight** problem. When he started working on the series in 1966, he would walk around the Desilu sound stage with twenty-pound weights strapped to his waist, ankles, and wrists to keep in top shape "so I can take my shirt off on camera." As any dedicated Trekkie knows, he did so often and enthusiastically. In the earliest episodes, scenes of Kirk working out in his quarters or being examined by Dr. McCoy were inserted for no discernible dramatic purpose. To prepare for these "money shots," Shatner kept a small gym in his dressing room to rein in his ballooning figure. [See **Appendix 2: A Shatnercentric Episode Guide** to *Star Trek*. Each episode is awarded "Kirk Points" based on the good captain having his shirt off, getting action from a female admirer, playing a dual role, etc.]

Shot in the Dark, A

Shatner played Paul Sevigne, the diligent examining magistrate, in the Broadway production of Harry Kurnitz's French farce from October 18, 1961 to February of 1963. The comedic mystery revolves around complications that follow the murder of a Parisian chauffeur. Julie Harris and Walter Matthau joined Shatner in the Harold Clurman-directed Leland Hayward production, which ran for 389 performances and earned a Tony Award for Matthau.

Adapted from the French comedy *L'Idiote* (1960) by Marcel Archard, *A Shot in the Dark* was distilled into a 1964 movie comedy starring Peter Sellers, Elke Sommer, and Herbert Lom. The role played by Shatner

Shatner cuddles up to Julie Harris in the Broadway production of A Shot in the Dark *(1961). [photo courtesy of Photofest]*

was somewhat rejiggered to accommodate Sellers' bumbling Inspector Clouseau series persona, which he originated in 1963's *The Pink Panther*.

Silent Betrayal, A   RATING: U U

This 1994 CBS-TV movie, directed by Robert Iscove, stars Richard Crenna, Helen Shaver, and Shatner. The latter appears as Bodosh, a martini-sipping Broadway producer who owns an apartment building where six gruesome murders have taken place. Richard Crenna is Frank Janek, a gruff New York City police detective called in to investigate. "Shatner's histrionics give the film a shot of much-needed energy," wrote Bruce Fretts of *Entertainment Weekly*. Ironically, Shatner's first scene requires him to make a 911 emergency call—something he has done repeatedly in real life (see **911 Calls**) and as host of the reality-based drama TV program *Rescue 911* (1989–92).

Skydiving

Shatner claims to have made a mid-air jump *once*, with comical results. "I went out of the airplane in total hysteria. When I landed, the instructor who'd been falling with me said, 'Were you aware that you were screaming all the way down?' I said I was and that was the only way I could get this terrible feeling out." Shatner calls skydiving "the most intense experience I've ever had, simply the most incredible, frightening, exhilarating experience I've ever had."

Sole Survivor   RATING: U U

The 1970 TV movie features the eclectic likes of Vince Edwards, Richard Basehart, Shatner, Brad Davis, and Patrick Wayne. In this CBS production, ghosts from a crashed World War II bomber in the Libyan desert return to haunt a surviving crew member, now (twenty-five years later) heading a team investigating the newly found wreckage. In this Paul Stanley-directed entry, Shatner is seen as Lt. Col. Joe Gronke, the spooked man's assistant. The film's ambiance mirrors that of the famed *The Twilight Zone* (1959–65), and this may not have been an accident. Its plot is highly derivative of two episodes, "The Arrival" and "King Nine Will Not Return," from the popular series.

Six Degrees of *Star Trek*

Lou Antonio (Tony) played Lokai, the black-white guy, in the *Star Trek* episode "Let That Be Your Last Battlefield" (January 10, 1969).

Spectre

This 1998 *Star Trek* novel, penned by Shatner, is the third in the sequence that began with *Ashes of Eden* and *The Return*. A sequel to the classic *Star Trek* second-season episode "Mirror, Mirror" (10/6/67), the novel follows the retired **James T. Kirk** on a mission of mercy to a parallel universe where humans live enslaved to the Klingons, Cardassians, and Bajorans. This time there seems to be some question whether Captain Kirk is up to the tasks set for him with, of course, the fate of the entire Federation dependent upon him.

Stage

Shatner began his career on stage and has never lost his love for the theater. The classical experience he received with the **Stratford Shakespeare Festival** in Canada clearly influenced his mature acting style. Early in his career, theatrical acting seemed to be Shatner's priority. He even backed out of a lucrative Hollywood movie deal in order to play the lead in *The World of Suzie Wong* on Broadway. For many years, he maintained his Canadian citizenship in case he wished to move to England and join that country's thriving theatrical community. However, the lure of big money in America kept him from exercising that creative option (see **Houses**).

Though he found success on Broadway, Shatner in the 1950s found **live television** an adequate substitute for the constant proving ground of stage performance. "American television in the early days gave an actor this kind of training," he later recalled. "There were so many dramatic productions at that time that an actor had a chance to try his hand at many roles. Nowadays, there's very little, and a young actor is hard put to find this kind of theatrical groundwork."

Most of Shatner's significant stage credits—*The World of Suzie Wong* (1958) and *A Shot in the Dark* (1961)—came before his days on *Star Trek*. However, he has maintained his ties to the theatrical community and worked regularly in that medium throughout his lengthy career. During his **lost years**, Shatner took to the road to seek out parts in regional summer stock productions. His credits during this period included *There's a Girl in My Soup* (1969), *Remote Asylum* (1970–71), and *Arsenic and Old Lace* (1973). In 1981, Shatner even fused his love of theater with his passion for directing when he put then-wife **Marcy Lafferty** through her paces as Maggie the Cat in a Los Angeles production of *Cat on a Hot Tin Roof.*

Ultimately, Shatner likes stage work for the same reason he loves **dual roles**—there's more room available for him to dominate the action. "It takes about a minute to overcome the image of Kirk on stage," he told the *New York Daily News* in 1982. "What I like about it is that the evening's entertainment is on my shoulders." Shatner performed the ultimate feat of solo gratification with his series of **one-man shows** on stage in the 1970s.

Star Trek (TV series)

This NBC science fiction television series is the one for which Shatner is best known. After replacing **Jeffrey Hunter** in time for the second pilot, he played **Captain James Tiberius Kirk** of the U.S.S. *Enterprise* from 1966 to 1969. His rough-and-tumble heroics provided the show with a solid action/adventure footing, from which its more philosophical pretensions could take flight.

The brainchild of writer/producer **Gene Roddenberry**, *Star Trek* was conceived as an attempt to bring the action and adventure of the western genre into an outer space setting. This was nothing new as earlier science fiction TV shows like *Captain Video* (1949–55), *Tom Corbett, Space Cadet* (1950–52), and *Space Patrol* (1951–52) had explored similar dramatic terrain. However, these primitive series were often childish in approach and amateurish in execution. Roddenberry's innovation was to bring humanistic values, sophisticated themes, and high production values to the science fiction genre. For much of *Star Trek's* TV run, the formula worked. Contrast it with its principal sci-fi competitor of the era, *Lost in Space* (1965–68), and most doubts will disappear. *Lost in Space* featured campy dialogue, over-the-top-performances, and godawful special effects—all geared to an audience of eight-year-olds or at least eight-year-old intellects. Stanley Adams, so entertaining as Cyrano Jones

Shatner—Ripe for Parody

William Shatner presents a large target for satirists—and not just physically. Ever since he exploded onto the national scene with TV's *Star Trek* in the 1960s, Shatner has been fodder for numerous comedy writers and performers looking to score a quick, easy laugh. Here are some of the barbs that hit their mark:

- John Belushi played Captain Kirk in a *Star Trek* sketch on *Saturday Night Live* in 1975.

- Fellow Canadian Jim Carrey donned Shatner's commander tunic for a 1990 *In Living Color* TV sketch called *The Wrath of Farrakhan*. Highlights included Kirk's wonderful query to Spock, "Are you out of your Vulcan mind?"

- On a 1993 installment of the satirical TV revue *The Edge*, two tiny aliens accidentally vaporize Captain Kirk's penis. "Call 911!" the emasculated spaceman shrieks when he learns the extent of the damage.

in the *Star Trek* episode "The Trouble with Tribbles" (12/29/67), played a walking, talking rutabaga in one particularly onerous *Lost in Space* installment.

Despite its artistic pretensions, *Star Trek* did make a few concessions to space opera convention. One was the presence of a rugged action hero in the person of the ship's captain. Enter William Shatner (after Hunter's departure and flirtations with casting Jack Lord and Lloyd Bridges) to take over the key assignment. Shatner was thirty-five when he took on the role of Captain Kirk. He considered it his last best chance at success in show business. If the new series failed, he told friends he planned to give up acting entirely, to try his hand at "selling ties at Macy's." But his confidence in his own abilities as a performer were at an all-time high. As he told interviewers in 1967, "I can learn lines without pain, I can gauge my performance, I can direct myself. I feel at the height of my powers at this moment, like a finely tuned racing machine."

The superfueled Shatner was able to hit a number of high personal notes with his initial work on *Star Trek*. He gives fine, subtle perfor-

- Joel Sherman's mother channel surfed her way to "William Shatner's Celebrity Autopsy" on the short-lived animated TV series *The Critic* in 1994.

- On a 1995 episode of TV's *The Simpsons*, an animated Shatner tried out for the role of Montgomery Burns in a pompous biopic about the slithery power plant magnate.

- That same year, *The Simpsons* annual Halloween special "Treehouse of Horror IV" spoofed Shatner's famous *Twilight Zone* appearance as "Nightmare at 5½ Feet"—set on a school bus instead of an airliner.

- In 1997, Fox's *Mad TV* satirized both *Star Trek* and cheesy 1970s variety specials with "The Kirk & Spock Variety Hour," a "long-lost" extravaganza starring Shatner and Nimoy.

mances in early episodes like "The Enemy Within" (10/6/66), "The Naked Time" (9/29/66), and "The City on the Edge of Forever" (4/6/67). As the series progressed, however, he grew anxious about the expanded role of **Leonard Nimoy** as Mr. Spock and began to lobby producers for more rock-'em sock-'em Kirk-centered action. Rumors abounded toward the end of the first season (1966–67) that Shatner would soon abandon the show which was suffering from low ratings. Somewhere in all of this an accommodation was reached and the program began to focus almost exclusively on the "Big Three" of Kirk, Spock, and McCoy—with Kirk the undisputed godhead of the trinity. The supporting players suffered the most from this subtle shift, as their already small number of lines dwindled appreciably.

In the show's second season (1967–68), violence and action became the order of the day, as subtlety flew out the window. *Enterprise* crew members engaged in gladiatorial combat in two separate episodes, as sure a sign of creeping creative sclerosis as anyone can name. An increasing number of installments adopted the high concept "*Star Trek*

Meets . . ." formula, with Kirk and his crew encountering the Romans ("Bread and Circuses," 3/15/68), the Nazis ("Patterns of Force," 2/16/68), and the very thinly veiled Vietnamese ("The Omega Glory," 3/1/68). Shatner himself seemed to be reveling in the change of direction. He got to take his shirt off a lot more (see **shirtlessness**), got a lot more play from the ladies, and even got to read the U.S. Constitution, tortuously, in "The Omega Glory." The giant sucking sound viewers heard was the show's artistic integrity flying out the window.

By *Star Trek*'s third season (1968–69), artistic integrity was the punch-line to a dirty joke. With a dramatically reduced budget and a time slot from hell on Friday nights at 10 P.M., new producer Fred Freiberger didn't even *try* to find good scripts anymore. Wind out of the ass of a simpleton could have served as a better shooting script than Shatner and his cohorts were saddled with in "Spock's Brain" (9/20/68), "The Way to Eden" (2/21/69), and "The Lights of Zetar" (1/31/69). Episodes like "That Which Survives" (1/24/69) and "The Empath" (12/6/68) were filmed on minimalist sets, not for artistic reasons, but merely because the show could no longer afford even the papier-mâché rocks constructed in previous seasons. Other installments were confined to the Starship *Enterprise* entirely. One stinker, "Let That Be Your Last Battlefield" (1/10/69), consisted almost entirely of actor Frank Gorshin chasing Lou Antonio down the corridors of the ship. By the time Abraham Lincoln appeared flying through space in a high-backed chair and stovepipe hat, it was clearly time to close up the shop. The show creaked to a halt on June 3, 1969, with one final Shatner show-stopper: the gender-bending dual role "Turnabout Intruder" (6/3/69), one of the campy gems of the series.

The seventy-nine original episodes have since been syndicated by 114 American stations and in 131 overseas markets. Today these episodes, classics and duds alike, are given lush packaging and presented on videocassette by Paramount Home Video, with many installments also available on RCA VideoDiscs.

While well received by critics, *Star Trek* was not an immediate hit with the TV viewing public. It never finished higher than fiftieth in the Neilsen ratings and was constantly on the brink of cancellation. Only a massive letter-writing campaign spearheaded by science-fiction author Harlan Ellison kept the show from being axed after its first season. This campaign that saved the TV show was the first evidence of *Star Trek*'s

legion of dedicated fans—now known as Trekkies. Today these passionate oddballs are organized into over 350 fan clubs whose members flock
to the over 400 conventions held annually. There are over 500 fanzines
focusing on such minutiae as Klingon syntax and possible homoerotic
undertones in the show. While Paramount always cited *Star Trek* as a loss
in its official financial filings (and denied Shatner and his costars any
residuals or merchandising royalties for much of the decade) *Star Trek*
in the 1970s became a syndicated rerun juggernaut. Its ten million-earth-
ling fan base exploded by seventy-seven percent between 1977 and 1979
alone. Buoyed by these numbers, and by the success of the 1977 sci-fi feature *Star Wars*, Paramount launched the *Star Trek* movie series in 1979
with **Star Trek: The Motion Picture**.

Various windbags in the worlds of journalism and punditry have
offered many different explanations for *Star Trek*'s enduring appeal.
Writing in *Stereo Review*, Steve Simels gave the simplest and best explanation, calling *Star Trek* "more consistently entertaining, on the most
basic level, than any other American TV action series before or since."

Not surprisingly, Shatner himself has weighed in on this question.
He observed that the TV show presented something for everyone: action
and adventure for kids, meaningful messages for adults, hard science for
technophiles, even a dash of psychedelia for the counterculture. An
unabashed apologist for the show's loftiest aspirations, he has offered,
predictably, a more hifalutin' explanation for *Star Trek*'s success in *USA
Today* (November 9, 1993).

SO SAYETH SHATNER

*"It sounds a little presumptuous, but I think
that* Star Trek *provides a mythology for people
in a culture that has no mythology. There
must have been a reason that . . . culture after
culture had mythological figures. It must have
satisfied some need. I think that's what this
does here."*

Star Trek (animated series)

Production on an animated *Star Trek* TV series began in June 1973 after demographic studies convinced NBC executives of the show's continued appeal to young viewers. A desperate Shatner signed up to provide voice-overs with the rest of the original cast. With scripts from many of the original *Star Trek* writers and creative input from series executive producer/creator **Gene Roddenberry**, the half-hour program had the potential to be respectable. However, the quality of the animation provided by Filmation Enterprises was execrable (a fact Shatner tacitly acknowledged by recording some of his voice-overs while sitting on the toilet). The principals tiredly mailed in their vocal performances for two years (September 8, 1973 to August 30, 1975) before the axe of cancellation mercifully fell. Astonishingly, the program won an Emmy Award for Outstanding Entertainment Children's Series—proof positive of the sad state of animation in the 1970s.

Star Trek: Generations   RATING: U U U

The seventh entry in the *Star Trek* big-screen film cycle, this 1994 release was Shatner's last on-camera appearance to date as Captain Kirk. He got to play a heroic death scene only after test audiences found the original ending unsatisfactory.

The feature film marked a passing of the torch from the original crew to the cast of TV's syndicated *Star Trek: The Next Generation* (1987–94). "We had gotten older," Shatner said of his original cast mates. "And the question, I guess, in Paramount's mind was how long would the audience pay to see elderly men trying to remember their lines?" Nevertheless, he was one "elderly man" who was invited back for a seventh go on the big screen.

"I really thought the sixth movie was the last for my character," Shatner said, curiously failing to mention that he had submitted a treatment for *Star Trek VII* that was rejected by Paramount. When Paramount decided to feature the *Next Generation* TV players in the new project, it appeared the original series regulars had reached the end of the gravy train at last. However, executive producer Rick Berman decided on his own initiative to write some of the old characters into his story treatment. Overtures were made to all the actors. Most of them declined to participate, but Shatner, **Walter Koenig**, and **James Doohan** eagerly signed on. As the story process went on, the death of Captain Kirk became a centerpiece of the movie.

Word soon leaked to the press that this would be Shatner's swan song as Kirk. "I thought it was a good dramatic idea until I realized it would turn out to be my funeral," Shatner quipped. But the chance to bring his most famous character full circle held undeniable appeal for the actor, who received a $6 million salary. "The whole idea of Kirk's death and my own seemed to combine," he said. "I wanted Kirk to die the way I would like to—at peace with himself and the life he had lived." Besides, killing off Kirk would make Shatner the focus of numerous national magazine and newspaper features, no small boost to his fledgling literary career.

Filming of *Star Trek: Generations* commenced in February of 1994. For Shatner, the shoot had an empty feeling about it. He missed having his TV and movie series friends **Leonard Nimoy** and **DeForest Kelley** around. Equally alienating was the attitude of the younger *Next Generation* actors, several of whom found it hard to perform in the presence of their childhood hero, Captain Kirk. "I felt like a guest on my own show," Shatner explained. "I could tell I no longer belonged, that my time had passed."

Adding to Shatner's vexation was the experience of sharing the lead with **Patrick Stewart**, Captain Jean-Luc Picard. Rumors swirled throughout production that the two men despised each other, though both chose to downplay their feud for the sake of the ongoing franchise. Especially upsetting to Shatner was a scene in which his character says to Picard, "Who am I to argue with the captain of the *Enterprise*?" "Those words stuck in my throat and I couldn't get the line out," Shatner admitted later. "By the third take, people were starting to get annoyed. But I had trouble saying those words. It was a very sad time for me."

The film opens on the bridge of the spanking new starship *Enterprise B*, where Kirk, Scotty, and Chekov are investigating a mysterious distortion in space-time known as the Nexus. When the ship becomes ensnared in one of the Nexus' energy tendrils, Kirk places himself in harm's way to save the vessel, but is apparently blasted into open space to his doom. Eighty years later, the crew of the *Enterprise D* is also swept up in the Nexus, where Captain Picard stumbles across Kirk living in a forest cabin in a paradisiacal dream world beyond time and space. He enlists Kirk's aid in stopping Soran, an evil scientist, from destroying the galaxy in a mad plan to harness the power of the Nexus for his own purposes. After many plot complications, the two *Enterprise* commanders foil Soran's designs. However, Kirk is killed in a climactic confrontation with the evil scientist in a desert wasteland.

Jonathan Frakes, Brent Spiner, Michael Dorn, LeVar Burton, Gates McFadden, and Marina Sirtis rounded out the *Next Generation* cast. Playing Soran was veteran British actor Malcolm McDowell, best remembered for his portrayal of Alex, the vicious, insolent hero of Stanley Kubrick's 1971 masterpiece *A Clockwork Orange*. He brought a special relish to his task of terminating **Captain James T. Kirk**. In the scene as originally shot, Soran blasts Kirk from behind with a phaser. "It felt lovely," McDowell cackled afterwards.

On September 14, 1994, the film was screened before a preview audience. The response was not exactly encouraging, especially concerning the ending. "The test audience told us a truth we should have known earlier," Shatner observed, namely that Kirk deserved better than to be shot in the back by a sneering McDowell. The principals returned to the desert to reshoot the sequence, at an additional cost of $4 million. In the revised ending, Kirk dies heroically, crushed to death after slugging it out with Soran on a high catwalk.

A curse dictates that all odd-numbered *Star Trek* feature films fall flat with critics, and this one was no exception. *Star Trek: Generations* reached theatres on November 18, 1994 and was savaged in most major publications as a tedious, convoluted mess. "The highly awaited time-travel teaming of Picard and Kirk," wrote Susan Wloszczyna in *USA Today*, "isn't quite the clash of the follicle-impaired titans that it's meant to be." The talented *Next Generation* ensemble was given little to do, while Malcolm McDowell's most significant contribution to the film was a stylish haircut, apparently on loan from Sting. Nevertheless, Trekkies dutifully lined up to watch the unimaginable, their childhood hero dying. *Generations* grossed $23 million in its opening weekend and $75 million overall—about the same as **Star Trek VI** made in 1991. For the first film with the new cast, it was a respectable showing, paving the way for the far superior *Star Trek: First Contact* in 1996. This film, in turn, is to be followed by a ninth film in the series, tentatively titled *Star Trek: Insurrection*, to be released in December of 1998. The screenplay for the new film is by **Star Trek** stalwart Michael Piller, and the film will be directed by Jonathan Frakes (Comdr. William Riker), who had already directed several episodes of TV's *Star Trek: The Next Generation* (1987–94) itself. Finally, the regular cast of that TV series (Patrick Stewart, Jonathan Frakes, LeVar Burton, Brent Spiner, Marina Sirtis, Gates McFadden, and Michael Dorn) will be joined by veteran actors F. Murray Abraham and Anthony Zerbe, presumably portraying the villains.

Star Trek Memories

This 1993 memoir, cowritten by Shatner with Chris Kreski, covered the years 1966 through 1969, during the filming of the original *Star Trek* TV series. Essentially a tepid collection of behind-the-scenes anecdotes, the book generated controversy due to the ill will that surfaced among the cast members whom Shatner interviewed.

In the years following *Star Trek Memories*, Shatner found himself hoisted on his own petard, as his costars released their own tell-all tomes. Always eager for a little camera time, they did not hesitate to take to the TV airwaves to publicly trash their former captain. "It's one thing to get on the phone and one friend says, 'You said this,' and you're privately on the line," Shatner grumbled. "But when they get on the national show and start talking about it, it's a little embarrassing."

"Doing the book made me tremendously nostalgic for when I was 25 years younger," Shatner told *TV Guide* shortly before the book's release. "It was pleasurable in that I was able to touch emotionally people I hadn't spoken to in 25 years." Refusing to be "touched" in any way by his former captain was **James Doohan**, who declined to be interviewed for the project. Other cast members merely took the occasion of the interview to inform Shatner how much they actually detested him. "Don't you want to hear how much we despise you?" **Nichelle Nichols** told him at the end of her interview session. Shatner claimed to have been blindsided by the outpouring of bile, likening the experience of interviewing

Shatner's curious choice of clothing patterns serves to distract attention from his controversial 1993 book Star Trek Memories. *[photo courtesy of AP Worldwide Photos]*

his costars to attending a high school reunion. "I've never gone back to a school reunion before," he said, "I guess, for that very reason."

The brouhaha in the press over these tensions helped make *Star Trek Memories* a runaway bestseller. Shatner was paid a $1.5 million advance to write a follow-up book, *Star Trek Movie Memories*, released in 1994 in a hardcover edition by HarperCollins (which was followed by a paperback edition in 1995).

In addition, back in 1979, Shatner collaborated with Sondra Marshak and Myrna Culbreath in an authorized biography of himself, covering his career to that date. Titled *Shatner: Where No Man*, this book is now an extremely rare paperback (New York: Ace Books, Grosset & Dunlap, 1979).

Star Trek: Phase II

This television series, commissioned by Paramount in 1977, was to reprise Shatner's role as **Captain James T. Kirk**. The proposed hour-long TV series would have reunited Shatner with his original show compatriots—with the conspicuous exception of **Leonard Nimoy**, who refused to don the cumbersome (and painful) Spock ears again on a weekly basis. To replace Nimoy, actor David Gautreaux was to be cast as Xon, a Vulcan science officer. However, a new weekly series was fated not to be until 1987, when *Star Trek: The Next Generation* revived the franchise.

Paramount abruptly canceled *Star Trek: Phase II*, already in pre-production, when its plans for launching a fourth broadcast network fell through. Script elements from the proposed *Star Trek: Phase II* episodes were later incorporated into **Star Trek: The Motion Picture** and the TV series *Star Trek: The Next Generation* (1987–94).

Star Trek: The Motion Picture RATING: U

The first of the **Star Trek** big-screen feature films, it was released in 1979. The on-again, off-again project began as a $3 million TV movie, was redesigned as a pilot for a new TV series **Star Trek: Phase II**, and ended up as a $44 million spectacle that was loathed by almost everyone who saw it. Shatner was on board every step of the way, astutely sensing that **Star Trek** was his only ticket out of TV game show and B-movie hell.

Robert Wise (*The Sound of Music*, 1965, *The Day the Earth Stood Still*, 1951, etc.) was signed on to direct the project, initially budgeted at $15 million. That figure would quickly swell, as special effects proceeded to consume almost two-thirds of all money spent on the screen project. The entire cast returned to play their original roles. Even **Leonard Nimoy** put aside bitterness over merchandising royalties (and after a successful settlement of his grievances) to reprise his Spock character.

At a press conference announcing his participation in the upcoming theatrical feature, Shatner tried hard to conceal his glee at finally being given a lead in a big-budget theatrical feature. "I somehow always felt that we would be back together," he crowed. "Regardless of what I was doing, or where my career was taking me at the moment, I knew Captain Kirk was *not* behind me."

As filming approached, Shatner saw an opportunity to bring a fresh perspective to his character. "Both Leonard and myself have changed over the years," he told reporters, "to a degree at any rate, and we will bring that degree of change inadvertently to the role we recreate." One of the changes Shatner had undergone was a twenty-five-pound weight gain that looked like forty-five pounds on camera. He knew that William Theiss' form-fitting pajama-style costumes would make him the butt (so to speak) of Hollywood jokes *if* he didn't do something quickly. So Shatner embarked on a grueling diet and weight training regimen under the supervision of "nutritionist to the stars" Dr. Ernst Wynder. The results can be seen in the finished film, as Shatner, of all the cast members, appears to have aged the least. Tinseltown gossip suggested the possibility that Shatner had resorted to more radical measures, such as face lifts and liposuction, to achieve the desired effect.

The production was beset by problems from the start. As many as four different writers had their fingerprints on the script, one of whom, Dennis Clark, lasted only three months. Two of these months, he later declared, "I spent hiding from Nimoy and Shatner because [the producers] didn't want me to talk to them. I'd have to leave my office when they were on the lot, because actors want to tell you, 'This is how I perceive the character,' and Gene [Roddenberry] didn't want their input. He didn't even like Bob Wise's input." The story everyone settled on, after countless rewrites, was ostensibly based on "In Thy Image," a **Gene Roddenberry** script for the abortive *Star Trek: Phase II* project. "In Thy Image," in turn, was a rehash of "Robot's Return," another unfilmed teleplay from Roddenberry's failed *Genesis II* series. The dirty little secret, however, which anyone who ever watched *Star Trek* could instantly perceive, was that *Star Trek: The Motion Picture* was a brazen copy of the original TV series episode "The Changeling." Expanded to almost three times the length and prettied up with special effects, yes, but still "The Changeling." Most galling of all, to the show's rabid fans, "The Changeling" (9/29/67) was actually *better!*

The film premiered in grand style on December 6, 1979, at the Kennedy Center in Washington, DC. However, in a portent of things to come, both Shatner and **Jimmy Doohan** fell asleep during the screening. Perhaps they were lulled into a stupor by one of the film's many interminable special effects sequences. A sure sign that the movie's mammoth effects budget had not been wisely allocated is an early sequence where Kirk and Scotty spend twenty minutes gazing out at the starship *Enterprise* as it sits in dry-dock. Try staring at a parked car for that length of time on your next lunch break and see if you don't get sleepy too.

Star Trek: The Motion Picture enjoyed a huge opening weekend, grossing $20 million—the second largest box-office splash to that point. However, it could not maintain that level of enthusiasm in the wake of a withering critical reception. The operative word was "soporific" as reviewer after reviewer lambasted the picture's plodding, deliberate pace. The promiscuous use of special effects enervated Richard Schickel of *Time*, who carped, "[T]he spaceships take an unconscionable amount of time to get anywhere, and nothing of dramatic or human interest happens along the way."

In purely financial terms, *Star Trek: The Motion Picture* can be judged a success. It grossed over $175 million, almost four times its budget. However, it did serious damage to the series' credibility with the show's most rabid fans—many of whom sat through it more than once out of sheer loyalty to the **Star Trek** ideal. "It was embarrassing to watch the fans," explained original series writer David Gerrold, "because they were all apologists for this picture: 'Well, it's not that bad. It's a different *kind* of **Star Trek**.' Instead of really just acknowledging that it was a bad movie, they tried to explain that it was wonderful and you were an idiot for not understanding it."

The stink from *Star Trek: The Motion Picture* lingered for a long time in the air. It took almost three years for Paramount to green light another **Star Trek** project. In addition, one of the film's early script iterations, *The God Thing*, about the *Enterprise*'s search for God at the end of the universe, would form the basis for the even more unwatchable **Star Trek V: The Final Frontier**. Still, for Shatner, the first movie was the beginning of a career renaissance. His credibility as a major star now restored, he largely gave up on the game show circuit and began to command more substantive parts. His bank account swelled thanks to a contract granting him a generous percentage of **Star Trek** movie merchandising royalties. Also, he had the satisfaction of knowing that, standing next to **Jimmy Doohan**, he looked positively svelte.

> "... *curiously smooth-skinned and hairy.*"
> —Newsweek's appraisal of Shatner's appearance
> in *Star Trek: The Motion Picture*

> "*Familiarity should not be permitted to undervalue Shatner's performance as Kirk; he grabs his role with relish, humour and solid sympathy.*"
> —Monthly Film Bulletin, February 1980

Star Trek II: The Wrath of Khan   RATING: U U U

This second film in the ongoing **Star Trek** movie saga was released in 1982. Directed by Nicholas Meyer, it returned the series to its action/adventure roots and won back the hearts of fans dispirited by 1979's **Star Trek: The Motion Picture**. Shatner had a particularly meaty part in the new installment. His epic verbal duels with costar Ricardo Montalban helped make *Star Trek II* a favorite among fans and general audiences alike.

The movie owed its positive vibe to one particularly smart pre-production decision. To ensure the mistakes of **Star Trek: The Motion Picture** were not repeated, Paramount executives promoted **Gene Roddenberry** to the post of executive consultant. This took the increasingly meddlesome **"Great Bird of the Galaxy"** out of the story development process. Creative control over the project was given to Harve Bennett, a former television producer whom Shatner later called "the man who got **Star Trek** back on track."

Despite the streamlined writing process, Shatner had his apprehensions about the new big-screen project. "I was nervous about it, especially after the first film," he admitted. "The success of your performance rests in the words. As this script developed, I swung wildly from awful lows to exalted highs." By the time filming began, however, Shatner was stoked. "I knew *The Wrath of Khan* would be great," he said.

Boosting everyone's spirits on the *Star Trek II* set was director Nicholas Meyer. The scenarist behind two inventive high concept movie hits, 1976's *The Seven-Per-Cent Solution* ("Sherlock Holmes Meets Sigmund Freud") and 1979's *Time After Time* ("H. G. Wells vs. Jack the Ripper in modern-day San Francisco") Meyer was a fledgling movie director (having only helmed *Time After Time*). Nevertheless, the cast and crew had full confidence in his abilities behind the camera. "Even though it was only the second picture he had directed," Shatner opined, "we felt that his imagination should be given full flower."

Production on *Star Trek II* got under way on November 9, 1981. The project went through several subtitle changes on its way to completion. Originally, it was to be called *Star Trek II: The Undiscovered Country*, after a line from Shakespeare's *Hamlet*. When that was scrapped as too erudite for mass audiences (though later revived as the subtitle of *Star Trek VI*) the producers switched to *Star Trek II: The Vengeance of Khan*. However, fears of competition from George Lucas' forthcoming third *Star Wars* movie—at that time called *Revenge of the Jedi*—forced Bennett, Meyer, and company to settle on the shorter, punchier *The Wrath of Khan*. Also downsized was the film's budget, to around $11 million, about a fourth of what was spent on **Star Trek: The Motion Picture**. The belt-tightening approach helped give the final movie some of the charming "slapped together in a week-and-a-half" quality of the original series.

As befit its cash constraints, the plot of *Star Trek II: The Wrath of Khan* was stripped to simplicity. A starship probing a distant sector of the galaxy stumbles upon ubermensch Khan Noonian Singh (Ricardo Montalban) and his cadre of genetic freaks stranded on the planet where Captain Kirk exiled them some fifteen years earlier (in the original series episode "Space Seed," February 16, 1967). The devious Khan hijacks the ship and steals The Genesis Device, an untested Federation innovation that creates life on barren planets. Kirk and the *Enterprise* crew (including **Kirstie Alley** as a Vulcan lieutenant) are dispatched to investigate. The ensuing violent confrontation claims the lives of Khan, his crew, and, in a moving climactic scene, beloved science officer Spock. All the regulars returned for another shift through space, although of all the subsidiary players only **Walter Koenig** (as Comdr. Pavel Chekov) is given anything substantive to say or do on camera.

While *Star Trek II* is best remembered by audiences as the **Star Trek** movie where Spock dies, it is also arguably the most Shatner-centered of the six original-crew motion pictures. After seemingly sleepwalking through much of **Star Trek: The Motion Picture**, Shatner seems rejuvenated here. He has many chewy scenes and does not miss a beat in his attempts to dominate all the action. Throughout the film, Kirk must wrestle with a mid-life crisis triggered by his birthday and the appearance of his estranged son David, played by Merritt Buttrick of TV's *Square Pegs* (1982–83). After doing his best to vacuum the lines off his face for the previous picture, Shatner finally accepts the realities of aging and change by donning granny glasses and ruing his misspent youth on screen.

However, *Star Trek II* was more than just *Steel Magnolias* (1989) in space. It was also a top-notch action romp in the tradition of old school episodes like "Arena" (1/19/67) and "The Doomsday Machine" (10/20/67). Shatner's byplay with costar Ricardo Montalban is particularly compelling. Squaring off exclusively via viewscreen (the chief flaw in the picture is their lack of a face-to-face confrontation) the two grand hams snarl and quote poetry to each other with a vigor that almost makes you forget what bad wigs they're both wearing. Especially affecting is the scene where Shatner finds the crew of a science station massacred by Khan and his followers, then excoriates him via communicator. "Like a poor marksman, you KEEP...MISSING...the TARGET!" Shatner rants in perhaps the finest cinematic exemplification of his acting style. Then, his head seeming to expand like a basketball being filled with air, his red cheeks bulging, he wails, "KHAAAAN! KHAAAAAAAAN!" with such a convulsive intensity that one might almost think a man's heart attack had been captured on camera. Theatre and television audiences invariably erupt into fits of laughter when this scene is played out, no matter how many times they've seen it before.

Viewers may have been laughing, *but* they were also paying. *Star Trek: The Wrath of Khan* grossed almost $80 million in the United States alone, easily earning back its relatively small budget. Critics were pleased with the scaled-down look and feel of the new entry, which in the eyes of many played like a feature-length television episode. No group was more pleased than **Star Trek**'s dedicated fans, who finally had a **Trek** film they could proudly proclaim their affection for after the debacle of **Star Trek: The Motion Picture**.

As for Shatner, he reveled in the return of the movie series to its Kirk-centric glory days. "I always knew there was a large audience that wanted to see me," he revealed to *People* magazine. He went on to designate himself the fulcrum of **Star Trek**.

Not so pleased with the functioning of their fulcrum were the other cast members, several of whom compared Shatner unfavorably with Ricardo Montalban. "It was great not having scenes reblocked by our leading man," **Walter Koenig** told *Starlog* magazine. "Montalban was always there for your close-up and always very giving. The two weeks I worked with Bill as the leading man weren't as much fun." There were the usual complaints among the cast about Shatner trimming their lines, even excising whole scenes designed to give their characters something more to do than stand around and say "Aye, sir." Also, Hollywood neo-phyte **Kirstie Alley** added her name to the list of actresses who report-edly have been the object of Shatner's romantic attentions off camera. For the record, she resisted his advances.

Walter Koenig explained the Shatner dilemma succinctly: "When you have one actor so dominating the proceedings in terms of partici-pation, regardless of how good he is, I don't think it's possible for the other actors to feel totally comfortable about the situation. The sense of ensemble playing wasn't there. In most cases, Bill dominated *every* scene he was in, and that's the way it was photographed."

For better or worse, Shatner's aggressive scene-hogging made *Star Trek II* what it was. And in the eyes of Paramount executives, that was a hit. They would repeat the same formula, with slightly less spectacular results, in 1984's *Star Trek III: The Search for Spock*.

Star Trek III: The Search for Spock   RATING: U U

The third entry in the *Star Trek* movie series was released in 1984. It was the feature film directorial debut of Leonard Nimoy, who appeared only briefly on screen as Spock, much of that in flashback to the previous the-atrical installment. *Star Trek III* wrapped up loose plot ends from *Star Trek II: The Wrath of Khan* (1982) and returned Spock to the land of the living, much to the delight of *Star Trek*'s ardent fans.

Production began on August 15, 1983. At first, Shatner chafed at hav-ing his longtime series' rival behind the cameras. "It was more awkward in the beginning than any of the other two [films]," he reported, liken-ing the experience of being directed by Nimoy to being ordered around by your brother. Elsewhere he placed their relationship in a marital con-text. "It's like your wife is suddenly earning more money than you. The relationship has changed and you have to make an adjustment. Once that adjustment is made, you might sit back and relax and enjoy it. Which is what I've begun to do."

Once the new power arrangements were sorted out, filming pro-ceeded briskly. Principal photography was completed in only forty-nine days at a relatively tight budget of $16 million. All the usual suspects returned to keep their SAG cards valid for another few years, although the disgruntled newcomer **Kirstie Alley** (of *Star Trek: The Wrath of Khan*) had been replaced by Robin Curtis. This time, the supporting cast even had a few scenes of their own to display their talents. Most amusing of these is a sequence in which Sulu dispatches a tall, burly security guard who had previously made fun of his short stature. "Don't call me Tiny," **George Takei** intoned, and the phrase soon began turning up on T-shirts and bumper stickers at *Star Trek* conventions throughout the world.

The real focus of *Star Trek III* was made plain in its subtitle, however. The plot concerns the efforts of the *Enterprise* crew to return Spock's body to his home planet of Vulcan for a ceremony that will reunite it with his still-living spirit, now inhabiting Dr. McCoy. Along the way, they encounter Klingons, led by Kluge (Christopher Lloyd), a vicious warrior who takes an instant disliking to Captain Kirk. Kirk's son David (Merritt Buttrick) is killed in a confrontation on the Genesis planet, and the starship *Enterprise* is destroyed by Kirk in an effort to foil the Klingon plans for galactic domination.

After dominating the action in *Star Trek II*, Shatner must have been salivating at the prospect of acting in a film in which Nimoy plays a corpse for most of the picture. However, while Kirk is given a few priceless scenes here, he does not command the same presence as he did in the previous entry. Reportedly Shatner had even less to do in the original script, but quickly made his objections known to Nimoy and producer Harve Bennett. More screen time for Kirk was added—as usual at the expense of the other actors.

In one of the more memorable scenes in this installment, Shatner has the opportunity for method hamming as Kirk learns his son David has been executed by a Klingon war party. Director Nimoy even cleared the set to get his star in the appropriate emotional state for this key sequence. He left it up to Shatner to decide how far to go in showing Kirk's grief, and Shatner went quite a way indeed. When given the news of David's death, he has Kirk stumble backwards and fall on his behind, croaking "You Klingon bastards, you've killed my *son!*" in a breakneck staccato. "He looks deeply hurt," Nimoy said of the performance, refusing to clarify whether he meant by the fall or the emotional blow. Shatner would later call it his finest piece of acting as Kirk.

Somehow, though, *Star Trek III*, as a piece, does not come off quite as well as it might have. For a film with such a simple plot, it moves at a snail's pace. The funereal mood set in the opening moments lingers throughout, accentuated by the death of David and the gratuitous destruction of the *Enterprise*. Shatner himself acknowledged the gimmicky nature of these developments by summing up the screenwriters' dilemma as "What else can we kill?" The concluding scenes on Vulcan, obviously meant to be moving and mystical, are merely tedious for many viewers. Even the action scenes fail to compel. The Klingon plot seems tacked on and perfunctory. Seriously damaging these sequences is Christopher Lloyd, who seems to be playing his *Taxi* (1979–83) role of Reverend Jim Ignatowski in Klingon makeup. His voice and demeanor are simply too mannered and recognizable to allow him to carry off such a villainous characterization.

Despite the picture's flaws, audiences eager for more **Star Trek** gave this installment the thumbs-up. Released in June of 1984, *Star Trek III: The Search for Spock* grossed more than $76 million in box-office receipts. "Installment three falls somewhere ahead of the first feature and way behind the high-water mark of [**Star Trek**] **II**," observed the *New York Daily News*, capturing the consensus opinion of fans and critics. Moviegoers were especially cheered by the return of Spock to the starship *Enterprise* fold. Many of the more rabid Trekkies threatened to boycott **Star Trek** films if the beloved Vulcan was not sprung from his space coffin. They had nothing to worry about. Spock and the rest of the crew would be back with full faculties engaged for 1986's **Star Trek IV: The Voyage Home**.

Star Trek IV: The Voyage Home   RATING: ∪∪∪(

The fourth of the **Star Trek** feature films found its release in 1986. A light-hearted time travel romp with an environmental twist, it was a much-needed change of pace for the big-screen series and proved to be a colossal hit with the public. Again, Leonard Nimoy took the reins as director, with creative assistance from screenwriters Harve Bennett and Nicholas Meyer.

Now regarded as one of the best **Star Trek** movies, *The Voyage Home* almost *did not* get produced. Shatner played hardball with Paramount before signing on for another voyage as Captain Kirk. Securely ensconced in prime-time as TV's *T. J. Hooker* (1982–86), he at last had the leverage to demand a sizable pay increase. Negotiations dragged on for months, and at one point Paramount was prepared to move *without* Shatner. Their contingency concept, a prequel called *Starfleet Academy*, was configured as a kind of "*Top Gun* [1986] in space," with young actors assuming the roles of the *Star Trek* regulars. To the relief of all concerned, that concept was scrapped when Shatner agreed to a $2 million contract. After a host of delays, *Star Trek*'s fourth feature was, as Sulu might have observed, "making good time."

Star Trek IV is quite a departure from the previous productions. After the gloomy goings-on in 1984's *Star Trek III*, Leonard Nimoy and Harve Bennett had a simple story prescription for the next entry: make 'em laugh. "We felt that we should lighten up," said Nimoy. "The picture should be fun in comparison to the previous three. The first movie had no comedy at all. That was intentional. It was intended to be a serious study of a problem. The second film had a little. The third film had a little. But there we were dealing with a lot of serious drama. There was a lot of life and death going on . . . I just felt it was time to lighten up and have some fun."

Originally slated to provide fun for the picture was comedy juggernaut Eddie Murphy, then fresh off his *Beverly Hills Cop* (1984) success. A longtime *Star Trek* fan, Murphy was to play a wacky college professor whose belief in UFOs is validated by the appearance of the *Enterprise* in modern-day San Francisco. However, Paramount was skittish about putting its major comedy star into its franchise science fiction series. Two great tastes do not necessarily blend well together. So Murphy's part was rewritten as a touchy-feely marine biologist, played in the finished film by Catherine Hicks. Producers were also eager to provide Kirk with a love interest after letting his hormonal urges go largely unattended on camera in the previous three pictures. In fact, two young screenwriters, Steve Meerson and Peter Krikes, were brought in to work on the project with explicit instructions to expand Shatner's screen role.

"The approach we were told to take is that Kirk really had to be the one to lead everyone," Meerson recalled. "Not necessarily that he had to actually have the idea to do something, but it had to appear as if he has the idea . . . . We were told Bill had to be the leader at all times."

Once Shatner had wrapped up work on ***T. J. Hooker*** for the 1985–86 television series, he joined the rest of the regulars for another round of intergalactic hijinks. *Star Trek IV* went before the cameras in February of 1986. Shooting took fifty-three days at a still relatively restricted budget of $23 million. Using modern-day exteriors like San Francisco's Golden Gate Park and that city's Presidio helped keep costs under control, while the production itself was almost completely devoid of expensive science fiction trappings.

The absence of special effects wizardry, however, did not detract at all from *Star Trek IV*'s entertainment quotient. That was provided by some snappy patter, inventive situations, and a humanistic theme that recalled the very best original TV series episodes. *The Voyage Home* opens with a gigantic probe paralyzing twenty-third century Earth in a misguided attempt to communicate with some long-extinct humpback whales. The starship *Enterprise* must travel back in time to 1986 and bring back two of the keening leviathans to keep the universe from being destroyed. Along the way there are a lot of the usual "how do we explain Spock's ears?" shenanigans. All of it might have seemed dreadfully familiar and clichéd in the hands of a different director and cast. But by this time the **Star Trek** repertory players had learned the secret of not taking themselves too seriously. Instead they play to the nostalgia of their audience, which feels as if it is in on the joke from the first scene to the last.

Shatner called the approach *joie de vivre*. "We discovered something in *Star Trek IV* that we hadn't pinpointed in any of the other movies," he said, "and it just shows how the obvious can escape you—that there is a texture to the best **Star Trek** hours that verges on tongue-in-cheek but isn't." True fans of **Star Trek**—and Shatner—have been grooving on this texture for years.

Star Trek IV: The Voyage Home reached theatres in time for Christmas of 1986. It was the most successful **Star Trek** big-screen excursion to date, grossing over $125 million, more than five times its budget! Critics lauded the movie's lighthearted tone and ensemble playing—particularly the Spock/McCoy byplay. "Nimoy and Kelley are at their most amusingly snippy," raved David Denby in *New York* magazine. "They appear to be playing two aging gays dishing at each other at a party while vying for the attention of William Shatner." As a rare novelty, the names of supporting cast members like **Walter Koenig** and **George Takei** were cited by reviewers as often as the so-called "Big Three." The seven dwarfs were delirious. "For the first time I felt the dialogue was indigenous to my character," explained Walter Koenig, "that only Chekov could say these lines." Never one to give up an old saw, he then added tellingly. "And I had the opportunity to work away from Bill Shatner."

Star Trek V: The Final Frontier   RATING:

This fifth entry in the *Star Trek* film series is the only one directed by Shatner. "Things don't turn out exactly the way you want them to," were the words Shatner used to sum up his participation in the 1989 project, and the show's fans mostly agreed. *Star Trek V* remains a notable failure in the *Star Trek* cinematic cycle, with turgid and amateurish direction often cited among the litany of critical complaints.

The *Star Trek V* story line germinated for almost ten years before taking root. It is loosely based on *The God Thing*, an early script for 1979's ***Star Trek: The Motion Picture***. That screenplay had the starship *Enterprise* encountering God at the far edges of the universe. It was rejected by Paramount as too pretentious, but Shatner found it fascinating. "It was a mind-boggling script," he gushed, "something along the lines of *2001* [1968]. The dialogue was incredible. Spock was questioning the logic of a supreme being whose actions appeared questionable and inconsistent. It would have made a classic science fiction film."

In the final screenplay, cowritten by Shatner from his original story, Sybok, a renegade Vulcan holy man, commandeers the *Enterprise* to take him on a search for God. Along the way, the charismatic guru manages to convert a number of the ship's crew to his philosophy of spiritual healing. Complications ensue when a Klingon vessel attacks the *Enterprise* to exact vengeance against Kirk. The film's climax takes place at the Great Barrier at the center of the galaxy, where God is found to be a large holographic head with a flowing white beard—in reality an evil alien projection. The film concludes with cosmic order restored and the star troika of Kirk, Spock, and McCoy warbling "Row, Row, Row Your Boat" around a campfire.

Shooting began on October 11, 1988. Anxious to bring his grand vision to fruition on time and under budget, Shatner was manic on the set, ordering people around in a nonsensical patter. "He thought that by talking fast it would speed up the schedule," observed Leonard Nimoy. "But you couldn't understand a word he was saying." Eventually, he got a hold of himself. Nevertheless, the production would not go smoothly. With a $30 million budget to work with (a third of which went to special effects), fledgling big-screen director Shatner was, understandably, like a kid in a candy store. Like any candy store, the set was plagued by petty thievery. In one instance $60,000 worth of costumes were stolen from a trailer. Cost overruns, labor disputes, and shoddy planning also dogged the project. In the end, *Star Trek V* came in $3 million *over* budget, a striking departure from the tidy and economical production on the previous theatrical trio. Shatner tried to write off the gaffes as the inevitable run-off of his boundless creative energy, but studio executives weren't buying it. "Directing multiple episodes of **T. J. Hooker** just did not prepare Bill Shatner for the wide screen's demands," opined Harve Bennett.

Following months of bad publicity, the film debuted in June of 1989 to eager if apprehensive audiences. Before long, moviegoers' worst fears were confirmed. If **Star Trek V** had any redeeming moments, they surely must have ended up on the cutting room floor. Most longtime **Star Trek** fans found themselves wincing through the movie's many embarrassing scenes, including a staggering sequence in which an aging **Nichelle Nichols** performs an ostensibly sexy striptease for a group of ogling barbarians. The other supporting characters were likewise stripped of all dignity. "Chekov and Sulu were supposed to be the best navigator and helmsman in Starfleet," an angry George Takei pointed out. Shatner's script has them get hopelessly lost in the forest. "Engineer Scott was supposed to know every inch of the *Enterprise* like 'the back of my hand.'" Yet Shatner depicts him bonking his head on a crossbeam. The humor, Takei concluded, "instead of being light and frolicsome, seemed only mean-spirited."

Shatner was apparently oblivious to these complaints. For him, *Star Trek V: The Final Frontier* represented a grand vision unrealized due to budget constraints, studio tinkering, and his own lack of experience as a director. "What the final result was, was the final result," he observed afterwards. "I have certain regrets but I feel in total that a lot of the vision was there. I made one major compromise at the beginning which was mitigating the original idea of the *Enterprise* searching for God and instead finding an alien pretending to be God. The enormous thrust of the idea was eviscerated and that was my first compromise. It seemed that was a necessary one due to the fact that everybody was very apprehensive about the obvious problem. I thought [the film] was flawed. I didn't manage my resources as well as I could have. I thought it was a meaningful *attempt* at a story and I thought it was a meaningful play. It carried a sense of importance about it."

Perhaps most damaging to **The Final Frontier** is its lackluster finale, in which the highly anticipated confrontation with God turns out to be nothing more than an encounter with a hologramatic head. In Shatner's original vision, Kirk is pursued by a legion of malevolent gargoyles let loose by the God creature. But special effects cost restrictions forced him to scuttle this idea. Detractors blasted Shatner for coming up with grandiose sequences that were impossible to film. But Shatner defended his unorthodox approach. "A first-time director knows no boundaries," he said, "and it's not knowing them that you shatter them. Rather than accepting the status quo, I tried to break the boundaries and make the camera do things that it wasn't supposed to, not because I didn't know how, but I thought that by standing firm and being as adamant as possible it would happen. But there came a point where I had to compromise."

One problem that did *not* plague *Star Trek V* was conflict between the director and his costars—despite initial reservations among the supporting players. "To say that most of us were dreading standing before a camera with Bill on the other side of it would be an understatement," was **Nichelle Nichols**' recollection of her return to playing her role as Communications Officer Uhura. "After twenty years of enduring his overbearing behavior on the set, our apprehensions about working on *Star Trek V* were not unfounded." Nevertheless, she found him to be "supportive, encouraging, [and] inspiring" as a director. **Leonard Nimoy** was equally effusive. "With us as actors, [Bill] was personable, charming, well-prepared, and boundlessly enthusiastic." Even stalwart Shatner enemies like **Jimmy Doohan** (Mr. Scott) agreed. "The man's not half as bad as I thought he'd be," he cracked.

Alone among the original crew members, **George Takei** (Commander Sulu) saw a darker motivation for Shatner's seeming change of heart. "It was not an unpleasant working experience to be directed by him," he remarked in his 1994 autobiography. "In fact, he was actually quite good at creating a positive environment on the set, marshalling his considerable reservoir of charm, loading into his weapon, and placing the setting at 'enchant'. . . . His charm was intended, however, always to burnish his own star. I knew I was only watching another acting performance—this time, he was acting the role of a cheerfully earnest and helpful director."

Earnest and helpful, perhaps, but ultimately unsuccessful. Shatner's compromised vision didn't transport with **Star Trek** fans. After a solid opening weekend, *Star Trek V* bombed with audiences, during a summer when *Batman* was setting huge box-office records. Its final box-office take was only $52 million, down by half from the previous film. Given its bloated budget, the profit margin for an unhappy Paramount was even smaller. Today it is widely considered the worst of the **Star Trek** films— with predictable objections from Shatner himself. "Regardless of where it ranked in anybody else's lexicon," he told the *Washington Post* in 1991, "*Star Trek V* was life-changing for me . . . . All the other films have special things about them. But *V* is very special to me."

> *"Oh my God. What are we going to do?"*
> —GEORGE TAKEI, on learning that Shatner
> was to direct *Star Trek V*

Star Trek VI:
The Undiscovered Country   RATING: U U U

The sixth film in the **Star Trek** cinematic cycle is the last numbered installment (thus far). This, the final journey of the original *Enterprise* crew is a story of intergalactic political intrigue inspired by the end of the Cold War. Released in time for Christmas of 1991, *Star Trek VI* was a hit with fans and critics alike, helping to erase the bitter taste left behind by **Star Trek V**.

In *Star Trek VI: The Undiscovered Country* the near geriatric *Enterprise* crew reunites for a diplomatic mission. It seems the Klingon high command has decided to seek peace with the Federation after years of galactic conflict. However, a renegade Klingon, General Chang

(Christopher Plummer), hatches a plan to disrupt the peace conference by assassinating the Klingon High Chancellor. Captain Kirk and Dr. McCoy are framed for the crime and sentenced to hard labor on a frigid prison planet. After a bizarre interlude in which Kirk enjoys a roll in the snow with a shape-shifting alien (played by supermodel Iman) the action ends up back at the peace conference. There, with some help from the newly commissioned Captain Sulu, our heroes foil Chang's plans to assassinate a Federation delegate.

While not high on theatrics, *Star Trek VI* benefited from a sound, politically relevant story line. "It's a really good idea," Shatner said. "It's a classic **Star Trek** idea in that the important issue of the day is incorporated into the story of **Star Trek**, and by doing so—and because we put it into the future—we're able to comment on it as though it has nothing to do with today, yet it makes a commentary."

The script was written by Nimoy and Dennis Martin Flinn, the latter a newcomer to **Star Trek**. Initially, Shatner was disappointed when the director's nod went to Nicholas Meyer. "I felt a sense of loss that I couldn't be the problem solver," he said. "I would have loved to have been immersed in those very same problems and bring to bear what I had learned on the previous film." Paramount, however, had no intentions of turning the reins over to their quixotic star. The studio was in a cost-cutting mode; in fact, the studio executives wrangled for tightening the movie's $26 million budget all through filming. The production could have been contentious and rocky—but somehow just the opposite happened.

Anyone who thought that Shatner would be a pain in the neck on the set after being passed over for the director's assignment was soon disabused of that notion. In fact, production on *Star Trek VI* rolled along with nary a hitch. "It went a lot smoother than I thought," said new producer Ralph Winter. "I had a great time with Bill. He was terrific and he was a lot of fun." Winter and Meyer even cast Shatner's daughter Melanie in a small role as a navigator.

Canadian actress Kim Cattrall was assigned the role of Valeris, a Vulcan who betrays the *Enterprise* crew to the Klingons. In keeping with the air of good feeling that pervaded the production, she had nothing but nice things to say about her leading man. "Shatner can technically do almost anything as an actor. He was a gentleman with me and it doesn't matter how I feel about him personally. We're both Canadians and I had a professional relationship.... I don't think anybody does better what he does. He is Captain Kirk and he's amazing in what he does."

Rounding out Canadian old home week was Christopher Plummer, Shatner's longtime friend from Stratford days in Ontario. He brought real Shakespearean heft to his performance as Chang, though his endless nonsensical quotations from *Hamlet* get a bit annoying after a while. His presence on the set obviously helped bring out the best in Shatner, who gives a delightfully chewy performance in this, his last go-round as a leading man in a ***Star Trek*** movie.

For the first time since ***Star Trek II***, Shatner actually was prompted into thinking seriously about his screen character. "The portrayal of Kirk attempts to show a man who has spent a lifetime imbued with the idea that his mission in life is to subdue, subvert, and make the enemy submit to his nation's or his Federation's view," he said. "That's his whole training and that is the military training. He learns differently and that is the classic dilemma that ***Star Trek*** has sought to present in its most successful shows."

Critics and audiences alike found *Star Trek VI: The Undiscovered Country* very satisfying indeed. "The crew's hairpieces are worse than ever, the bags under their eyes could hold a week's worth of groceries," wrote Leah Rozen in her review for *People*, but, she conceded, "hard-core Trekkies will get their rockets off *with Star Trek VI.*" In fact, hard-core and other Trekkies poured out almost 150 million of their hard-earned dollars to watch the *Enterprise* crew zoom off into the sunset. The movie's powerhouse performance helped convince Paramount to continue the movie series, now focusing upon the characters from the *Star Trek: The Next Generation* TV show (1987–94).

Star Trek VI ends with one final touching creative flourish, as all the original series actors sign their names in the *Enterprise*'s last log book. Majestic orchestral music plays appropriately in the background. "They reversed the order of the names so Shatner's is last, like an opera," said composer Cliff Eidelman. "It's a minute of signing off, which is real emotional music." A baton of sorts had been passed, to the cast and crew of *Star Trek: The Next Generation*, who would soldier on in ***Star Trek: Generations*** in 1994.

Star Trek VII

The film that was ultimately made as **Star Trek: Generations** lost its Roman numeral only after Shatner gave up on a campaign to write and direct the feature, á la 1989's **Star Trek V**. Shatner's treatment differed substantially from the finished on-screen product. His version had Kirk falling in love with a younger woman and Kirk and Spock were to suffer a falling-out then spend the entire movie bickering with each other. Paramount disliked the concept and told Shatner to pitch it elsewhere. He later reworked the older man/younger woman romance angle into his 1995 **Star Trek** novel **Ashes of Eden**.

The Shatnerific Trivia Challenge
PART TWO: THE LIFE AND CAREER OF WILLIAM SHATNER

1. In what space fantasy is Shatner's character mutating into a lizard-like creature?

2. Name the actor who appeared on screen with both William Shatner and Sean Connery.

3. Which of these did Shatner *not* play: Tom Sawyer, Tinnitus, Tamburlaine, T. J. Hooker.

4. The failure of which TV project aided the success of another important project?

5. On what occasion did Shatner appear on television with Steve McQueen?

6. Name William Shatner's big-screen movies which featured these actors: (Caution: nobody's saying Shatner *co*starred with them)
   a. Judy Garland
   b. Yul Brynner
   c. Paul Newman
   d. Marlene Dietrich
   e. Edward G. Robinson
   f. John Travolta
   g. Ava Gardner
   h. Sonny Bono

7. True or false: *Star Trek* was Shatner's first appearance in a TV sci-fi series.

8. Which of these TV game shows did Shatner *not* appear on?
   a. *Celebrity Bowling*
   b. *Hollywood Squares*
   c. *Masquerade Party*
   d. *Match Game*
   e. *Pyramid*

9. Say that you're William Shatner. You married three of these women, and were sued for palimony by the other two. Do you remember who's who?
   a. Eva Marie Friedrick
   b. Nerine Kidd
   c. Marcy Lafferty
   d. Vira Montes
   e. Gloria Rand

10. What does William Shatner have in common with the Tennessee Williams heroine Blanche DuBois (of *A Streetcar Named Desire*)?

11. Operation Lazarus sounds like a movie title but it's not. Shatner got a lot of attention for it—and could have gone to jail! What's going on?

12. Follow carefully: What's the Shatner movie that's adapted from a classic Japanese movie... by the director of another classic Japanese movie that was adapted into Hollywood's *The Magnificent Seven* (1960)?

13. *Today Show* TV host Jane Pauley thought it demeaning for Captain Kirk to be promoting a food product. Retorted Shatner, "For Captain Kirk maybe, but for William Shatner it was perfectly feasible!" What was the product in question?

14. Match the name of the character on the left with the name of the TV movie or feature film in which Shatner played him.

    1. Rack Hansen   A. *Airplane II: The Sequel*
    2. Mark Preston   B. *Want a Ride, Little Girl?*
    3. Buck Murdock   C. *Secrets of a Married Man*
    4. Chase Prescott   D. *Kingdom of the Spiders*
    5. Chris Jordan   E. *The Barbary Coast*
    6. Jeff Cable   F. *Dead Man's Island*
    7. Matt Stone   G. *The Devil's Rain*

15. Who was producer Gene Roddenberry's first choice for the role of TV's Captain Kirk?

16. Which one of Shatner's daughters appeared with him in a movie?

17. Match the movie or episode title to the plot line:
    a. *The Land of No Return*
    b. "Nightmare at 20,000 Feet"
    c. *Horror at 37,000 Feet*
    d. *Sole Survivor*
    e. *The Crash of Flight 401*

    1. Ghosts from a World War II bomber return to haunt a surviving crew member.
    2. A plane full of wild animals crashes in the wilderness.
    3. There's a gremlin sitting on the wing of an airplane.
    4. A plane goes down in the Everglades.
    5. A plane is haunted by ghosts.

18. Which two *Fantasy Island* stars has Shatner appeared with on screen?

19. A canine appears in the title of which Shatner TV project?

20. Who are Dunhill, Stirling, and China?

Answers on page 280

Starvation Years

Shatner's term for his five years (1952-56) of struggle as a young actor in Canada. "I'm talking about rope mattresses in attics and saving two dollars if I wanted to eat," he once explained, "or not doing my laundry if I wanted to eat." The low point came during Shatner's days with the **Canadian National Repertory Theatre** in Ottawa. Here Shatner lived alone, scraping by on $31 a week through the long, frigid winters of 1952 and 1953. Shatner developed his distaste for **fruit salad** during these years, because he had to eat it every day at the local Woolworth's in order to economize.

"Those days were hell. I got through them because in front of me was a dream. I hoped to become as fine an actor as Laurence Olivier."

—SHATNER, on his starvation years

Stewart, Patrick (B. 1940)

This bald, lean, sharp-featured British actor, with his distinctive stentorian voice, played the role of Captain Jean-Luc Picard on TV's *Star Trek: The Next Generation* from 1987 to 1994. He also appeared in the feature **Star Trek: Generations** with Shatner in 1994, as well as the continuation of the series feature films with *Star Trek: First Contact* (1996) and the projected new **Star Trek** film. A well-known member of the English stage, Stewart had an impressive Shakespearean pedigree before taking on the role of the commander of the starship *Enterprise* NCC-1701-C. He had also appeared in such feature films as *Hedda* (1975), *Excalibur* (1981),

Shatner and Patrick Stewart show evidence of the warm personal relationship they developed on the set of Star Trek: Generations *(1994). [photo courtesy of AP Worldwide Photos]*

Lifeforce (1985), and *The Doctor and the Devils* (1985), and was familiar to American audiences from his part (Sejanus) in the famed BBC television production of Robert Graves' *I Claudius* (1980), which had Derek Jacobi in the title role. However, there any and all similarities to Shatner end.

A thinking man's captain who plays the flute and sends his burly first officer out to do his fighting for him, Picard was the polar opposite of the brash, impulsive **James T. Kirk**. Yet Stewart brought an intelligence and dignity to the ongoing role that endeared him to TV viewers over the long haul. One man not charmed was Shatner, who saw his successor on the *Enterprise* bridge as a rival, *not* a friend. In interviews during the years when the syndicated *Next Generation* was on the air, Shatner took every opportunity to compare Stewart unfavorably to himself—or damn him with faint praise. "Stewart is not the captain, he's just a wonderful actor," was a typical remark. At other times, like a fan arguing with his buddies, Shatner would take up the "my captain is better than your captain" argument. "Kirk was the better captain," he once told a TV interviewer, "because he was more three dimensional"—though he declined to reveal which other two dimensions he had in mind. While he was aware of such comments, Stewart largely remained above the fray.

Sparks were expected to fly when the two performers worked together on **Star Trek: Generations** in 1994. According to Shatner, however, "instant liking and respect transpired" when the duo first met at the ShoWest movie exhibitors' convention that year in Las Vegas. "Patrick told me that he felt very lost among all these people neither one of us knew, so we held hands and kind of clung together like two howler monkeys might." That evening, the two men shared a corporate jet back to Los Angeles.

Shatner denied rumors that he and Stewart fought on the movie set of **Star Trek: Generations**. In fact, he says they bonded on their mutual love of horses. Before long, Shatner was sharing his **panty hose** with the cerebral Shakespearean. "We became very friendly," Shatner explained to *TV Guide*. The two captains have since teamed up to promote **pre-paid phone cards** together and have made numerous joint *Star Trek* convention appearances. Since leaving the daily grind of *Star Trek: The Next Generation*, Stewart has appeared in such theatrical and television features as *Jeffrey* (1995), *The Canterville Ghost* (1996), *Conspiracy Theory*

(1997), and a television remake of Melville's classic 1851 novel, *Moby Dick* (1998). In addition, of course, he was on hand for the next theatrical entry of **Star Trek** entitled *Star Trek: First Contact* (1996). After the successful filming of that entry and the enthusiastic response of its fans, it has been reported that Stewart will receive $12 million to reprise his role as Captain Picard in the next entry, *Star Trek: Insurrection* (1998).

Stiller, Ben (B. 1965)

Actor-director, the son of the comedy team of Jerry Stiller and Anne Meara, whose screen directing and/or acting efforts have included *Reality Bites* (1994), *Zero Effect* (1998), and *There's Something about Mary* (1998). As a child, idolized Shatner. In 1975, Stiller actually met his hero, but like many such fantasy encounters this one ended in disillusionment. Stiller had a guest spot on his mother's short-lived TV drama *Kate McShane* (1975) on the Paramount lot. Shatner was shooting his series **The Barbary Coast** on the next sound stage. "I thought it couldn't get any better," recalled Stiller, "One day I went up to him and yelled, 'Captain Kirk!' He turned around and had a handlebar mustache. I felt so gypped. It was an early lesson on the bitter disappointments of Hollywood."

Shatner in makeup for The Barbary Coast *(1975). Could this be the mustache that scared a youthful Ben Stiller? [photo courtesy of* The Everett Collection]

Stratford Shakespeare Festival

In 1953 Shatner joined this Shakespearean repertory company, which was founded by the renowned English director **Tyrone Guthrie**. The company staged the Bard's works in a huge earthen pit underneath a tent in Stratford, Ontario, Canada. For $80 a week, Shatner had the opportunity to appear in sixty plays during his three-year stint with the festival, learning his trade alongside such established stars as James Mason, Alec Guinness, and Anthony Quayle. Among the nearly one hundred parts Shatner undertook at Stratford were Lucentio in *The Taming of the Shrew*, Gratiano in *The Merchant of Venice*, and Lucius in *Julius Caesar*. He received positive notices and gradually claimed bigger and bigger acting assignments.

"When I was 21, it was a very good year," Shatner seems to be saying in this early publicity portrait. [photo courtesy of Archive Photos]

One of Shatner's greatest triumphs at Stratford came as a surprise to everyone—including the actor himself. He was serving as understudy to Christopher Plummer (later his on-screen nemesis General Chang in 1991's ***Star Trek VI: The Undiscovered Country***) in a Stratford production of *Henry V* (not a fifth sequel, but the name of an English king). It was early in the season, before Shatner had had an opportunity to rehearse with the cast, when Plummer suddenly became ill and checked into the hospital. With only a few hours notice, Shatner found himself having to play Henry, one of Shakespeare's most demanding stage roles, in front of 2,300 people and a gaggle of influential critics. He carried it off splendidly until the final scene, when he suddenly could not remember his lines. Frantically, he huddled around the actor playing Henry's brother. "What's the line?" Shatner asked, but the response was an unintelligible garble. The audience took it as a sign that Henry was weary and depleted after a monumental battle. Only as Shatner walked away did the forgotten bit of dialogue come back to him, all too late. "Looking back, it was a marvelous piece of staging," he crowed. The performance garnered rave reviews, serving as a major boost to Shatner's burgeoning career.

T. J. Hooker

Shatner played the title role in this hour-long television police drama from 1982 to 1986. The ABC network series, picked up in its final season by CBS, concerned a gruff but lovable police detective (Shatner) who relinquishes his gold shield for a job on uniformed patrol. One-time *Dance Fever* (1985–87) TV host **Adrian Zmed** plays Hooker's wisecracking partner, Officer Vince Romano, while buxom **Heather Locklear** is Officer Stacy Sheridan.

Originally the series was to be called *The Protectors*, with Shatner portraying a hardnosed police academy instructor whose young cadets would see most of the chase-and-gun action. "*Dallas* with cops" was how executive producer Rick Husky framed the initial concept. When test audiences responded positively to the Hooker character, however, the cadets were expelled and the series reconfigured around the now stocky Shatner. For the record, Hooker worked from the mythical Los Angeles County Police Department (LCPD).

The project soon became renowned for its spectacular action sequences. In fact, the lasting image of the character of T. J. Hooker in most viewers' minds—famously parodied in a *Saturday Night Live* sketch—is Shatner clinging on to the hood of a speeding car. To prepare for the role, Shatner worked out daily in his home and ran three to five miles a day. Typically, he lost so much weight that his police uniform had to be taken in at the start of each season—only to be let out again as he ballooned over the course of the year.

Shatner plays Hooker as a tough but tender man squeezed by the constraints of the system. When asked what his character's greatest fear was, he replied, "feeling too much for the victims." Unwilling to be part

Old friend Leonard Nimoy plays a cop haunted by his son's drug addiction on an episode of T. J. Hooker. *[photo courtesy of Photofest]*

of just another TV cop show, Shatner consistently lobbied for more character development amidst the weekly mayhem. Over the course of the show's four-year run, Hooker loses a partner in the line of duty, divorces his wife, and stares down the barrel of a different ethical crisis every installment. The series gave Shatner a chance to play another complex on-camera hero—without falling prey to typecasting. "Viewers think of Hooker as the archetypal conservative cop fighting for justice," Shatner said of his creation, "which Kirk does, but on a higher plane. They are both universal characters doing what they can to preserve peace and justice. They share similar qualities, but there are differences, too. Kirk has a thoughtful, analytical approach to problems. Hooker is an angry man who reacts to stress with action. Actually, the core of each of them, of course, is within myself."

Besides playing the lead, Shatner also directed ten episodes of *Hooker* during the course of its TV run. His dominance of the show alienated some of his costars, particularly **Locklear**. Reportedly, she also resented Shatner's habit of rubbing himself up against her during episode rehearsals. The Beach Boys, Jerry Lee Lewis, and

Leonard Nimoy all had memorable guest-starring roles on the program over the years. *T. J. Hooker* remains Shatner's longest-running television drama series to date.

Takei, George (B. 1939)

This bantam Japanese-American actor played navigator extraordinaire Hikaru Sulu for all three seasons (1966–69) of *Star Trek*. Takei (pronounced Ta-KAY) endured four years in a Japanese-American internment camp during World War II before embarking on an acting career in the late 1950s. He brought to the role of Sulu an understated integrity and dry sense of humor. Around the set, Takei was known for his wickedly funny Shatner impersonation, which he invariably uncorked immediately after having his lines cut by the domineering star. "Hail...ing...Fre...quencies...O...pen...Cap...tain...Fas...Cin... a...ting!" Takei would say, aping Shatner's trademark staccato style. He believed Shatner's ultimate dream was to play all the characters on the TV show, so rankled was the star at having to share dialogue with the supporting players. "Shatner was the one who made life trying for all of us," Takei said, speaking for his fellow **"seven dwarfs."**

Over the years, Takei has been frequently miffed at Shatner's attempts to undercut him in small ways, such as sleepwalking through an important scene in *Star Trek II* (1982) in which Sulu receives his captain's commission. "When we shot the scene, Bill played it as he had rehearsed it, disinterested, murmuring some trivia about my captaincy, looking straight out into the void. There was no eye contact. No emotion. No relationship. Nothing....I was not surprised when I later learned that the scene was cut."

For all of the tension between them, however, Takei has never regarded Shatner with the same strong, unrelenting resentment as, say, fellow series regular **Jimmy Doohan**. Takei has maintained a fairly clear-headed view of Shatner as a charmer, not an ogre. "He always managed to keep that smiling, charming façade up, as if nothing out of the ordinary had happened, joking, giggling, and bantering. And always that sunny, oblivious, rankling smile. That smile as bright, as hard, and as relentless as the headlights of an oncoming car. You just had to get out of its way." Perhaps Takei gained insight into Shatner's personality type because of his experience in the political arena. He spent eleven years on the board of directors of the Southern California Rapid Transit District and ran unsuccessfully for a seat on the Los Angeles City Council in 1973. His autobiography, *To the Stars*, was published in 1994. On the screen scene, he has appeared, over the decades, in such non-**Star Trek** films as *Ice Palace* (1960), *The Green Berets* (1968), *Prisoners of the Sun* (1991), *Oblivion* (1994), and *Kiss* (1996), the latter a TV docudrama about Henry Kissinger and President Nixon.

> *"Like any large family, you have that Uncle Bill that you just can't stand."*
> —GEORGE TAKEI, on the dysfunctional *Star Trek* clan

Tamburlaine the Great

This classic Christopher Marlowe tragedy (1590) was adapted by Tyrone Guthrie and Donald Wolfit for a production at the Stratford (Ontario,

Shatner (top of cage) makes his Broadway debut opposite Anthony Quayle in Tamburlaine the Great *(1956). [photo courtesy of Photofest]*

Canada) Festival. In their new rendition of this production for New York, also directed by Guthrie, Shatner made his Broadway debut on January 19, 1956. The play follows the rise and fall of Tamburlaine (c. 1336–1405), the king of Persia. Anthony Quayle played the title role in the drama, which had a short run of twenty-one performances, despite great critical acclaim, at the Winter Garden Theatre. As **Usumcasane**, one of Tamburlaine's faithful attendants, Shatner had little to do beyond lugging a sedan chair around the stage, but he apparently lugged it well. A Twentieth Century-Fox official who saw him perform offered Shatner a seven-year movie contract with the studio, but he rejected it, reportedly on the advice of a mysterious stranger. "I thought there was nothing to be gained from signing and everything to lose," he told *TV Guide* in 1966. "Mainly my youth."

Tek

This addictive brain stimulant serves as the focal point of Shatner's *Tek* science-fiction cycle. The popular and prolific series, launched in 1989 with the publication of the novel *TekWar*, has grown to include comic books, trading cards, and a syndicated television series. "I wrote them as the sort of books you could read on airplanes and throw away afterwards," Shatner commented to *Entertainment Weekly*, "but they've become this phenomenon."

Set in the twenty-second century, the Tek series chronicles the exploits of **Jake Cardigan**, a rough-and-tumble hero whom Shatner likens to his *T. J. Hooker* character. Jake's future world is one of nefarious corporations, killer androids, and cryogenic prison chambers. Shatner originally envisioned Tek as the basis of a screenplay for a movie in which he could then star, but decided to expand the concept into a series of novels. His consultant for the ongoing project is veteran science fiction writer **Ron Goulart**.

Tek Book Series

An ongoing science fiction book series by the prolific Shatner, featuring private investigator Jake Cardigan. To date, the literary franchise, which spawned audiocassette versions of some of the entries as well as cable TV movies and a 1995 cable TV series (*TekWar*), includes:

TekWar (1989)
TekLords (1991)
TekLab (1991)
Tek Vengeance (1992)
Tek Secret (1993)
Tek Power (1994)
Tek Money (1995)
Tek Kill (1996)
Tek Net (1997)

Tek Kill

The eighth book in Shatner's popular *Tek* series was published in 1996. In this futuristic detective thriller, private investigator **Jake Cardigan** tries to clear his boss of a murder charge. Unfortunately, the telepathic visions of a **Tek** addict are the only evidence he has in the case.

TekLab

The third installment in Shatner's *Tek* book series came out in 1991. Herein, hero **Jake Cardigan** is on the trail of a serial killer in the blasted ruins of twenty-first century London. "Shatner's future world is as generic and unconvincing as his characters," wrote *Kirkus Reviews*, summing up the general critical reaction to the series.

TekLords

This second 1991 installment in the *Tek* book series has private eye **Jake Cardigan** investigating the murder of a drug-control agent and the release of a synthetic plague in San Francisco. The critic for *Kirkus Reviews* concluded the book was "okay for existing fans, but won't win many new converts."

Tek Money

The seventh book in Shatner's *Tek* series was published in 1995. Series hero **Jake Cardigan** is found racing to solve the murder of an old friend—with his own son the prime suspect. "This book does not add any new dimensions to the future world of the series," observed *Booklist*. "It is, however, as readable as any of its predecessors."

Tek Net

The ninth book in Shatner's *Tek* series was distributed in 1997. This high body count thriller has **Jake Cardigan** and his partner Sid Gomez targeted for elimination by the Teklords after a new computerized form of **Tek** threatens to wipe out their market share. "A workmanlike piece of action sf" was how *Booklist* summarized the contents. More entries, obviously, will follow in this highly lucrative book series.

Tek Power

The sixth installment in Shatner's popular *Tek* series is a wry parable on drug legalization. In this 1994 offering, the evil Teklords hatch a plot to replace the president of the United States with an android replica, paving the way for the legitimization of **Tek**. As always, supersleuth **Jake Cardigan** intervenes to foil their plans. "The series has become predictable in the best sense of the term," opined the reviewer for *Booklist*. "Each book offers fast action, a well-drawn, grittily realistic future world, some characters we know and like, some new ones, and, increasingly, a pleasant, dry wit."

Tek Secret

The fifth of Shatner's *Tek* sci-fi book series is again set in a grim world of the future controlled by evil drug lords. Published in 1993, *Tek Secret* follows **Jake Cardigan** on the trail of a missing industrial heiress. Along the way, he uncovers a web of corruption and covert operations involving the U.S. government. This book signals a grittier direction for the **Tek** series.

Tek Vengeance

The fourth installment in Shatner's *Tek* series was published in 1992. The novel finds **Jake Cardigan**'s girlfriend assassinated by a Jake robot replica while he is in Berlin to testify against the evil Teklords. Jake and his partner Sid Gomez seek revenge, in a book *Kirkus Reviews* grudgingly called "the best since the series began."

TekWar (book)

The first book in Shatner's *Tek* series, published in 1989. Set in the year 2043, *TekWar* concerns **Jake Cardigan**, an ex-cop who is framed for dealing in the addictive brain stimulant called Tek. He is sentenced to fifteen years in cryogenic freeze, but escapes after four years to confront his accusers.

TekWar (television movie series)   RATING: U U L

The 1995 cable TV series based on Shatner's *Tek* book cycle. The first of four TV movies, part of the USA (cable) Network's "Action Pack" anthology, debuted in January of 1994. Shatner coproduced and directed the ninety-two minute film and essayed the role of Walter Bascom, one of the enigmatic mandarins of the Tek universe. Budgeted at a tidy $4

Shatner as Walter Bascomb, one of the enigmatic mandarins of his TekWar *universe. [photo courtesy of The Everett Collection]*

million, the movie stars Greg Evigan, TV's beloved B. J. McCay (of the comedy adventure series *B. J. and the Bear*, 1979 to 1981), as futuristic sleuth **Jake Cardigan**. Scottish pop star Sheena Easton appears as Warbride, the leader of a band of radical environmentalists.

"It is all fairly lightweight, not to mention convoluted," wrote the reviewer for *Maclean's*. "Shatner manages to keep the plot flowing, and there are occasional flashes of a movie—odd camera effects and angles—lurking amid the TV truisms and idiot-box dialogue." The critic went on to laud the film for its top-notch special effects. "All its visual gewgaws, however, cannot mask the lack of a plausible script."

The cable television movies **TekLords**, **TekLab**, and **Tek Justice** followed in rapid succession in 1994. On January 7, 1995, a one-hour USA Network series was launched, with Greg Evigan again starring as **Jake Cardigan**. Shatner appeared frequently as Bascom, along with Eugene Clark as Sid Gomez, Maria Del Mar as Sam Houston, Leya Doig as Cowgirl, and Ernie Gruenworld as Spaz. "In retooling *TekWar* into one-hour form," wrote David Bianculli in the *New York Daily News*, "the series has regained some energy and vitality, and relied much less on special effects 'stun gun' footage." Filmed in Toronto by Atlantis Films, Ltd., the action-filled *TekWar* series represented Shatner's attempt to draw on "a Canadian pool of talent . . . that is as good as the best I've ever worked with." The series version lasted for eighteen episodes over the 1984–85 TV season.

Tek Nepotism

In the summer of 1995, Shatner's *TekWar* cable television series was on a ventilator. The USA Network had already pulled the plug, and the show was winding down in obscurity on the Sci-Fi Channel. What better time for Shatner to squeeze in a little work for his daughters? The series' final episode, "Betrayal," was a veritable family affair.

Plot: Walter Bascom (William Shatner) suspects Jake Cardigan as the source of a security leak within the Cosmos Agency. Meanwhile, therapist Janet Blake (Melanie Shatner) attempts to help Jake deal with his recurring nightmares.

Writer: Lisabeth Shatner
Director: William Shatner
Guest Stars: William Shatner (Walter H. Bascom)
Melanie Shatner (Dr. Janet Blake)

Television

From *Star Trek* in the 1960s to *T. J. Hooker* in the 1980s, Shatner's greatest successes have come on the small screen. Partly it stems from his ability to control the creative process on series where all the action revolves around him. "I've gotten a great insight into the omnipotence of the series lead," he observed from his high chair of power on the *Star Trek* set in 1966. "Everybody does his best not to upset the *star*. It's an almost unique position few in the entertainment world achieve.... It's like absolute power."

The fact that the vast majority of his acting gigs have been in television has never stopped Shatner from criticizing the medium that Lilliputian science fiction author **Harlan Ellison** once called "the glass teat." "Television, by its nature, has to appeal to as many people as possible," Shatner has said. "Which means the lowest common denominator. Occasionally— and those are the occasions I watch TV for—television will do something extraordinary." Among the extraordinary TV shows Shatner has said he watches are "reality program-

Shatner captained ABC's Battle of the Network Stars *team for several years in the late 1970s. [photo courtesy of* The Everett Collection*]*

ming, *National Geographic* specials, sports, and CNN." The list of shows he *doesn't* watch includes *Star Trek* reruns, *Star Trek: The Next Generation*, or any of the other series offshoots. Shatner finds television useful mainly for its soporific effects. "It provides a rhythm that puts me to sleep." Unless he has to tape something, that is. "I still can't figure out my VCR," he boldly revealed in 1993.

$10,000 Pyramid

This 1970s ABC-TV game show was variously hosted by Bill Cullen and Dick Clark, and Shatner occasionally appeared on the program as a celebrity player. The concept was simple: contestants paired with celebrities to solve seven word association puzzles in six categories displayed on an enormous pyramid.

Shatner appeared on many incarnations of this long-running game program. His most famous guest shot came in 1979, and ended in an orgy of violent mayhem. The setting was New York's Ed Sullivan Theatre at Broadway between Fifty-third and Fifty-fourth streets. Shatner was appearing alongside fellow celebrity **Leonard Nimoy**, taping one of the five days' worth of shows they would complete in a single afternoon, thanks to the magic of wardrobe changes. Shatner's dexterity with a clue had carried his partner into the playoff round, earning her a chance at $10,000. However, he froze up on the final answer, blowing the victory at the last possible second. Then, still on camera, Shatner, seemingly, went berserk, lifting up his plush swivel chair from the show's futuristic set and heaving it over a railing. The show quickly cut to a commercial. The nervous gasps of the audience soon turned to laughter, however, as the camera cut back in on Shatner and Nimoy standing together holding the broken bits of chair between them, with broad smiles on their faces. Pressure from a grueling schedule, frustration over his moribund career, and his own fondness for **practical jokes** offer some rationale for Shatner's outburst, but a completely satisfactory explanation has never been offered yet.

Tenth Level, The   RATING: U U

This two-hour CBS television drama special, directed by Charles S. Dubin and starring Shatner, aired on August 26, 1976. Shatner plays a psychologist, Professor Stephen Turner, who conducts mind control experiments on human subjects. (The title refers to a study in which over ninety percent of the participants would obey a researcher to the point of inflicting the tenth level of pain on another person.) Calling the TV film "repulsive and pointless," *Variety* recommended it only "for people who like to pull the wings off flies."

Apparently, the subject matter hit a little close to home. "It has been suggested to me," Shatner said of the project, "that this whole play was a gigantic scientific experiment to see how far they could push actors...just another little case of manipulation. The actor is constantly manipulating himself, and the director and writer are always there to guide his way." Others in the cast include Lynn Carlen, Viveca Lindfors, Ossie Davis, Estelle Parsons, and Stephen Macht.

Testimony of Two Men   RATING: U U

This 1977 TV miniseries, adapted from the Taylor Caldwell novel (1968), follows the lives of two surgeon siblings in post-Civil War Pennsylvania. Shatner has a supporting role as Adrian Ferrier, a relative of the two heroes. Shown in three parts, the sweeping six-hour **costume drama** was part of Operation Prime Time, a joint initiative by independent television stations to produce high-quality programming. Like the subsequent telefilm *The Bastard* (1979), also starring Shatner, this ambitious entry features more sex than absorbing history. Others in the large eclectic cast include David Birney, Barbara Parkins, Ralph Bellamy, Theodore Bikel, Tom Bosley, Ray Milland, Margaret O'Brien, and Dan Dailey.

Third Walker, The   RATING: U L

This 1978 feature is set in Ireland, and features Shatner as the trouble-plagued Munro Maclean. The murky, flashback-laden drama concerns twins who are mixed up at birth and raised by different mothers. Colleen Dewhurst plays Shatner's shrewish wife. The first-time director was Teri McLuhan, daughter of hip philosopher Marshall McLuhan.

This Was America

This twelve-part historical documentary PBS-TV series had Shatner as host for its run in 1979–80. The Emmy Award-winning program used early photographs to recreate the lives of Americans at the turn of the twentieth century. Historian and author Martin Sandler gathered the material for this offering, which was produced by the Boston-based BBI Communications group. The *Boston Herald-American* called Shatner "the best documentary narrator since Basil Rathbone." *Variety* praised the "earnest, almost impassioned reading by Shatner."

Tinnitus

This medical condition is characterized by a hissing or ringing in the ears. Shatner was diagnosed with it in the early 1990s after he noticed a hissing in his ears while walking on a beach in Malibu, California, with his second wife, **Marcy Lafferty**. The condition, which is incurable, became so serious that it helped wreck Shatner's marriage and made him contemplate suicide.

"There was a time when I thought, 'I don't think I can deal with this anymore,' Shatner said of the ssshhhhhh-like drone that constantly played in his head. "And I began to actively think of what means you could use that—that you could end your life."

Relief finally came in January 1996 in the form of hearing-aid-like devices prescribed by Dr. Pawel Jastreboff of the University of Maryland Tinnitus and Hyperacusis Center. The devices continuously feed white noise into Shatner's ear, drowning out the annoying drone. A relieved Shatner now serves as a spokesperson and fundraiser for the Baltimore-based center.

It wasn't until later that Shatner realized the cause of his condition. "**Leonard Nimoy**, who also has the problem, reminded me that there had been an explosion on the *Star Trek* movie set. We both got this ringing in the ears. My ringing is in my left ear, and his ringing is in his right ear." Other celebrities who suffer from tinnitus include David Letterman, Barbra Streisand, Steve Martin, and Tony Randall.

"I wanted to run and escape the sound. And that only increased the panic because there was no place to run."

—SHATNER, on his tinnitus

Tom Sawyer

The title role played by Shatner, in his first public performance, in a stage production of the Mark Twain classic (1876) for the Montreal Children's Theatre in 1939. He was eight years old. He remained with the acting group for five years, appearing in children's plays every weekend.

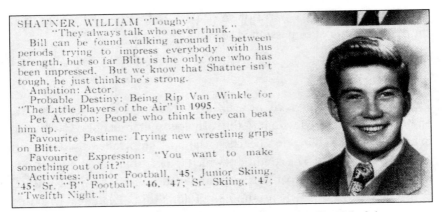

SHATNER, WILLIAM "Toughy"
"They always talk who never think."
Bill can be found walking around in between
periods trying to impress everybody with his
strength, but so far Blitt is the only one who has
been impressed. But we know that Shatner isn't
tough, he just thinks he's strong.
    Ambition: Actor.
    Probable Destiny: Being Rip Van Winkle for
"The Little Players of the Air" in 1995.
    Pet Aversion: People who think they can beat
him up.
    Favourite Pastime: Trying new wrestling grips
on Blitt.
    Favourite Expression: "You want to make
something out of it?"
    Activities: Junior Football, '45; Junior Skiing,
'45; Sr. "B" Football, '46, '47; Sr. Skiing, '47;
"Twelfth Night."

"Toughy" Shatner's yearbook photo from Montreal's West Hills High. [photo courtesy of Seth Poppel's Yearbook Archives]

Toughy

The nickname Shatner earned for his tenacity in fighting off anti-Semitic classmates at Montreal's West Hill High School. The sobriquet appeared beside his name in his high school yearbook. "But we know that Shatner isn't tough," the yearbook writers added, "he just thinks he's strong." The yearbook cut-ups apparently found Shatner's pugnacity quite amusing. They listed the actor/jock's pet aversion as "People who think they can beat him up" and his favorite expression as "You want to make something out of it?" For the record, Shatner's own yearbook quotation was "They always talk who never think."

Toupee

Speculation has run rampant in the science fiction community about the true nature of Shatner's impeccably coifed hair. While some deluded fans still maintain it is nothing but an expensive permanent (and Shatner himself denies it is anything but one hundred percent real), words like weave, plugs, and rug are more frequently used to account for the ever-changing shape and color of Shatner's mane over the recent decades.

Because his personal wigs were too ratty-looking, *Star Trek*'s producers had two custom hairpieces made for Shatner at the beginning of each television season in the late 1960s. That way, he could wear one while the other was being cleaned. Unfortunately, somewhere along the line the reserve hairpiece disappeared from the makeup department. A search was conducted, the usual inquiries were made, but the missing item was never recovered. Suspicions began to turn toward Shatner himself, who, some allege, may have preferred the top-quality $200 workplace wigs to his own substandard collection.

By the 1980s, Shatner had opted for a fuller, wavier hairstyle. Reports had him spending as much as $2,000 a month to maintain his hair weave. The curly monstrosity he wore in the late 1980s earned him recognition in a *National Enquirer* feature rating worst celebrity hairpieces. Together with the tight bodice that Shatner wears to restrain his distended belly, the hair weave is one of Shatner's few concessions to vanity. "I don't like to see youth slipping away," he admitted to *Playboy* in 1989. "Seeing old

Gene Roddenberry and Shatner compare hair care solutions at a Star Trek *convention in the 1970s. [photo courtesy of Photofest]*

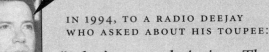

SO SAYETH SHATNER

IN 1994, TO A RADIO DEEJAY
WHO ASKED ABOUT HIS TOUPEE:

*"I don't wear a hairpiece. That's the stupidest
question I ever heard."*

photographs, buried in the attic someplace, that's one thing. But to see yourself walking around on a television screen in one instant and then to compare that with your present-day form in the next is tough."

In 1991, Shatner had to deal with more than just seeing his image reflected in old reruns, when placards featuring doctored photos of him—along with five other bewigged celebrities—began appearing on walls and lampposts around lower Manhattan. The posters were part of a baldness outing campaign conducted by writer Ed Leibowitz and graphic designer Lorraine Heffernan, whose stated purpose was to "wrest the toupees from the chrome domes of America's leading celebrities." For the record, the other shineheads exposed in the campaign were Charles Bronson, Ted Danson, Larry Hagman, "Broadway" Joe Namath, and John "Duke" Wayne.

Shatner's hair has become an icon of *fin de siecle* pop culture mythology. In 1997, the irreverent Comedy Central cable network game show *Win Ben Stein's Money* captured the zeitgeist with a category called "Synthetic Fabrics Not Found on William Shatner's Head." In another bizarre sidelight, the 1997 New York Underground Film Festival saw the premiere of *William Shatner Lent Me His Hairpiece (An Untrue Story)*, a thirteen-minute film written and directed by Ken Hegan. The vicious parody stars Hegan as an obsessed Trekkie who battles Shatner for control of the actor's wig.

Town Has Turned to Dust, A

This live television play, starring Shatner and Rod Steiger, aired on CBS-TV's *Playhouse 90* on June 19, 1958. Shatner is the ringleader of a lynching party in the Rod Serling-penned drama, which earned rave reviews from *Variety* and the *New York Journal American*. Jack Gould, writing in the *New York Times*, called Shatner "the embodiment of hate and blind physical passion," and termed his portrayal "[one] of the season's superlative performances."

Not surprisingly, the only detractor from the chorus of kudos was Rod Serling, the archetypal skunk at the garden party. He had intended *A Town Has Turned to Dust* to be a mordant commentary on racism in the South, specifically the actual Emmett Till lynching case. However, by the time of the TV production filming, Serling said, "my script had turned to dust" thanks to jittery network censors. The racial element was largely removed, and the story was transplanted from the present-day south to 1870s New Mexico. A scene where a sheriff commits suicide had to be excised because one of the program's sponsors was an insurance company. The final script was almost unrecognizable from the one Serling had submitted. "They chopped it up like a roomful of butchers at work on a steer," he wailed.

The disheartening experience of *A Town Has Turned to Dust* helped turn Serling away from topical drama and into the realm of science fiction and fantasy. The ultimate result was ***The Twilight Zone*** (1959–65), a CBS-TV series on which Shatner was to make two memorable guest appearances.

Traffic incidents

Over the decades, Shatner has had a number of strange encounters involving moving vehicles, none stranger than his motorcycle trek in the Mojave Desert that ended in an **alien encounter**. Detractors will contend that the lack of corroborating witnesses to these incidents indicates that they did not, in fact, take place. Whatever one's opinion of the author of these accounts, however, Shatner's ability to generate media coverage cannot be denied.

In what may have been a sign that he should stay away from the highways of North America, Shatner had a near-death experience while driving from Montreal to Toronto during his early days as an actor in the 1950s. A truck sideswiped his car, propelling it into a deep canal and leaving Shatner flailing to escape as the vehicle filled with water. As his life flashed before his eyes, Shatner heard Macbeth's speech on the futility of life echoing in his head: "It is a tale, told by an idiot, signifying nothing." Just then the truck driver appeared and freed Shatner from the sinking automobile. A shaken Shatner decided on the basis of this experience to redouble his efforts to do something meaningful with his life.

By 1977, Shatner had exorcised those demons of inadequacy and become a famous actor. However, that status brought no relief from his propensity for strange situations on the roadway. That year, Shatner found himself in a limousine with a talkative driver. "I thought, Oh my God, what a place to be hung up with a Trekkie." But the man turned out to have a fascinating tale to tell. As P.O.W.s in Vietnam, he and his army buddies had kept themselves from going berserk in captivity by acting out episodes of **Star Trek**. "One of us would pretend to be Captain Kirk and others Spock, McCoy, and the rest of the crew.... We did that for the length of time that I was a prisoner of the Vietnamese." The man went on to thank Shatner for inspiring him with his portrayal of Kirk. "We came from different places all over the United States and we had nothing in common except our love of **Star Trek**. It was the only thing that kept us sane." Both men ended up crying at the recollection.

A third situation occurred in the 1980s. In an early example of the phenomenon known as road rage, Shatner left his vehicle to accost a fellow motorist who had given him the finger. But his experience playing a hero on TV did not serve him well in the ensuing confrontation. "He got out of the car and got taller," Shatner told *Playboy* in 1989. "At that point, I think 'Beam me up, Scotty' would have been a good phrase."

Continuing on the theme of auto hijinks, *People* magazine reported in 1989 about the time Shatner got caught in the rain while jogging in Baltimore. "I was on a busy road, and at every stoplight I came to I'd knock on windshields and say, 'Would you mind giving me a ride?' But they all drove off. Here I was, running along the side of the road banging on windows and looking for a lift. I was down to begging, 'Haven't you ever seen **Star Trek**?'"

Perhaps he would have earned more respect had he been wearing his **T. J. Hooker** costume. Actually, that worked for Shatner in 1982 when he caused and then settled a traffic accident. He was crossing a Los Angeles street in his show's police sergeant's uniform when the driver of a Jeep stopped to stargaze. The car behind then plowed into the Jeep's rear. "It was the fault of the person behind," said Shatner, not stopping to consider his own role in the collision. "So when the driver of the Jeep came out to look, I said, 'There's no damage to you. Move on.' And I told the other driver, 'It was your fault. You got a little damage. Keep moving. Don't block traffic.' And they all really thought I was a policeman."

Shatner's penchant for moving violations has even extended to the golf course. One time, he plowed his golf cart into someone else's, then screamed at its occupants that he had the right of way. The three men got out to confront Shatner, who found he was both outnumbered and outsized. Nevertheless, he offered one man a flying dropkick. When that didn't work, he assumed a supine position and apologized feverishly. The incident is similar in its particulars to a story Shatner has told about a bloodbath on a miniature race car course. For details of that particular confrontation, see **Fights**.

Transformed Man, The

This Decca Records album was recorded by Shatner in 1968. The phrase "a collection of songs and dramatic readings set to music" does not begin to describe the contents of this bizarre, visionary recording. Shatner has said he tried to perform certain songs "as though I were drugged" and one listen to the LP confirms the veracity of that statement.

Produced by music industry veteran **Don Ralke**, *The Transformed Man* is an intensely personal aural journey through the works of playwrights, poets, and pop lyricists. The album is highlighted by Shatner's staccato talk-singing style on such cuts as Bob Dylan's "Mr. Tambourine Man" and The Beatles' "Lucy in the Sky with Diamonds." "I wanted to show the various ways writers express themselves at different times on universal themes," Shatner said soon after its release. Three decades later, he was still explaining his artistic method to a baffled world. "When a cut is played without any context you'll be puzzled by what I'm doing, but my hope is that you'll know what I'm doing if you listen to the whole record."

Some have suggested the record was Shatner's attempt to assimilate through speech and song his deeply-felt reactions to an **alien encounter** in the Mojave Desert. A satisfied Shatner compared its September 1968 release with such other career milestones as the first time he received star billing and the rave notices he received for *The World of Suzie Wong* (1960) on Broadway. "When I listen to this record, I have the same thrill," he said.

Dismissed as the product of a bad acid trip by most listeners at the time, *The Transformed Man* is today considered a camp classic. Rhino Records included two of the cuts on *Golden Throats*, a 1990 novelty album celebrating rancid celebrity caterwauling. In 1991, authors Jimmy Guterman and Owen O'Donnell included the record in their book *The Worst Rock 'n' Roll Records of All Time*. The American Booksellers Association even offered Shatner $100,000 to sing "Mr. Tambourine Man" at its 1991 convention. He wisely declined.

The complete track list for the album is as follows:

(1) "King Henry the Fifth," (2) "Elegy for the Brave," (3) "Theme from Cyrano," (4) "Mr. Tambourine Man," (5) "Hamlet," (6) "It Was a Very Good Year," (7) "Romeo and Juliet," (8) "How Insensitive (Insensatez)," (9) "Spleen," (10) "Lucy in the Sky with Diamonds," (11) "The Transformed Man."

Entertainment Weekly called the record, "The most ear splitting album of all the former cast members [of *Star Trek*]." Mike Wilkins in *TV Guide* noted that the album was "the most bizarre record," and that "Shatner interprets 'Mr. Tambourine Man' as if he were some crazed drug addict."

A Transformed Opinion?

Over the years, Shatner's opinion of his only studio album has changed dramatically—and then changed back again. Below is a sampling of his many thoughts about *The Transformed Man*:

"This, to me, is a work of art."
—SHATNER to biographers in 1979

"Some cuts worked, some didn't. I haven't heard it in a long time."
—SHATNER to *Playboy* in 1989

"I think the album is very meritorious. I'm not embarrassed by The Transformed Man *at all. Am I living in a fool's paradise?"*
—SHATNER to the *Rocky Mountain News* in 1997

Trinity and Beyond   RATING: U U L

A feature-length 1995 documentary, directed by Peter Keiran and narrated by Shatner, commemorating the detonation of the atomic bombs on Hiroshima and Nagasaki fifty years earlier. The spectacular examination of the nuclear age relies on impressive visual effects and a score by the Moscow Symphony Orchestra, with Shatner's subdued voice-overs as an appropriate counterpoint. Nuclear scientists Edward Teller and Frank H. Shelton provide commentary for the footage, much of it previously classified government material, as well as fresh interviews with surviving scientists who helped to create the atom and hydrogen bombs. *Variety* judged the ninety-two-minute film to be a "factually solid, visually stunning, informative documentary...."

Trusk, J. (B. 1951)

This William Shatner lookalike frequently performs at roasts, bar mitzvahs, and corporate functions. A burly former auctioneer, Trusk began impersonating Shatner after friends told him he was a dead ringer for the famous actor. He went on to make a splash at Trek Con '96 in Hartford, Connecticut, appearing alongside original crew members **George Takei**, **Nichelle Nichols**, **Jimmy Doohan**, and **Walter Koenig**, and was featured in *Trekkies*, a 1997 documentary about **Star Trek** fandom. Perhaps Trusk's finest moment of celebrity imposture came on May 31, 1995, when he appeared on TV's *The Tonight Show* with Shatner himself. Those interest-

Shatner with J. Trusk, America's pre-eminent Shatner lookalike. Or is that J. Trusk with Shatner? [NBC photo from The Tonight Show with Jay Leno, *courtesy of Margaret Norton]*

ed in contacting Trusk should visit his Internet Web site at http://www.jtrusk.com.

Twenty-Five Year Mission Tour

This series of joint appearances made by Shatner and **Leonard Nimoy** celebrated twenty-five years of *Star Trek*. The shows played to sellout crowds in eleven cities across the United States in the summer of 1992. Engaging in lighthearted banter designed to play off commonly held perceptions of themselves (Shatner as an overbearing egotist, Nimoy as a brooding iceman), Shatner and Nimoy developed an extemporaneous rapport that left audiences howling with approval. The duo regaled fans with anecdotes from their days on the TV and movie series, including the oft-repeated **bicycle story**. "We're in the smelling-of-the-roses phase

Shatner encounters a pesky gremlin on the wing of an airliner in the classic Twilight Zone *episode "Nightmare at 20,000 Feet." (1964). [photo courtesy of Photofest]*

of our life," Shatner said of the tour. "So we're enjoying each other more and more. He makes me laugh, and I get him to giggle sometimes."

Twilight Zone

Shatner appeared in two episodes of the classic fantasy TV anthology series, hosted by Rod Serling on CBS-TV from 1959 to 1965. In "Nick of Time," which aired on November 18, 1960, Shatner plays Don Carter, a newlywed who becomes obsessed with a bobbing-head fortune-telling machine in an Ohio diner. The half-hour, black-and-white episode, tidily scripted by master fantasist Richard Matheson, is one of the understated gems of the series. Even better known is "Nightmare at 20,000 Feet," which debuted on October 11, 1963. In this thirty-minute shocker, Shatner gives a twitchy performance as Bob Wilson, a disturbed airline passenger who keeps spotting a gremlin on the wing of the airborne plane. Incredibly cheap make-up effects are the only blemishes in this otherwise gripping episode, also written by Richard Matheson. The story line would be revamped for *Twilight Zone: The Movie* (1983) in the segment directed by George Miller and featuring John Lithgow in Shatner's old TV role.

Ultimate Survivors: Winning Against Incredible Odds

This 1991 inspirational videotape, hosted by Shatner, profiles law enforcement officers who survived devastating career-related incidents. The eighty-five-minute program plays against Shatner's reassuring *Rescue 911* (1989-92) TV persona. Re-enactments depict such real-life situations as a police officer being shot in the face by a deranged motorist, a U.S. marshal escaping an armed ambush, and a state trooper trapped inside a burning squad car. The cumulative effect, as the *Hollywood Reporter* observed, is to promote the idea that "a long-term outlook on life and its rewards is necessary to recover from physical and psychological trauma."

Universe

This 1976 documentary, narrated by Shatner, examines man's place in the cosmos. The twenty-eight-minute, NASA-sponsored film uses animation to chronicle cosmic history forward from the Big Bang moment, theorized as the cosmic explosion that scientists believe created the universe as we know it. *Universe* was nominated for an Academy Award for Best Documentary Short.

Usumcasane

This role was played by Shatner in his January 1956 Broadway debut, in the **Stratford Shakespeare Festival**'s production of Christopher Marlowe's **Tamburlaine the Great**.

Vanished
RATING: U U L

Billed as a long-form TV movie, this four-hour, two-part 1971 NBC production, directed by Buzz Kulik, is actually one of the first of an entertainment species known as a "miniseries." Based on the novel (1968) by Fletcher Knebel, the plot concerns the sudden disappearance of a top presidential advisor. Shatner plays Dave Paulick, a military aide, but he is just a small part of an all-star cast that includes Richard Widmark as

Shatner and Lee Grant must outwit a psycho on the loose in a hospital in the slasher cheapie Visiting Hours *(1982). [photo courtesy of Archive Photos]*

the President, Tom Bosley, E. G. Marshall, and Robert Young (playing a stereotypical southern senator). Widmark and Young received Emmy nominations for their work in this entry. Somewhere in the sea of familiar faces is Neil Hamilton, who played the police commissioner on TV's *Batman* (1966–68).

Visiting Hours

RATING:

This repugnant 1982 R-rated slasher movie, directed by Jean-Claude Lord, provided Shatner with a supporting role as the employer of a TV reporter who is hounded by a psychotic viewer. The plot concerns a misogynistic killer who likes to photograph his victims in their death throes. Most of the action takes place in a hospital, hence the title. Michael Ironside appears as the killer, who goes by the less-than-terrifying moniker of Colt Hawker. Lee Grant and Linda Purl also costar in this Canadian-made stinker. The film is also known as *The Fright* and *Get Well Soon*.

Voice of the Planet

In this ten-hour ecological television special, Shatner stars as a writer whose computer channels Gaia, the spirit of Planet Earth. As the deliciously named William Hope Planter, Shatner appears from his home in a Himalayan monastery. Faye Dunaway provides the voice of Gaia, who rails against animal experimentation while espousing the benefits of mandatory sterilization for Third World citizens.

"All matter is part of Mother Earth and we have to start cleaning our act up immediately or we're all going to die," Shatner warned in an interview prior to *Voice of the Planet*'s completion. Filmed on location in Nepal, the bizarre new age "documentary"—which *People* magazine dubbed "the longest infomercial ever made"—aired over five nights on Turner Broadcasting System beginning October 15, 1990. Shatner was proud of his work on the series, going so far as to cite *Voice of the Planet* as the one performance of his that he would most like to pass on to his grandchildren. In an ironic sidelight, the monastery where the series was filmed burned down a short time later when a group of American visitors blew out a circuit while hooking up an electrical generator.

Ten Lousy Feature Movies William Shatner Would Probably Like to Forget

1. *Big Bad Mama* (1974)
2. *Deathdream* (1972)
3. *The Devil's Rain* (1975)
4. *Incubus* (1965)
5. *The Land of No Return* (1978)
6. *The Outrage* (1964)
7. *The Third Walker* (1978)
8. *Visiting Hours* (1982)
9. *Want a Ride, Little Girl?* (1972)
10. *White Comanche* (1968)

(see individual entries for more details)

Von Puttkamer, Jesco (B. 1919)

This scientist, futurist, and space flight planner was interviewed extensively by Shatner for the actor's *Mysteries of the Gods*. A *Star Trek* aficionado (he actually penned his own Trek novella), Von Puttkamer also served as a technical adviser on *Star Trek: The Motion Picture* (1979).

Born in Germany, von Puttkamer emigrated to the United States in 1961 to be a part of Wernher von Braun's renowned rocket development team. He worked on the Apollo, Skylab, and Space Shuttle programs, wrote a number of books on space flight and in 1971 served as chairman of the first international congress on "Space for Mankind's Benefit."

In the late 1970s, von Puttkamer was employed as Program Manager of Space Industrialization and Integrated Long-Range Planning Studies for the National Aeronautics and Space Administration (NASA), where he was responsible for the agency's long-range studies in space flight.

Vulcan Salute

Fictitious hand gesture used on *Star Trek* (both in the TV series of the 1960s and the feature films), in which the thumb and forefinger, middle and ring fingers are held apart. It first appeared in the second season's opening episode "Amok Time" (9/15/67). **Leonard Nimoy** originated the salute, which he based on a rabbinical blessing offered to Jewish congregations during prayer. A little-known fact about Shatner is his inability to perform the Vulcan Salute, which he was required to give for a humorous scene in ***Star Trek III: The Search for Spock*** (1989). Director **Leonard Nimoy**'s solution was to tie Shatner's fingers into the proper positions using fishing line.

Want a Ride, Little Girl?   RATING:

This exploitative 1972 feature film, directed by William Grefe, highlights Shatner as a psychotic murderer. Filmed on the cheap in Poland Springs, Florida, the movie opens with Shatner's character, Matt Stone, hacking his mother's lover to death with a sword. Things go dramatically downhill from there. As an adult, and now released from prison, Stone develops a twisted fascination with women who resemble his dead mother. **Harold Sakata**, the hulking Japanese wrestler who played Odd Job in the James Bond film *Goldfinger* (1964) also stars. Shatner's future wife,

As Mark Preston, Shatner prepares to confront the servants of Satan in The Devil's Rain *(1975). [photo courtesy of Photofest]*

Marcy Lafferty, has a small role as a horny motel clerk who gives in to Stone's advances. She had sense enough to appear under an assumed name, something Shatner should have considered. In 1974, the PG-rated picture was re-released under a new title, *Impulse*, and it is also known as *I Love to Kill*. Shatner has disavowed the tawdry project in subsequent interviews.

> *"I've forgotten why I was in it. I probably needed the money. It was a very bad time for me. I hope they burn it."*
> —SHATNER on *Want a Ride, Little Girl?*

Weight

Shatner has long struggled to keep down his earthly body weight. Early in his career, it was not even an issue. "I never thought much about having a good body," he recalled of his younger days, "because I was gifted by *having* a good body. I didn't do much in the way of care, nor did I ever abuse it by drinking or smoking very much."

By the time Shatner started working on TV's **Star Trek** in the mid-1960s, however, his Battle of the Bulge indeed was raging. On the set, he carped constantly about his captain's tunics, which seemed to get smaller each time they were cleaned. But the problem was just as often the result of Shatner's getting larger. While he exercised strenuously during the summer months to arrive fit and trim for the start of each season,

SO SAYETH SHATNER

ON AGING AND WEIGHT GAIN:

"Two things happen as you get older: Not only does gravity take its toll, but you think, is it worth missing this great-tasting dessert for the narcissism of taking off your shirt, or is life too short?"

over the course of the season's filming he allowed his waistline to balloon. The problem became so serious by the show's third season (1968–69) that memos were exchanged between staff producers about the possibility of putting together a clip reel of Shatner at his heaviest to show to him in order to shame him into slimming down. Even though the reel was never made, Shatner did embark on a crash diet after viewing some unflattering dailies.

Certainly the plush velour costuming favored by **Star Trek** wardrobe man William Theiss did not help matters any. But then uncomfortably-tailored outfits have followed Shatner wherever he has gone in his career, from the skin-tight pajamas he had to pour himself into for **Star Trek: The Motion Picture** (1979) to the bulging police sergeant's uniform he wore on **T. J. Hooker** (1982–86). "We had twelve shirts made for Shatner [for *Star Trek III*]," explained costume designer Robert Fletcher "He diets before a movie and shows up looking terrific. But he would slip as it went along." Later in his career Shatner addressed the problem of extra tonnage by donning a cumbersome corset to hold in his enormous belly. "Every inch of bloat shows on camera," he told the *Washington Post* in 1991.

West Hill High School

The Montreal high school attended by Shatner (class of 1948).

The archetypal jock, Shatner was at one time or another a member of the skiing, wrestling, and football teams. "I had aspirations of being a football player and at the same time I wanted to act," he once said. "As a result, I was torn in two directions. The actors don't play football and the football players think the actors are sissies." Only his religious commitments kept him from advancing on the gridiron, where he once missed being chosen for the team because of his observance of the Jewish holy days. Not that Shatner has any regrets about the way things turned out. "I was a bit small for a pro football career," he has said.

Whale of a Tale, A   RATING: U U

Truly, Shatner must have been hard up to take part in this low-budget 1976 children's feature about a boy and his whale. Filmed at Marineland in California, the little-known movie was also released as *Joey and the*

West Hills High in Montreal, which Shatner attended from 1944 to 1948. [photo courtesy of Seth Poppel's Yearbook Archives]

Whale. Young Joey (Scott Kolden) gets a job hauling buckets of chum for marine biologist Shatner. The lad gets lost at sea and is rescued by a trained porpoise. This G-rated, ninety-minute feature was directed by Ewing Malis Brown, and costarred the insipid trio of Abby Dalton, Andy Devine, and Marty Allen.

"I'm not terribly proud of some of the features I've made," Shatner explained to an interviewer, "but they were offered to me at various times when better movies weren't being offered." Shatner could have been speaking of *A Whale of a Tale* or any of a half dozen other movies he made during these, his **lost years** of the 1970s.

"Whales Weep Not"

This erotic poem by British author D. H. Lawrence was written in 1930–31, and published, posthumously, in the writer's collection, *Last Poems*, in 1932. At **Star Trek** conventions in the mid-1970s, Shatner would call attention to the plight of whales by reciting "Whales Weep Not" to throngs of sexually retarded men wearing Spock ears. The poem, full of phallic imagery, combines Shatner's love of whales with another of his passions, male **sexuality**. Maybe that's why Shatner agreed to appear in the substandard *A Whale of a Tale* (1976). On second thought, maybe not.

Wheaton, Will (B. 1973)

This slim, babyfaced teen actor played Ensign Wesley Crusher on *Star Trek: The Next Generation* (1987–94). Intensely disliked by most fans of that syndicated follow-up TV series, Wheaton also once suffered the wrath of Shatner. He ambled onto the set of **Star Trek V: The Final Frontier** (1989), which Shatner was directing, hoping to pay his respects and schmooze with the original starship *Enterprise* crew. However, an imperious Shatner ordered him off the sound stage, bellowing "If this were my bridge and my ship, you wouldn't be allowed on!" A distressed Wheaton complained to *Star Trek* creator **Gene Roddenberry**, who by that time had little control over the series or its temperamental star. Shatner later apologized to the adolescent actor. Wheaton also has appeared in such diverse feature films as *Stand By Me* (1988), *Toy Soldiers* (1991), *The Liar's Club* (1993) and *Mr. Stitch* (1995).

White Comanche   RATING: U L

This 1968 western feature has Shatner in a **dual role** as half-breed Indian twins bent on destroying each other. Shatner is the white Comanche of the title, Johnny Moon, a half-breed raised by white settlers, as well as Notah, the brother who stayed with his tribe. All hell breaks loose when Johnny Moon is charged with a murder committed by Notah. Joseph Cotten is on hand to help sort it all out. Shatner spent three months in Spain filming the low-budget production, putting considerable strain on his already creaky marriage to **Gloria Rand**.

Whitney, Grace Lee (B. 1930)

This shapely blonde actress played Yeoman Janice Rand during the first TV season (1966–67) of *Star Trek*. The original Chicken of the Sea mermaid in the well-known commercials, Whitney had an impressive résumé but an alleged reputation for wild behavior on the set. She quickly soured on the way her character was developed on the mid-1960s show. "I was hired as a sexy, ballsy woman," she told an interviewer. Nevertheless, most of her screen time was spent in menial tasks, such as bringing Kirk soup or preparing his uniform shirts for wear. Before the first episode even aired, *Trek*'s creators were working on ways to write her out of the sci-fi program. One of her only supporters on the set was Shatner. When he lobbied for her not to be fired, rumors began to circulate that the two were, perhaps, lovers. Both parties have always denied those claims. In effect, Whitney says, their relationship was a lot like the one their fictional characters enjoyed. "There was no sexuality between Rand and Kirk. The relationship was never consummated. He was married to the ship. Supposedly, she was in love with him, and supposedly he was very fond of her, but I don't think they ever really got together." After being let go from the show midway through the first season, Whitney went into an emotional tailspin, before finally righting herself in the late 1970s.

William Shatner Ate My Balls

This Internet Web site home page features captioned pictures of Shatner expressing his desire to ingest other people's testicles. *The William Shatner Ate My Balls* page is one of over 400 Ate My Balls Web sites devoted to various celebrities. A thorough site list is available on the World Wide Web at http://www.yahoo.com/Entertainment/Humor_Jokes_and_Fun/Tasteless_Humor/Ate_My_Balls.

William Shatner: Live

This 1977 live album captures Shatner's performance of his **one-man show** in the mid-1970s. Recorded at Hofstra University, the two-disc set was produced by Shatner and released through his company, Lemli Music (named after his daughters Leslie, Melanie, and Lisabeth). A remarkable performance before a mostly stoned college audience. A track listing for the double LP follows:

SIDE ONE: (1) "Earthbound," (2) "Go with Me," (3) "High Flight," (4) "The Flight of Man," (5) "Galileo";

SIDE TWO: (1) "6 Ways to the Moon," (2) "War of the Worlds";

SIDE THREE: (1) "The Movie";

SIDE FOUR: Short Takes: (1) "William Shatner—Audience," (2) "Starship's Facilities," (3) "Peter," (4) "Summer Spaceship," (5) "Three-way Alchemy—The Brain," (6) "Finale."

William Shatner mask

Mask worn by crazed slasher Michael Myers (NO, not the *Saturday Night Live* comedian and film star) in the classic 1978 horror movie *Halloween*. Because of the film's shoestring budget, the prop department had to use the cheapest mask that they could locate in the costume store: a William Shatner mask. They then spray-painted the face white and teased out the hair to create the eerie effect required.

In a case of life imitating art, Shatner himself has taken to donning two William Shatner masks on Halloween trick or treat excursions with his grandchildren. "I take one off, and I've still got the mask on," Shatner told carrot-topped late-night TV talk show host Conan O'Brien in 1997. "Then I take the other off," he continued, pointing to his face, "and I've still got the mask on!"

Shatner tries to horn in on some of Bryan Ferry's action with this publicity shot for his 1977 album William Shatner—Live! *[photo courtesy of The Everett Collection]*

William Shatner's A Twist in the Tale

This syndicated television series, hosted by Shatner, consists of high-concept ghost stories for children. Shatner personally introduced the new series at the MIP-TV market in Cannes in March of 1998. Filmed in New Zealand, the fifteen-part series is a joint venture between Cloud 9, the British production company, and the German entertainment giant Bertelsmann (CLT-UFA International). According to Shatner, the series will provide parents with spooky dramas "that you can enjoy with your youngster, secure in the knowledge there will be nothing you would not want the child to see." He will supply narration and commentary for the stories from an armchair setting. "The challenge is not to moralize but to be dramatic and to be fun," the host/creator told the *Hollywood Reporter* in 1998.

A *Twist in the Tale* is the opening salvo in Shatner's campaign to conquer the lucrative international syndicated market. Such hugely successful TV series as *Xena: Warrior Princess* (1995–), also filmed in New Zealand, have shown the potential for profit in this arena. "There's a whole new world out there in syndication," Shatner cackled, "and I'm glad to be surfing the wave."

Women

Shatner has never been coy about spelling out the attributes he desires in a woman. He once defined a good female figure as "the Greek ideal. Venus de Milo. 36-24-36." And in 1989, when asked which heavenly body he'd like most to visit, Shatner replied, "How about Melanie Griffith?" He's even detailed hairstyle and fashion guidelines for his potential conquests. "I am definitely in favor of the long hair trend in women," he told *Photoplay* in 1968. "One of the glories of being a woman is long, luxuriant hair, whether it is used to run barefoot through or tie in pigtails. A girl who is particularly well built should wear miniskirts, *if* she has the right legs. If not, she should consider getting clothes to *overcome* these defects, not show them off for all to see."

Beyond good looks and a spectacular body, to hold Shatner's attention, a woman, apparently must possess a quality he calls "magnetism."

Shatner escorts actress Nancy Novak to the west coast premiere of the Francis Ford Coppola turkey Finian's Rainbow *in 1968. [photo courtesy of AP Worldwide Photos]*

"If a woman is *not* pretty, but she has that magnetism, that special something, it can be dynamite. And if she's pretty *and* she has that special something—that's wild." A certain homey orientation and a few shared interests catch his eye as well. Shatner looks for "a girl who's capable of giving love as well as receiving. One who can cook but also eat her own food with relish, one who plays tennis, has a sense of humor to counter my straitlaced manner, and one who likes to go horseback riding."

Shatner claims to have been a male chauvinist even in his high school and college years. "During my day and age one took a girl out and tried to make a pass and tried to make out. That was the big deal," he once remembered. However, by the late 1970s, Shatner believed he had arrived at "a point beyond women's lib" where his belief in the dominance of society by alpha males and the imperatives of equality could harmonize. "I really do intrinsically and insightfully believe in the quality of a woman and a man's mind," he told biographers in 1979. "I do also believe that there is greater upper body strength in a man, that nature gave him more musculature. But while there are those few areas where nature has provided variations in our bodies—I really do believe in the equality of man and woman, and in equal pay for equal work."

There is one area where Shatner claims to be skittish about equal opportunity, however—television news. "I find it hard to accept a young girl as a newscaster," he declared, "as against an older man with gray hair telling me the news." In 1989, Shatner, by then an older man with *fake* hair, began telling viewers the news about emergency phone calls and rescue operations as host of the television reality program **Rescue 911**.

World of Suzie Wong, The

Shatner won numerous awards in 1958 for his performance in this Broadway play. Then twenty-seven, he abandoned his burgeoning Hollywood career to take the lead role in the stage production, which opened at the Broadhurst Theatre on October 14, 1958.

Based on the novel (1957) by Richard Mason, **The World of Suzie Wong** concerns a Canadian architect who falls in love with a Chinese prostitute while living in Hong Kong. Shatner won the part of Robert Lomax after a fifteen-minute audition. His female lead was France Nuyen, a twenty-two-year-old ingenue with whom he clashed repeatedly over preparation and approach. In fact, it was commonplace for actors on the **Wong** set to be bullied by Shatner, who took control of the elaborately mounted show with the tenacity of a man who believed this play could make or break his entire career. The atmosphere became so poisonous that director Joshua Logan simply stopped showing up for rehearsals.

The ill wind of backstage strife no doubt affected the critical reception as well. "It opened as a turkey," Shatner remembered years later. "It got seven bad notices. It was directed as a turgid drama. People walked out in the middle of it—you could hear whole rows of people getting up and walking out." At best, the players were damned with faint praise. "William Shatner gives a modest performance that is also attractive," wrote Brooks Atkinson in the *New York Times*, "a little wooden, perhaps, which is one way of avoiding maudlin scenes."

Shatner shows off his big stick on stage in The World of Suzie Wong *(1958). [photo courtesy of Photofest]*

The play seemed destined for the scrap heap. However, Shatner had too much at stake to let it slide into oblivion. He began subtly changing the pace and tenor of the show, turning it from a turgid drama into a fluffy romantic confection. Audiences began to respond. A play that was slated to close after three months got a new lease on life. Amazingly, *The World of Suzie Wong* lasted a year and a half on Broadway. For his part, Shatner was rewarded with acting honors from *Theater World*, the Theater Guild, and the Drama Circle. Thereafter, he never could shake the reputation of being a behind-the-scenes control freak, and that may have factored into the decision not to cast him in the ensuing 1960 film version, directed by Richard Quine and featuring Nancy Kwan in France Nuyen's role. Shatner's leading man part went to William Holden, who, at any rate, was a bigger star than Shatner at the time. Shatner was crushed at being passed over, but would soon get used to seeing plum roles go to screen actors with more bankability.

In a strange case of chickens coming home to roost, two disgruntled members of the *Suzie Wong* cast would cross paths with Shatner later in life. William Windom, Shatner's understudy in the role of Lomax—whom he reportedly mistreated badly—returned to grind his gears as Captain Decker in the classic second season **Star Trek** installment "The Doomsday Machine" (10/20/67). France Nuyen, whom Shatner warred with constantly during the Broadway run, would spar with him once more, this time in the role of Elaan, a petulant alien princess who beams aboard the starship *Enterprise*, in the third-season **Trek** episode "Elaan of Troyius" (12/20/68). Both she and Shatner most certainly must have drawn on their *Suzie Wong* experience in playing many scenes of bickering and recrimination. They were able to work past the bad blood, however, and went on to do two more television projects together in the early 1970s.

World Peace

Shatner has a simple solution to the problems of war and injustice: brain power. "Most of the human brain is unused," he explained to biographers a few decades ago. "From that the thought could be extended: the brain is there, waiting to be used in manners that we haven't yet begun to see—toward the kinds of thinking and the kinds of actions that would stop the idiocies you see around you.

"Why is it better for a man in Lebanon to kill another man now, today, than to work out some kind of arrangement? Why is it the Irish are bombing each other with such a bloodthirst as to be bestial? Why is there so much strife when common sense can show you what's to happen? In Africa—I mean, we're about to see a bloodbath. Things are going to happen that are really going to be terrible, unless something is done—and common sense—the use of the *head*—could prevent it and do something else.

"And if I were able to do anything about people, I would point to their heads and say, 'There is that large mass sitting on top of your shoulders of which ten percent is being used. The rest is lying fallow, waiting for ideas and functions that have not yet been given to it. And that, maybe, is what the next three hundred years will do.'"

Amen to that. And God bless you, William Shatner.

Writing

A true Renaissance man, Shatner has pursued writing in addition to **acting**, **directing**, and **producing**. Throw in his musical dabblings on such LP albums as ***The Transformed Man*** (1968) and you have the entertainment industry equivalent of baseball's rare five-tool player. His aspirations in this arena go back to his earliest days in show business.

Shatner began submitting script ideas for *Star Trek* soon after he was hired for the TV series in 1966. Creator **Gene Roddenberry** related one instance when the actor forced him, as executive producer, to read one of his story treatments. "He wouldn't let me take it home to read," Roddenberry recalled. "He insisted on reading it right there. So I fortified myself with a Scotch and prepared to suffer. But the story flowed and was so damned poetic I caught myself wishing I could write that well." Nevertheless, Roddenberry passed on the script, for reasons he left unstated. Beyond piddling script changes, Shatner did not get a chance to put words into the mouths of *Star Trek* characters until 1989, when he cowrote and directed the feature film ***Star Trek V: The Final Frontier***.

For Shatner, writing, acting, and the other disciplines form one gorgeous artistic mosaic. "I've learned a great deal about acting from writing," Shatner explained back in 1967. "An actor interprets a writer's work just as a musician interprets a composer's work. The criterion of a good actor is how well he interprets the work of the writer. Even the writer may not know exactly what he has written—this is the nebulous area in which the actor works."

Wynder, Dr. Ernst (B. 1922)

Nutritionist and exercise promoter who served as Shatner's health guru for a time during the late 1970s. Shatner met Wynder, the director of the American Health Foundation, at a dinner party in 1978. At the time, the actor was desperately trying to get in shape for his triumphant return to the big screen in ***Star Trek: The Motion Picture*** (1979). Wynder convinced him to abandon such luxuries as sugar and coffee and embrace a rigorous workout regimen. By the next year, Shatner was noticeably trimmer (though some have hinted that other methods, such as liposuction, may have had something to do with that). In 1979, the star served as celebrity spokesperson for Wynder's "Know Your Body" program, which endeavored to help young people stay fit. Wynder is the author of *The American Health Foundation Guide to Lifespan Health* (1984) and a leading proponent of the link between cancer and diet.

Zmed, Adrian (B. 1954)

This swarthy boyish actor played the brash patrolman, Officer Vince Romano, alongside Shatner on ABC-TV's **T. J. Hooker** from 1982 to 1985. A virtual unknown when he joined the show, Zmed went on to star in the feature film *Grease 2* (1982) and to serve as host of the syndicated televised disco party *Dance Fever* from 1985 to 1987. His other film credits include *Bachelor Party* (1984), *The Other Woman* (1992), and *Improper Conduct* (1994). He is included here *only* because his name begins with the letter "z."

Shatner and costar Adrian Zmed explore the world behind the badge in the TV series T. J. Hooker (1982 to 1985) [photo courtesy of Photofest]

Appendix 1

∼

A Shatnerography

Behold, the great man's credits...

FEATURE FILMS

The Brothers Karamazov (Metro-Goldwyn-Mayer, 1958). Color, 146 minutes. No rating.
DIRECTOR/WRITER: Richard Brooks
CAST: Yul Brynner (Dmitri Karamazov); Lee J. Cobb (Fyodor Karamazov); Richard Basehart (Ivan Karamazov); William Shatner (Alexei Karamazov); Albert Salmi (Smerdyakov); Claire Bloom (Katya); Maria Schell (Grushenka)

Judgment at Nuremberg (United Artists, 1961). B&W, 178 minutes. No rating.
DIRECTOR: Stanley Kramer; WRITER: Abby Mann
CAST: Spencer Tracy (Judge Dan Haywood); Marlene Dietrich (Madame Bertholdt); Burt Lancaster (Ernst Janning); Richard Widmark (Captain Harry Buyers); Maximilian Schell (Hans Rolfe); William Shatner (Captain Byers); Judy Garland (Irene Hoffman); Montgomery Clift (Rudolf Peterson); Werner Klemperer (Emil Hahn)

The Explosive Generation (United Artists, 1961). B&W, 89 minutes. No rating.
DIRECTOR: Buzz Kulik; WRITER: Joseph Landon
CAST: William Shatner (Peter Gifford); Billy Gray (Bobby Herman); Lee Kinsolving (Dan Carlyle); Patricia McCormack (Janet Sommers)

The Intruder (Pathe American, 1961). B&W, 84 minutes. No rating.
DIRECTOR: Roger Corman; WRITER: Charles Beaumont
CAST: William Shatner (Adam Cramer); Frank Maxwell (Tom Mc-Daniel); Beverly Lunsford (Ella McDaniel)

The Outrage (Metro-Goldwyn-Mayer, 1964). B&W, 97 minutes. No rating.
DIRECTOR: Martin Ritt; WRITER: Michael Kanin
CAST: Paul Newman (Juan Carrasco); Edward G. Robinson (the con-man/narrator); Laurence Harvey (the husband); Claire Bloom (the wife); William Shatner (the preacher)

The Incubus (Daystar Independent, 1965). B&W, 78 minutes. No rating.
DIRECTOR/WRITER: Leslie Stevens
CAST: William Shatner (Marc); Allyson Ames (Kia); Milos Milos (Incubus)

White Comanche (Spanish International, 1968). Color, 90 minutes. No rating.
DIRECTOR: Jose Briz; WRITERS: Frank Gruber, Manuel Gomez, Rivera Robert Holt, and Jose Briz
CAST: William Shatner (Johnny Moon/Notah); Joseph Cotten (a cauca-soid); Luis Prendes (Grimes)

Want a Ride, Little Girl? (Conqueador, 1972). Color, 91 minutes. PG-rated.
Director: William Grefe; WRITER: Tony Grechales
CAST: William Shatner (Matt Stone); Ruth Roman (Julia Marstow); Jennifer Bishop (Ann Moy); Kim Nicholas (Tina Moy)

Deathdream (Europix, 1972). Color, 88 minutes. PG-rated.
DIRECTOR: Bob Clark; WRITER: Alan Ormsby
CAST: John Marley (Charles Brooks); Lynn Carlin (Christine Brooks); Richard Backus (Andy Brooks); William Shatner (the friend)

Big Bad Mama (New World, 1974). Color, 85 minutes. R-rated.
DIRECTOR: Steve Carver; WRITERS: William Norton and Frances Doe
CAST: Angie Dickinson (Wilma McClatchie); William Shatner (William J. Baxter); Tom Skerritt (Fred Diller); Susan Sennett (Billy Jean); Robbie Lee (Polly)

The Devil's Rain (Bryanston, 1975). Color, 86 minutes. PG-rated.
DIRECTOR: Robert Fuest; WRITERS: James Ashton, Gabe Essoe, and Gerald Hopman
CAST: Ernest Borgnine (Jonathan Corbis); Ida Lupino (Mrs. Preston); Tom Skerritt (Tom Preston); Joan Prather (Julie Preston); William Shatner (Mark Preston); Eddie Albert (Dr. Richards); Keenan Wynn (Sheriff Owens); John Travolta (Danny)

Mysteries of the Gods (Hemisphere, 1976). Color, 93 minutes. G-rated.
DIRECTOR: Charles Romine; WRITER: Erich von Daniken
CAST: William Shatner (narrator); Jeane Dixon; Dr. Jesco von Puttkamer

A Whale of a Tale (Luckris, 1976). Color, 90 minutes. G-rated.
DIRECTOR/WRITER: Ewing Miles Brown
CAST: William Shatner (Dr. Jack Fredericks); Marty Allen (Louie); Scott C. Kolden (Joey Fields)

Kingdom of the Spiders (Dimension, 1977). Color, 94 minutes. PG-rated.
DIRECTOR: John "Bud" Cardos; WRITERS: Richard Robinson and Alan Caillou
CAST: William Shatner (Dr. Robert "Rack" Hansen); Tiffany Bolling (Diane Ashley); Woody Strode (Walter Colby); David MacLean (Sheriff Smith); Lieux Dressler (Emma Washburn)

The Land of No Return (International Picture Show, 1978). Color, 84 minutes. PG-rated.
DIRECTOR: Kent Bateman; WRITERS: Kent Bateman and Frank Ray Perilli
CAST: William Shatner (Curt Benell); Mel Tormé (Zak O'Brien); Donald Moffat (Air Traffic Controller)

The Third Walker (Quadrant, 1978). Color, 90 minutes. PG-rated.
DIRECTOR: Teri McLuhan; WRITER: Robert Thom
CAST: Colleen Dewhurst (Kate MacLean); William Shatner (Munro MacLean); Frank Moore (James MacLean); Monique Mercure (Marie Blanchard); Tony Meyer (Etienne Blanchard); David Meyer (Andrew MacLean); Marshall McLuhan (Voice of the Judge)

Riel (Prism Films, 1979). Color, 150 minutes. PG-rated.
DIRECTOR: George Bloomfield; WRITER: Gary Teubner

CAST: Raymond Cloutier (Louis Riel); Christopher Plummer (John A. MacDonald); Roger Blay (Dumont); Lloyd Bochner (Dr. Schulz); William Shatner (Canadian Army Officer); Arthur Hill; Leslie Nielsen

Star Trek: The Motion Picture (Paramount, 1979). Color, 132 minutes. G-rated.
DIRECTOR: Robert Wise; WRITER: Harold Livingston
CAST: William Shatner (Adm. James T. Kirk); Leonard Nimoy (Comdr. Spock); DeForest Kelley (Lt. Comdr. Leonard "Bones" McCoy); James Doohan (Comdr. Montgomery "Scotty" Scott); George Takei (Lt. Comdr. Hikaru Sulu); Majel Barrett (Dr. Christine Chapel); Walter Koenig (Comdr. Pavel Chekov); Nichelle Nichols (Lt. Comdr. Nyota Uhura); Stephen Collins (Captain William Decker); Persis Khambatta (Lieutenant Ilia)

The Kidnapping of the President (Bordeaux Films, 1980). Color, 105 minutes. R-rated.
DIRECTOR: George Mendeluk; WRITER: Richard Murphy
CAST: Hal Holbrook (President Adam Scott); Van Johnson (Vice President Ethan Richards); William Shatner (Jerry O'Connor); Ava Gardner (Beth Richards)

Visiting Hours (Filmplan International, 1982). Color, 105 minutes. R-rated.
DIRECTOR: Jean Claude Lord; WRITER: Brian Taggert
CAST: Michael Ironside (Colt Hawker); Lee Grant (Deborah Ballin); Linda Purl (Sheila Munroe); William Shatner (Gary Baylor)

Star Trek II: The Wrath of Khan (Paramount, 1982). Color, 113 minutes. PG-rated.
DIRECTOR: Nicholas Meyer; WRITER: Jack B. Sowards
CAST: William Shatner (Adm. James T. Kirk); Leonard Nimoy (Mr. Spock); DeForest Kelley (Dr. Leonard "Bones" McCoy); James Doohan (Chief Engineer Montgomery "Scotty" Scott); Walter Koenig (Comdr. Pavel Chekov); George Takei (Comdr. Hikaru Sulu); Nichelle Nichols (Comdr. Nyota Uhura); Bibi Besch (Dr. Carol Marcus); Merritt Butrick (Dr. David Marcus); Kirstie Alley (Lieutenant Saavik); Ricardo Montalban (Khan Noonian Singh)

Airplane II: The Sequel (Paramount, 1982). Color, 85 minutes. PG-rated.
DIRECTOR/WRITER: Ken Finkleman
CAST: Julie Hagerty (Elaine Dickinson); Robert Hays (Ted Striker); Lloyd Bridges (McCroskey); Peter Graves (Captain Oveur); William Shatner (Comdr. Buck Murdock); Sonny Bono (Joe Salucci); Raymond Burr (Judge); Chuck Connors (Sarge); Chad Everett (Simon); Rip Torn (Kruger); John Dehner (Commissioner); Jack Jones (Singer)

Star Trek III: The Search for Spock (Paramount, 1984). Color, 105 minutes. PG-rated.
DIRECTOR: Leonard Nimoy; WRITER: Harve Bennett
CAST: William Shatner (Adm. James T. Kirk); Leonard Nimoy (Captain Spock); DeForest Kelley (Dr. Leonard "Bones" McCoy); James Doohan (Comdr. Montgomery "Scotty" Scott); Walter Koenig (Comdr. Pavel Chekov); George Takei (Captain Hikaru Sulu); Nichelle Nichols (Comdr. Nyota Uhura); Robin Curtis (Lieutenant Saavik); Merritt Butrick (Dr. David Marcus); Mark Lenard (Ambassador Sarek of Vulcan); Dame Judith Anderson (High Priestess); Christopher Lloyd (Lord Kruge)

Star Trek IV: The Voyage Home (Paramount, 1986). Color, 119 minutes. PG-rated
DIRECTOR: Leonard Nimoy; WRITERS: Steve Meerson, Peter Krikes, Harve Bennett, and Nicholas Meyer
CAST: William Shatner (Adm. James T. Kirk), Leonard Nimoy (Captain Spock); DeForest Kelley (Dr. Leonard "Bones" McCoy); James Doohan (Captain Montgomery "Scotty" Scott); George Takei (Captain Hikaru Sulu); Walter Koenig (Comdr. Pavel Chekov); Nichelle Nichols (Comdr. Nyota Uhura); Mark Lenard (Ambassador Sarek of Vulcan); Robin Curtis (Lieutenant Saavik); Brock Peters (Admiral Cartwright); Grace Lee Whitney (Comdr. Janice Rand); Majel Barrett (Comdr. Christine Chapel); Catherine Hicks (Dr. Gillian Taylor)

Star Trek V: The Final Frontier (Paramount, 1989). Color, 107 minutes. PG-rated.
DIRECTOR: William Shatner; WRITER: David Loughery
CAST: William Shatner (Captain James T. Kirk); Leonard Nimoy (Mr. Spock); DeForest Kelley (Dr. Leonard "Bones" McCoy); James Doohan

(Chief Engineer Montgomery "Scotty" Scott); Walter Koenig (Comdr. Pavel Chekov); Nichelle Nichols (Communications Officer Nyota Uhura); George Takei (Comdr. Hikaru Sulu); David Warner (St. John Talbot); Charles Cooper (General Korrd); Cynthia Gouw (Caithlin Dar); Todd Bryant (Captain Klaa); Lawrence Luckinbill (Sybok)

Star Trek VI: The Undiscovered Country (Paramount, 1991). Color, 113 minutes. PG-rated.
DIRECTOR: Nicholas Meyer; WRITERS: Denny Martin Flinn and Nicholas Meyer
CAST: William Shatner (Captain James T. Kirk); Leonard Nimoy (Captain Spock); DeForest Kelley (Dr. Leonard "Bones" McCoy); James Doohan (Captain Montgomery "Scotty" Scott); Walter Koenig (Comdr. Pavel Chekov); Nichelle Nichols (Comdr. Nyota Uhura); George Takei (Captain Hikaru Sulu); Mark Lenard (Ambassador Sarek of Vulcan); Brock Peters (Admiral Cartwright); David Warner (Chancellor Gorkon); Christopher Plummer (General Chang)

Bill & Ted's Bogus Journey (Orion, 1991). Color, 93 minutes. PG-rated.
DIRECTOR: Peter Hewitt; WRITERS: Christ Matheson and Ed Solomon
CAST: Keanu Reeves (Ted Logan); Alex Winter (Bill S. Preston); William Shatner (Captain James T. Kirk); Joss Ackland (De Nomolos); Pam Grier (Mrs. Wardroe); William Sadler (Grim Reaper)

National Lampoon's Loaded Weapon I (New Line, 1993). Color, 83 minutes. PG-13 rated.
DIRECTOR: Gene Quintano; WRITERS: Don Holley and Gene Quintano
CAST: Emilio Estevez (Jack Colt); Samuel L. Jackson (Wed Lugar); Jon Lovitz (Tim Beckard); William Shatner (Gen. Curtis Mortars); Tim Curry (Jigsaw); Kathy Ireland (Destiny Demeanor); Bruce Willis (Home Owner); Dr. Joyce Brothers (Coroner); Denis Leary (Mike McCracken); Whoopi Goldberg (Sergeant York)

Star Trek: Generations (Paramount, 1994). Color, 123 minutes. PG-rated.
DIRECTOR: David Carson; WRITERS: Ronald D. Moore and Brannon Braga
CAST: Patrick Stewart (Captain Jean-Luc Picard); Jonathan Frakes (Comdr. William T. Riker); Brent Spiner (Lieutenant Commander

Data); LeVar Burton (Eng. Georgi LaForge); Michael Dorn (Lieutenant Commander Worf); Gates McFadden (Dr. Beverly Crusher); Marina Sirtis (Counselor Deanna Troi); William Shatner (Captain James T. Kirk); James Doohan (Captain Montgomery "Scotty" Scott); Walter Koenig (Comdr. Pavel Chekov); Guinan (Whoopi Goldberg); Barbara March (Lursa, House of Duras); Gwynyth Walsh (B'Etor, House of Duras); Malcolm McDowell (Dr. Tolian Saran)

Trinity and Beyond (Visual Concept Entertainment, 1995). Color, 93 minutes. No rating.
DIRECTOR: Peter Kuran; WRITERS: Scott Narrie and Don Pugsley
CAST: William Shatner (narrator); Frank H. Shelton; Edward Teller

TV MOVIES AND MINISERIES

Sole Survivor (CBS, 1/9/70). Color, 100 minutes.
DIRECTOR: Paul Stanley; WRITER: Guerdon S. Trueblood
CAST: Vince Edwards (Maj. Michael Devlin); Richard Basehart (Gen. Russell Hamner); William Shatner (Lt. Col. Joe Gronke); Brad Davis (Elmo); Patrick Wayne (Mac); Lou (Antonio Tony)

Vanished (NBC, 3/8/71, 3/9/71). Color, 190 minutes.
DIRECTOR: Buzz Kulik; WRITER: Dean Riesner
CAST: Richard Widmark (President Paul Roudebush); Skye Aubrey (Jill Nichols); William Shatner (Dave Paulick); Robert Young (Sen. Earl Gannon); Tom Bosley (Johnny Cavanaugh); James Farentino (Gene Culligan); Larry Hagman (Jerry Fraytag); Arthur Hill (Arthur Greer); Eleanor Parker (Sue Greer); E. G. Marshall (Arthur Ingram); Steven McNally (General Palfrey); Betty White (herself)

Owen Marshall, Counselor at Law (ABC, 9/12/71). Color, 120 minutes.
DIRECTOR: Buzz Kulik; WRITER: Jerry McNeely
CAST: Arthur Hill (Owen Marshall); Vera Miles (Joan Baldwin); William Shatner (D.A. Dave Blankenship); Tim Matheson (Jim McGuire); Bruce Davison (Cowboy Leatherberry); Joseph Campanella (Dr. Eric Gibson); Rick Lenz (Baird Marshall); Dana Wynter (Judge Lynn Oliver)

The People (ABC, 1/22/72). Color, 90 minutes.
DIRECTOR: John Korty; WRITER: James M. Miller
CAST: Kim Darby (Melodyne Anderson); William Shatner (Dr. Curtis);

Diane Varsi (Valency); Dan O'Herlihy (Sol Diemus); Chris Valentine (Francker)

The Hound of the Baskervilles (ABC, 2/12/72). Color, 90 minutes.
DIRECTOR: Barry Crane; WRITER: Robert E. Thompson
CAST: Stewart Granger (Sherlock Holmes); Bernard Fox (Dr. Watson); William Shatner; (George Stapleton); Anthony Zerbe (Dr. John Mortimer); Ian Ireland (Henry Baskerville); Sally Ann Howes (Laura Frankland); Alan Calliou (Inspector Lestrade); June Merrow (Beryl Stapleton)

Incident on a Dark Street (NBC, 1/13/73). Color, 120 minutes.
DIRECTOR: Buzz Kulik; WRITER: E. Jack Neumann
CAST: James Olson (Joseph Dubbs); David Canary (Pete Gallagher); William Shatner (Deaver Wallace); Robert Pine (Paul Hamilton); Richard Castellano (Frank Romeo); Murray Hamilton (Edmund); Gilbert Roland (Dominic Leopold); John Kerr (Attorney Gallagher)

Go Ask Alice (ABC, 1/24/73). Color, 90 minutes.
DIRECTOR: John Korty; WRITER: Ellen Violett
CAST: Jamie Smith-Jackson (Alice); William Shatner (Sam); Ruth Roman (the psychiatrist); Wendell Burton (Joel Clements); Julie Adams (Dorothy); Andy Griffith (the priest)

The Horror at 37,000 Feet (CBS, 2/13/73). Color, 90 minutes.
DIRECTOR: David Lowell Rich; WRITERS: James D. Buchanan and Ronald L. Austin
CAST: Chuck Connors (Captain Ernie Slade); Buddy Ebsen (Len Farlee); William Shatner (Paul Kovalik); France Nuyen (Annalik); Roy Thinnes (Alan O'Neill); Tammy Grimes (Mrs. Pinder); Lyn Loring (Manya); Jane Merrow (Sheila O'Neill); Paul Winfield (Dr. Enkalla)

Pioneer Woman (ABC, 12/19/73). Color, 90 minutes.
DIRECTOR: Buzz Kulik; WRITER: Suzanne Clauser
CAST: Joanna Pettet (Maggie Sergeant); William Shatner (John Sergeant); Helen Hunt (Sarah Sergeant); David Janssen (Robert Douglas); Lance Le Gault (Joe Wormser)

Indict and Convict (ABC, 1/6/74). Color, 100 minutes.
DIRECTOR: Boris Sagal; WRITER: Winston Miller
CAST: George Grizzard (Bob Mathews); Reni Santoni (Mike Belano); William Shatner (Sam Belden); Susan Howard (Joanna Garret); Eli Wallach (DeWitt Foster); Harry Guardino (Mel Thomas); Ed Flanders (Timothy Fitzgerald); Myrna Loy (Judge Christine Taylor); Ruta Lee (Phyllis Dorfman); Kip Niven (Norman Hastings)

Pray for the Wildcats (ABC, 1/23/74). Color, 100 minutes.
DIRECTOR: Robert Michael Lewis; WRITER: Jack Turley
CAST: Andy Griffith (Sam Farragut); William Shatner (Warren Summerfield); Robert Reed (Paul McIlvian); Marjoe Gortner (Terry Maxon); Angie Dickinson (Nancy McIlvian); Lorraine Gary (Lila Summerfield); Janet Margolin (Krissie Kincaid)

The Barbary Coast (ABC, 5/4/75). Color, 120 minutes.
DIRECTOR: Bill Bixby; WRITER: Douglas Heyes
CAST: William Shatner (Jeff Cable); Dennis Cole (Cash Conover); Lynda Day George (Clio Du Bois); Neville Brand (Florrie Roscoe); Richard Kiel (Moose Moran); Bill Bixby (Philippe Despard); John Vernon (Templar)

Perilous Voyage (NBC, 7/29/76). Color, 120 minutes.
DIRECTOR: William A. Graham; WRITERS: Oscar Millard, Robert Weverka, and Sidney L. Stebel
CAST: Michael Parks (Antonio De Leon); Lee Grant (Virginia Monroe); William Shatner (Steve Monroe); Frank Silvera (General Salazar); Victor Joy (Dr. Merrill); Charles McGraw (Captain Humphreys); Stuart Margolin (Rico)

The Tenth Level (CBS, 8/26/76). Color, 120 minutes.
DIRECTOR: Charles S. Dubin; WRITER: George Bellak
CAST: William Shatner (Dr. Stanley Milgram)

Testimony of Two Men (Syndicated, 5/9/77, 5/16/77, 5/23/77). Color, 300 minutes.
DIRECTORS: Larry Yest and Leo Penn; WRITERS: James Miller, Jennifer Miller, and William Hanley
CAST: David Birney (Jonathan Ferrier); David Huffman (Harold Ferrier); William Shatner (Adrian Ferrier); Barbara Parkins (Marjorie Fer-

rier/Hilda Eaton); Ralph Bellamy (Dr. Spaulding); Theodore Bikel (Peter Heger); Tom Bosley (Dr. Hedler/Narrator); Ray Milland (Jonas Witherby); Margaret O'Brien (Flora Eaton); Dan Dailey (Father McGuire); Linda Purl (Mavis Eaton); Cameron Mitchell (Jeremiah Hadley)

The Bastard (Syndicated, 5/22/78, 5/23/78). Color, 200 minutes.
DIRECTOR: Lee H. Katsin; WRITER: Guerdon Trueblood
CAST: Andrew Stevens (Philippe Charboneau/Philip Kent); Tom Bosley (Benjamin Franklin); William Shatner (Paul Revere); William Daniels (Sam Adams); Buddy Ebsen (Benjamin Edes); Lorne Greene (Bishop Francis); Patricia Neal (Marie Charboneau); Eleanor Parker (Lady Amberly); Cameron Mitchell (Captain Plummer); Harry Morgan (Captain Caleb); Donald Pleasance (Solomon Sholto); Barry Sullivan (Abraham Ware)

Little Women (NBC, 10/2/78, 10/3/78). Color, 200 minutes.
DIRECTORS: Leo Penn, Gordon Hessler, John Newland, and Philip Leacock; WRITER: Suzanne Clauser
CAST: Meredith Baxter Birney (Meg March); Susan Dey (Jo March); William Shatner (Professor Friedrich Bhaer); Ann Dusenberry (Amy March); Eve Plumb (Beth March); Greer Garson (Aunt March); Dorothy McGuire (Marmee); Robert Young (Grandpa Lawrence); Cliff Potts (John Brooke); William Schallert (Reverend March)

Crash (aka *The Crash of Flight 401*) (ABC, 10/29/78). Color, 104 minutes.
DIRECTOR: Barry Shear; WRITERS: Donald S. Sanford and Steve Brown
CAST: William Shatner (Carl Tobias); Adrienne Barbeau (Veronica Daniels); Ron Glass (Jerry Grant); Sharon Gless (Lesley Fuller); Artie Shaw (Elderly Passenger); Lorraine Gary (Emily Mulwray); George Maharis (Evan Walsh); Ron Glass (Jerry Grant)

Disaster on the Coastliner (ABC, 10/28/79). Color, 120 minutes.
DIRECTOR: Richard Sarafian; WRITER: David E. Ambrose
CAST: Lloyd Bridges (Al Mitchell); Raymond Burr (Estes Hill); William Shatner (Stuart Peters); E. G. Marshall (Roy Snyder); Yvette Mimieux (Paula Harvey); Robert Fuller (Matt Leigh); Pat Hingle (John Marsh)

The Babysitter (ABC, 11/28/80). Color, 100 minutes.
DIRECTOR: Peter Medak; WRITER: Jennifer Miller

CAST: Patty Duke Astin (Liz Benedict); William Shatner (Dr. Jeff Benedict); Quinn Cummings (Tara Benedict); John Houseman (Doc Lindquist); Stephanie Zimbalist (Joanne Redwine); David Wallace (Scotty)

Secrets of a Married Man (NBC, 9/24/84). Color, 100 minutes.
DIRECTOR: William A. Graham; WRITER: Dennis Nemec
CAST: William Shatner (Christopher Jordan); Michelle Phillips (Katie Jordan); Cybil Shepherd (Elaine); Glynn Turman (Jesse); Jackson Davies (Terry); Kevin George (Brian Jordan); Tiffany Michas (Beth Jordan); Daemon Clark (Alex Jordan)

North Beach and Rawhide (CBS, 11/12/85, 11/13/85). Color, 120 minutes.
DIRECTOR: Harry Falk; WRITERS: Jimmy Sangster, John Beaird, and George Yanok
CAST: William Shatner (Rawhide McGregor); Tate Donovan (Sean "North Beach" Connelly); Christopher Penn (Dan Donnelly); Leo Penn (Mr. Donnelly); Ron O'Neal (Kyle Weston); Conchata Ferrill (Doc Norman); James Olsen (Bill Cassidy); Lori Loughlin (Candy Cassidy)

T. J. Hooker: Blood Sport (CBS, 5/21/86). Color, 104 minutes.
DIRECTOR: Vincent McEveety; WRITERS: Rudolph Bochert, Don Ingalls, Bruce Reisman, Stan Berkowitz, and Rick Husky
CAST: William Shatner (Sgt. T. J. Hooker); James Darren (Officer Jim Corrigan); Heather Locklear (Officer Stacy Sheridan); Don Murray (Senator Grayle); Kim Miyori (Barbara Grayle); Henry Darrow (Gus Kalioki); Keye Luke (Dr. Makimura)

Broken Angel (ABC, 3/14/88). Color, 96 minutes.
DIRECTOR: Richard T. Heffron; WRITER: Cynthia Cherbak
CAST: William Shatner (the husband); Susan Blakely (the wife); Erika Eleniak (the daughter); Roxanne Biggs (Gang Counselor)

Voice of the Planet (TBS, 2/18/91). Color, 600 minutes.
DIRECTOR/WRITER: Michael Tobias
CAST: William Shatner (William Hope Planter); Faye Dunaway (Gaia)

A Family of Strangers (CBS, 2/21/93). Color, 120 minutes.
DIRECTOR: Sheldon Lary; WRITERS: Anna Sandor and William Gough
CAST: Melissa Gilbert (Julie Lawson); Patty Duke (the mother); William Shatner (the father)

TekWar (Syndicated, 1/23/94). Color, 97 minutes.
DIRECTOR: William Shatner; WRITERS: Westbrook Claridge and Alfonse Ruggiero
CAST: Greg Evigan (Jake Cardigan); William Shatner (Walter Bascom); Eugene Clark (Sid Gomez)

TekWar: TekLords (Syndicated, 2/20/94). Color, 96 minutes.
DIRECTOR: George Bloomfield; WRITER: Morgan Gendel
CAST: Greg Evigan (Jake Cardigan); William Shatner (Walter Bascom); Eugene Clark (Sid Gomez)

TekWar: TekLab (Syndicated, 2/27/94). Color, 105 minutes.
DIRECTOR: Timothy Bond; WRITER: Chris Haddock
CAST: Greg Evigan (Jake Cardigan); William Shatner (Walter Bascom); Eugene Clark (Sid Gomez)

TekWar: TekJustice (Syndicated, 5/14/94). Color, 99 minutes.
DIRECTOR: Gerard Ciccoritti; WRITERS: Morgan Gendel and Jim Macak
CAST: Greg Evigan (Jake Cardigan); William Shatner (Walter Bascom); Eugene Clark (Sid Gomez)

A Silent Betrayal (CBS, 12/20/94). Color, 100 minutes.
DIRECTOR: Robert Iscove; WRITER: Edward DeBlassio
CAST: Richard Crenna (Lt. Frank Janek); Helen Shaver (Monique Dessier); William Shatner (Bodosh)

Columbo: Butterfly in Shades of Gray (ABC, 1/10/95). Color, 96 minutes.
DIRECTOR: Dennis Dugan; WRITER: Peter S. Fischer
CAST: Peter Falk (Lieutenant Columbo); William Shatner (Fielding Chase); Molly Hagan (Victoria Chase)

Prisoner of Zenda, Inc. (Showtime 9/29/96). Color, 101 minutes.
DIRECTOR: Stefan Scaini; WRITERS: Richard Clark and Rodman Gregg
CAST: Jonathan Jackson (Rudy/Oliver); Jay Brazeau (Professor Wooley); William Shatner (Michael Gatewick)

Dead Man's Island (CBS, 3/5/96). Color, 97 minutes.
DIRECTOR: Peter Hunt; WRITER: Peter S. Fischer
CAST: Christopher Atkins (Roger Prescott); Morgan Fairchild (Valerie St. Vincent); William Shatner (Chase Prescott)

TELEVISION SERIES (DRAMATIC)

For the People (as David Koster; CBS, 1965)
Star Trek (as Captain James T. Kirk; NBC, 1966 to 1969)
Star Trek animated series (voice of Captain James T. Kirk; NBC, 1973 to 1975)
The Barbary Coast (as Jeff Cable; ABC, 1975 to 1976)
T. J. Hooker (as Sgt. T. J. Hooker; ABC, 1982 to 1985; CBS, 1985 to 1986)
TekWar (occasional, as Walter Bascom, USA Network, 1994 to 1995)

TELEVISION SERIES (AS HOST/NARRATOR)

Challenge (host, ABC, 1972)
Flick Flack (host, Global Network of Canada, 1974)
Breakaway (narrator, syndicated, 1977)
This Was America (host/narrator; syndicated, 1979 to 1980)
Rescue: 911 (host/narrator; 1989 to 1992)

TELEVISION APPEARANCES (EPISODIC)

Goodyear TV Playhouse: "All Summer Long" (NBC, 10/28/56)
Omnibus: "School for Wives" (ABC, 11/11/56)
Kaiser Aluminum Hour: "Gwyneth" (NBC, 12/18/56)
Omnibus: "Oedipus Rex" (ABC, 1/6/57)
Studio One: "The Defender" (CBS, 2/25/57, 3/4/57)
Kaiser Aluminum Hour: "The Deadly Silence" (NBC, 5/21/57)
Alfred Hitchcock Presents: "The Glass Eye" (CBS, 10/6/57)
Studio One: "The Deaf Heart" (CBS, 10/21/57)
Studio One: "No Deadly Medicine (CBS, 12/9/57, 12/16/57)
Kraft Theater: "The Velvet Trap" (NBC, 1/8/58)
U.S. Steel Hour: "Walk with a Stranger" (CBS, 2/26/58)
U.S. Steel Hour: "A Man in Hiding" (CBS, 5/7/58)
Suspicion: "Protégé" (NBC, 5/12/58)
Climax: "Time of the Hanging" (CBS, 5/22/58)
Playhouse 90: "A Town Has Turned to Dust" (CBS, 6/19/58)
Kraft Mystery Theater: "The Man Who Didn't Fly" (NBC, 7/16/58)
U.S. Steel Hour: "Old Marshals Never Die" (NBC, 8/13/58)
Sunday Showcase: "The Indestructible Mr. Gore" (NBC, 12/13/59)
Alfred Hitchcock Presents: "Mother, May I Go Out to Swim?" (CBS, 4/10/60)
Play of the Week: "Night of the Auk" (syndicated, 5/2/60)

Robert Herridge Theater: "Story of a Gunfighter" (CBS, 8/25/60)
Family Classics: "The Scarlet Pimpernel" (CBS, 10/28/60)
The Twilight Zone: "Nick of Time" (CBS, 11/18/60)
Alcoa Presents One Step Beyond: "The Promise" (ABC, 11/29/60)
The Outlaws: "Starfall" (NBC, 11/24/60, 12/1/60)
Thriller: "The Hungry Glass" (NBC, 1/3/61)
Thriller: "The Grim Reaper" (NBC, 6/13/61)
The Defenders: "Killer Instinct" (CBS, 9/23/61)
Dr. Kildare: "Admitting Service" (NBC, 11/2/61)
Naked City: "Portrait of a Painter" (ABC, 1/10/62)
Naked City: "Without Stick or Sword" (ABC, 3/28/62)
The Defenders: "The Invisible Badge" (CBS, 11/24/62)
The Nurses: "A Difference of Years" (CBS, 1/3/63)
The Dick Powell Show: "Colossus" (NBC, 3/12/63)
The Nurses: "The Quality of Mercy" (CBS, 3/21/63)
Alcoa Premiere: "Million Dollar Hospital" (ABC, 4/18/63)
77 Sunset Strip: "Five" (ABC, 9/20/63, 9/27/63, 10/4/63)
The Twilight Zone: "Nightmare at 20,000 Feet" (CBS, 10/11/63)
Channing: "Dragon in the Den" (ABC, 10/23/63)
Route 66: "We Build Our Houses with Their Backs to the Sea" (CBS, 10/26/63)
The Defenders: "The Cruel Hook" (CBS, 11/2/63)
Arrest and Trial: "Onward and Upward" (ABC, 1/19/64)
Burke's Law: "Who Killed Carrie Cornell?" (ABC, 2/14/64)
The Defenders: "Uncivil War" (CBS, 6/27/64)
The Outer Limits: "Cold Hands, Warm Heart" (ABC, 9/26/64)
The Reporter: "He Stuck in His Thumb" (CBS, 10/30/64)
The Man from U.N.C.L.E.: "The Project Strigas Affair" (NBC, 11/24/64)
Bob Hope Chrysler Theater: "The Shattered Glass" (NBC, 12/11/64)
The Defenders: "Whipping Boy" (CBS, 1/31/65)
Doctors and Nurses: "Act of Violence" (CBS, 2/23/65)
Lamp Unto My Feet: "The Cape" (CBS, 3/8/65)
The Virginian: "The Claim" (NBC, 10/6/65)
12 o'Clock High: "I Am the Enemy" (ABC, 11/8/65)
Insight: "Locusts Have No Kings" (syndicated, 11/21/65)
The Fugitive: "Stranger in the Mirror" (ABC, 12/7/65)
The Big Valley: "A Time To Kill" (ABC, 1/19/66)

Dr. Kildare: "The Encroachment" (NBC, 2/21/66)

Dr. Kildare: "A Patient Lost" (NBC, 2/22/66)

Dr. Kildare: "What Happened to All the Sunshine and Roses" (NBC, 2/28/66)

Bob Hope Chrysler Theater: "Wind Fever" (NBC, 3/2/66)

Dr. Kildare: "The Taste of Crow" (NBC, 3/7/66)

Dr. Kildare: "Out of a Concrete Tower" (NBC, 3/8/66)

Gunsmoke: "Quaker Girl"(CBS, 12/10/66)

Alexander the Great (ABC pilot, 1/26/68)

CBS Playhouse 90: "The Shadow Game" (CBS, 5/7/69)

Prudential on Stage: "The Skirts of Happy Chance" (PBS, 5/28/69)

The Virginian: "Black Jade" (NBC, 12/31/69)

The Name of the Game: "Tarot" (NBC, 2/13/70)

Paris 7000: "The Shattered Idol" (ABC, 3/5/70)

Ironside: "Little Jerry Jessup" (NBC, 3/12/70)

Medical Center: "The Combatants" (CBS, 3/18/70)

Hollywood Television Theater: "The Andersonville Trial" (PBS, 5/17/70)

The FBI: "Antennae of Death" (ABC, 11/29/70)

The Name of the Game: "The Glory Shouter" (NBC, 12/18/70)

Men at Law: "One American" (CBS, 4/14/71)

Ironside: "Walls Are Waiting" (NBC, 4/15/71)

Mission: Impossible: "Encore" (CBS, 9/25/71)

Cade County: "The Armageddon Contract" (CBS, 11/7/71)

Sixth Sense: "Can a Dead Man Strike from the Grave?" (ABC, 2/26/72)

Sixth Sense: "Death at the Top of the Stairs" (ABC, 3/23/72)

NET Playhouse: "The '40s: The Last GI's" (narrator) (PBS, 5/25/72)

Hawaii Five-O: "You Don't Have to Kill to Get Rich—But It Helps" (CBS, 9/26/72)

Mission: Impossible: "Cocaine" (CBS, 10/21/72)

Owen Marshall, Counselor at Law: "Five Will Get You Six" (ABC, 10/26/72)

Marcus Welby, M.D.: "Heartbeat for Yesterday" (ABC, 12/12/72)

The Bold Ones: The Doctors: "A Tightrope to Tomorrow" (NBC, 1/9/73)

Barnaby Jones: "To Catch a Dead Man" (CBS, 2/4/73)

Mannix: "Search for a Whisper" (CBS, 2/18/73)

Police Surgeon: "Bad Apple" (syndicated, 3/27/73)

Police Surgeon: "Fifty Kilos to Nowhere" (syndicated, 9/23/73)

The Magician: "The Illusion of the Queen's Gambit" (NBC, 2/4/74)

The Six Million Dollar Man: "Burning Bright" (ABC, 4/12/74)
Ironside: "Amy Prentiss: aka The Chief" (NBC, 5/23/74)
Kung Fu: "A Small Beheading" (ABC, 9/21/74)
Petrocelli: "Edge of Evil" (NBC, 10/2/74)
Kodiak: "The Last Enemy" (ABC, 10/4/74)
Police Woman: "Love, Mabel" (NBC, 11/26/74)
Amy Prentiss: "Baptism of Fire" (NBC, 12/1/74)
Police Woman: "Smack" (NBC, 12/174)
The Rookies: "The Hunting Ground" (ABC, 1/20/75)
Columbo: "Fade in to Murder" (NBC, 10/10/76)
The Oregon Trail: "The Scarlet Ribbon" (NBC, 11/30/77)
How the West Was Won (ABC, 3/5/78, 3/12/78)
Mork and Mindy: "Mork, Mindy, and Mearth Meet Milt" (ABC, 2/18/82)
Police Squad: "Revenge and Remorse (The Guilty Alibi)" (ABC, 3/25/82)
Mork and Mindy: "Midas Mork" (ABC, 4/23/82)
Ray Bradbury Trilogy: "The Playground" (PBS, 2/85)
Max Headroom (ABC, 11/87)
Friday Night Surprise (NBC pilot, 2/26/88)
The Larry Sanders Show: "The Promise" (HBO, 8/22/92)
seaQuest DSV: "Hide and Seek" (NBC, 2/27/94)
Eek! The Cat Christmas Special (Fox, 12/5/94)
Eek! The Cat: "Eek Space 9" (Fox, 2/19/96)
The Fresh Prince of Bel-Air: "Eye, Tooth"(NBC, 5/13/96)
Cosby: "Pilot, Not the Pilot" (CBS, 11/10/97)

TELEVISION APPEARANCES (SPECIALS/VARIETY)

The John Wayne Special: Sing Out, Sweet Land (NBC, 4/8/71)
The Amazing World of Kreskin (syndicated, 9/18/71)
Secrets of the Deep (syndicated, 1973)
Space Age (syndicated, 9/27/73)
Benjamin Franklin: The Statesman (CBS, 1/28/75)
Mitzi and a Hundred Guys (CBS, 3/24/75)
Battle of the Network Stars V (NBC team member, 1976)
Junior Almost Anything Goes (ABC, 1977)
Star Trek: The Superfans, The Superstars (syndicated, 1977)
Anyone for Tennyson: "A Poetic Portrait Gallery" (PBS, 4/13/77)
Photoplay Gold Medal Awards (syndicated, 6/18/77)

Science Fiction Film Awards (host, syndicated, 1/21/78)
Battle of the Network Stars VII (ABC team member, 11/18/78)
The 52nd Annual Academy Awards (ABC, 4/14/80)
Training Dogs the Wodehouse Way (syndicated, 1/81)
Celebrity Challenge of the Sexes (CBS, 5/25/81)
Circus of the Stars VI (CBS, 12/13/81)
Battle of the Network Stars XII (ABC team captain, 5/7/82)
Fridays (ABC, 6/15/82)
Battle of the Network Stars XIII (ABC team captain, 10/1/82)
Madame's Place (syndicated, 11/82)
Celebrity Daredevils (ABC, 1983)
The I Love TV Test (syndicated, 1983)
US Awards (syndicated, 2/83)
The Magic Planet (ABC, 3/17/83)
The 55th Annual Academy Awards (ABC, 4/11/83)
The 35th Annual Emmy Awards (NBC, 9/25/83)
The Love Boat Fall Preview Special (ABC, 9/17/83)
Battle of the Network Stars XV (ABC team captain, 11/3/83)
Foul-Ups, Bleeps, and Blunders (ABC, 1/10/84)
The Love Boat Fall Preview Party (ABC, 9/15/84)
Heroes and Sidekicks: Indiana Jones and the Temple of Doom (host) (CBS,
    11/27/84)
Battle of the Network Stars XVII (ABC team captain, 12/20/84)
Circus of the Stars IX (CBS, 1984)
World of Tomorrow (syndicated, 1984)
The Real Trivial Pursuit (ABC, 1985)
TV's Funniest Game Show Moments (ABC, 1985)
Lifestyles of the Rich and Famous (syndicated, 3/85)
The Night of 100 Stars II (ABC, 3/10/85)
The 37th Annual Emmy Awards (ABC, 9/22/85)
Cinemax Comedy Experiment: The Canadian Conspiracy (Cinemax,
    1/15/86)
Saturday Night Live (host) (NBC, 12/20/86)
The 44th Annual Golden Globe Awards (host) (syndicated, 1987)
The 22nd Annual Academy of Country Music Awards (NBC, 4/6/87)
The 59th Annual Academy Awards (ABC, 3/30/87)
Happy Birthday, Hollywood! (ABC, 5/18/87)

Top Flight (CBS, 10/27/87)
The Search for Houdini (host) (syndicated, 10/31/87)
The 40th Annual Emmy Awards (Fox, 8/28/88)
This Is Your Life (syndicated, 11/20/89)
Alaska's Killer Whales: Between Worlds (host) (PBS, 1989)
The 2nd Annual Valvoline National Driving Test (CBS, 1990)
The 25th Annual Academy of Country Music Awards (NBC, 4/25/90)
Amazon, Land of the Flooded Forest (narrator) (PBS, 1990)
Happy Birthday, Bugs: 50 Looney Years (CBS, 5/9/90)
Voices That Care (Fox, 1991)
The Horror Hall of Fame (syndicated, 1991)
The Star Trek 25th Anniversary Special (syndicated, 1991)
Sea World Star-Spangled Summer (San Diego host) (ABC, 1991)
An Evening at the Improv (A&E, 4/27/91)
Hollywood Charity Horse Show (ESPN, 2/92)
What About Me? I'm Only Three! (CBS, 1992)
The MTV Movie Awards (MTV, 6/8/92)
The 49th Annual Golden Globe Awards (TBS, 1992)
Eek! The Cat Christmas Special (Fox, 12/5/93)
Coming Up Roses (CBS, 1994)
CBS Sneak Peek (CBS, 1994)
The 1994 Billboard Music Awards (Fox, 12/12/94)
Star Trek: A Captain's Log (CBS, 1994)
The Museum of Television & Radio Presents: Science Fiction, A Journey into the Unknown (Fox, 1994)
The 105th Tournament of Roses Parade (grand marshal) (ABC, CBS, NBC, 1/1/94)
The 52nd Annual Golden Globe Awards (TBS, 1995)
The Roger Corman Special (Sci-Fi Channel, 1995)
Star Trek: 30 Years and Beyond (UPN, 1996)
Muppets Tonight! (syndicated, 1996)

TELEVISION APPEARANCES (GAME SHOWS)

(syndicated *except* where noted)
What's My Line (CBS, 1965)
Don Adams' Screen Test (1975, 1976)
Masquerade Party (1975)

Hollywood Squares (NBC, 1968. 1970, 1976)
Rhyme and Reason (ABC, 1976)
$20,000 Pyramid (1976, 1977)
$25,000 Pyramid (1976)
Liar's Club (1977)
Tattletales (1977)
Celebrity Sweepstakes (1977)
Celebrity Bowling (1978)
The Cross-Wits (1978)
Masquerade Party (1978)
Match Game (1978)
Rhyme and Reason (1978)
To Tell the Truth (1978)
$10,000 Pyramid (1979)

CORPORATE/PUBLIC SERVICE FILMS AND VIDEOS

American Enterprise (Phillips Petroleum, 1975)
Microworld (AT&T, 1980)
Robotics: The Future Is Now (AIMS Media, 1984)
The Vegetarian World (Bullfrog Films, 1984)
Nature's Systems (Concord Video, 1987)
The Color of Safety (Barr Films, 1987)
Fitness for Wellness (AIMS Media, 1987)
Lifestyles for Wellness (AIMS Media, 1987)
Nutrition for Wellness (AIMS Media, 1987)
Wellness—Health and Stress (AIMS Media, 1987)
Wellness—Moderation in Eating (AIMS Media, 1987)
Lake Powell and Canyon County (TVI Inc., 1988)
Ultimate Survivors: Winning Against Incredible Odds (Calibre Press, 1991)
It Didn't Have to Happen: Drinking and Driving (Perennial Education, 1994)
Lennar Home of the Future Marketing Video (Lennar Realty Corporation, 1997)

STAGE APPEARANCES

Measure for Measure (Stratford Shakespeare Festival, 1954)
The Taming of the Shrew (Stratford Shakespeare Festival, 1954)
Oedipus Rex (Stratford Shakespeare Festival, 1954)

Julius Caesar (Stratford Shakespeare Festival, 1955)
The Merchant of Venice (Stratford Shakespeare Festival, 1955)
King Oedipus (Stratford Shakespeare Festival, 1955)
The Merry Wives of Windsor (Stratford Shakespeare Festival, 1956)
Henry V (Stratford Shakespeare Festival, 1956)

Tamburlaine the Great (Winter Garden Theatre, New York, 1956). Opened January 19, 1956; closed February 4, 1956; twenty-one performances
DIRECTOR: Tyrone Guthrie; AUTHOR: Christopher Marlowe.
CAST: Anthony Quayle (Tamburlaine); Eric House (Mycetes); William Shatner (Usumcasane)

The World of Suzie Wong (Broadhurst Theatre, New York, 1958–60). Opened October 14, 1958; closed January 24, 1960; 508 performances.
DIRECTOR: Joshua Logan; AUTHOR: Paul Osborn
CAST: France Nuyen (Suzie Wong); William Shatner (Robert Lomax); Sarah Marshall (May Fletcher).

A Shot in the Dark (Booth Theatre, New York, 1961–63). Opened October 18, 1961; closed February 1, 1963; 389 performances
DIRECTOR: Harold Clurman; AUTHOR: Harry Kurnitz
CAST: Julie Harris (Josefa Lantenay); William Shatner (Paul Sevigne); Walter Matthau (Benjamin Beaurevers)

The Hyphen (University of Utah, Salt Lake City, Utah, 1966)
There's a Girl in My Soup (East coast cities, 1969)
The Tender Trap (Papermill Playhouse, Millburn, NJ, 1970)
Remote Asylum (Ahmanson Theatre, Los Angeles, 1970–71)
Period of Adjustment (Midwest cities, 1971)
Arsenic and Old Lace (Ohio cities, 1973)
The Seven Year Itch (Centre Stage Playhouse, Milwaukee, WI, 1974)
An Evening with William Shatner (U.S. cities, 1976–77)
Tricks of the Trade (East coast cities, 1977)
Symphony of the Stars (U.S. tour, 1978)
Star Traveler (U.S. and Canada, 1978)
Otherwise Engaged (Solari Theatre, Los Angeles, 1979)
Deathtrap (U.S. cities, 1981)
Cat on a Hot Tin Roof (director only) (Melrose Theatre, Los Angeles, 1981)

BOOKS

Shatner: Where No Man (written with Sondra Marshak and Myrna Culbreath) (Grosset & Dunlap, 1979)
TekWar (Putnam, 1989)
TekLords (Putnam, 1991)
TekLab (Putnam, 1991)
Believe (Putnam, 1992)
Tek Vengeance (Putnam, 1993)
Tek Secret (Putnam, 1993)
Star Trek Memories (HarperCollins, 1993)
Star Trek Movie Memories (HarperCollins, 1994)
Tek Power (Putnam, 1994)
Tek Money (Putnam, 1995)
Ashes of Eden (Pocket Books, 1995)
Tek Kill (Putnam, 1996)
Man o' War (Putnam, 1996)
Star Trek: The Return (Wheeler, 1997)
Star Trek: Avenger (Pocket Books, 1997)
Tek Net (Putnam, 1997)
Delta Search (HarperPrism, 1997)
In Alien Hands (HarperPrism, 1997)
Star Trek: Spectre (Pocket Books, 1998)
The Law of War (Ace, 1998)

RECORDINGS

- *The Transformed Man* (Decca Records, 1968). DL-75043
  Produced by Don Ralke
  "King Henry the Fifth," "Elegy for the Brave," "Theme from Cyrano," "Mr. Tambourine Man," "Hamlet," "It Was a Very Good Year," "Romeo and Juliet," "How Insensitive (Isensatez)," "Spleen," "Lucy in the Sky with Diamonds," "The Transformed Man"
- *Mimsy Were the Borogoves* (Caedmon Records, 1976)
- *Asimov: Foundation—The Psychohistorians* (Caedmon Records, 1976)
- *William Shatner: Live* (Lemli Records, 1977). Lemli-00001A-D
  Produced by Richard Canoff
  "Earthbound," "Go With Me," "High Flight," "The Flight of Man,"

"Galileo," "6 Ways to the Moon," "War of the Worlds," "The Movie," "William Shatner—Audience," "Starship's Facilities," "Peter," "Summer Spaceship," "Three-way Alchemy—The Brain," "Finale."

AWARDS

Tyrone Guthrie Award, Most Promising Actor, 1956
Theater World Award, Best Actor, *The World of Suzie Wong*, 1959
Theater Guild, Best Actor, *The World of Suzie Wong*, 1959
Drama Circle, Best Actor, *The World of Suzie Wong*, 1959
Academy of Science Fiction, Horror and Fantasy Films, Life Career Award, 1980
Golden Raspberry Award, Worst Actor, *Star Trek V: The Final Frontier* (1989)
Golden Raspberry Award, Worst Director, *Star Trek V: The Final Frontier* (1989)

Appendix 2

~

Star Trek:
A Shatnercentric Episode Guide

I have awarded "Kirk Points" for each episode on the following basis:

One (1) point if **Kirk gets action** (KGA) from a female admirer.

One (1) point if Kirk is seen with his **shirt off** or his shirt partially torn (SO).

One (1) point if **Kirk's blood** is spilt during the episode (KB).

One (1) point if Kirk engages in **hand to hand combat** (HHC).

One (1) point if Shatner plays a **dual role** (DR).

One (1) point if Kirk unplugs or outwits a **supercomputer** (SC)

One (1) point if Kirk gives a **long, moralizing speech** to an alien or enemy (LMS)

One (1) point if Kirk is annoyed by the presence of a **persnickety bureaucrat** (PB)

One (1) point if Kirk **refuses to kill** an enemy for moral reasons (RTK)

One (1) point if Kirk commits an **egregious violation** of the Prime Directive (EV)

Because Shatner has set the bar so high, I have added a five-point bonus for episodes where five of the above conditions apply. A perfect "ten" represents the ultimate in Shatner performances, the nirvana of Shatnerica.

FIRST SEASON, 1966–67

(NBC-TV, each episode 60 minutes)
REGULAR CAST: William Shatner (Captain James T. Kirk); Leonard
Nimoy (Mr. Spock); DeForest Kelley (Dr. Leonard "Bones" McCoy);
George Takei (Lt. Hikura Sulu); Nichelle Nichols (Lt. Nyota Uhura);
James Doohan (Engineer Montgomery "Scotty" Scott)

EPISODE 1: "The Man Trap"
ORIGINAL AIR DATE: 9/8/66
DIRECTOR: Marc Daniels; TELEWRITER: George Clayton Johnson
GUEST CAST: Grace Lee Whitney (Yeoman Janice Rand); Alfred Ryder
(Professor Crater)
SYNOPSIS: A shapeshifting "salt vampire" begins stalking the corridors of
the *Enterprise*, draining crewmembers of their sodium chloride.
KIRK POINTS: 0 (More of a McCoy episode)
FRIENDS OF BILL: Telewriter George Clayton Johnson costarred with
Shatner in the 1962 film *The Intruder*.

EPISODE 2: "Charlie X"
ORIGINAL AIR DATE: 9/15/66
DIRECTOR: Lawrence Dobkin; TELEWRITER: D.C. Fontana
GUEST CAST: Grace Lee Whitney (Yeoman Janice Rand); Robert Walker
Jr. (Charlie Evans)
SYNOPSIS: Charlie Evans, an insufferable brat with super powers, tries to
take over the *Enterprise*.
KIRK POINTS: 1 (LMS)

EPISODE 3: "Where No Man Has Gone Before"
ORIGINAL AIR DATE: 9/22/66
DIRECTOR: James Goldstone; TELEWRITER: Samuel A. Peeples
GUEST CAST: Gary Lockwood (Lt. Comdr. Gary Mitchell); Sally
Kellerman (Dr. Elizabeth Dehner)
SYNOPSIS: A mysterious force field at the edge of the galaxy gives Comdr.
Gary Mitchell awesome destructive powers.
KIRK POINTS: 4 (SO, KB, HHC, LMS)
FRIENDS OF BILL: Paul Fix (Dr. Piper) appeared with Shatner in the 1964
film *The Outrage*.

EPISODE 4: "The Naked Time"
ORIGINAL AIR DATE: 9/29/66
DIRECTOR: Marc Daniels; TELEWRITER: John D. F. Black
GUEST CAST: Grace Lee Whitney (Yeoman Janice Rand); Majel Barrett (Nurse Christine Chapel); Bruce Hyde (Lt. Kevin Riley)
SYNOPSIS: A strange disease infects the *Enterprise*, bringing out the emotional insecurities of the crewmembers.
KIRK POINTS: 1 (SO)

EPISODE 5: "The Enemy Within"
ORIGINAL AIR DATE: 10/6/66
DIRECTOR: Leo Penn; TELEWRITER: Richard Matheson
GUEST CAST: Grace Lee Whitney (Yeoman Janice Rand)
SYNOPSIS: A transporter malfunction splits Kirk into two people: "Good" Kirk is kind and gentle; "Bad" Kirk is rude, boorish, and steals McCoy's brandy.
KIRK POINTS: 4 (KGA, SO, HHC, DR)

EPISODE 6: "Mudd's Women"
ORIGINAL AIR DATE: 10/13/66
DIRECTOR: Harvey Hart; TELEWRITER: Stephen Kandel
GUEST CAST: Roger C. Carmel (Harry Mudd)
SYNOPSIS: Intergalactic rapscallion Harry Mudd and his crew of Amazon beauties cause a commotion on a remote mining planet.
KIRK POINTS: 0

EPISODE 7: "What Are Little Girls Made Of?"
ORIGINAL AIR DATE: 10/20/66
DIRECTOR: James Goldstone; TELEWRITER: Robert Bloch
GUEST CAST: Majel Barrett (Nurse Christine Chapel); Michael Strong (Dr. Roger Korby)
SYNOPSIS: Dr. Korby, a mad scientist, fashions an android duplicate of Kirk in an effort to win the love of Nurse Chapel.
KIRK POINTS: 1 (DR)

EPISODE 8: "Miri"
ORIGINAL AIR DATE: 10/27/66
DIRECTOR: Vincent McEveety; TELEWRITER: Adrian Spies

GUEST CAST: Grace Lee Whitney (Yeoman Janice Rand); Kim Darby (Miri); Michael J. Pollard (Jahn)

SYNOPSIS: Kirk and his crew encounter a group of ragamuffins who have a strange disease that kills them at puberty.

KIRK POINTS: 8 (SO, KB, LMS, plus a special 5-point bonus for the priceless scene in which the children surround Kirk and chant "Bonk bonk on the head" in unison).

FRIENDS OF BILL: Kim Darby (Miri) went on to costar with Shatner in the 1972 TV movie *The People*.

EPISODE 9: "Dagger of the Mind"

ORIGINAL AIR DATE: 11/3/66

DIRECTOR: Vincent McEveety; TELEWRITER: Shimon Wincelberg

GUEST CAST: James Gregory (Dr. Tristan Adams); Morgan Woodward (Dr. Simon van Gelder); Marianna Hill (Dr. Helen Noel)

SYNOPSIS: Kirk must outwit the sadistic director of a Federation penal colony.

KIRK POINTS: 0

EPISODE 10: "The Corbomite Maneuver"

ORIGINAL AIR DATE: 11/10/66

DIRECTOR: Joseph Sargent; TELEWRITER: Jerry Sohl

GUEST CAST: Grace Lee Whitney (Yeoman Janice Rand); Clint Howard (Balok)

SYNOPSIS: The fearsome alien who has been menacing the *Enterprise* turns out to be the child-like Balok. Once he discards his disguise, he kicks back a brew with Kirk and his crew and teaches everyone a lesson about prejudice.

KIRK POINTS: 1 (SO)

EPISODE 11: "The Conscience of the King"

ORIGINAL AIR DATE: 12/8/66

DIRECTOR: Gerd Oswald; TELEWRITER: Barry Trivers

GUEST CAST: Arnold Moss (Anton Karidian); Barbara Anderson (Lenore Karidian); Bruce Hyde (Lt. Kevin Riley)

SYNOPSIS: The lead player in a troupe of actors traveling on board the *Enterprise* turns out to be a notorious mass murderer.

KIRK POINTS: 1 (KGA)

EPISODE 12: "Balance of Terror"
ORIGINAL AIR DATE: 12/15/66
DIRECTOR: Vincent McEveety; TELEWRITER: Paul Schneider
GUEST CAST: Grace Lee Whitney (Yeoman Janice Rand); Paul Comi (Lt. Andrew Stiles); Garry Walberg (Commander Hansen)
SYNOPSIS: Kirk engages in a duel of wits with a Romulan commander during an encounter in the Neutral Zone.
KIRK POINTS: 0 (Still a great episode)
FRIENDS OF BILL: Larry Montaigne (Decius) had appeared with Shatner in the *Outer Limits* episode "Cold Hands, Warm Heart" in 1964.

EPISODE 13: "The Menagerie"
ORIGINAL AIR DATES: 12/17/66, 12/24/66
DIRECTOR: Marc Daniels; TELEWRITER: Gene Roddenberry
GUEST CAST: Jeffrey Hunter (Captain Christopher Pike); Susan Oliver (Vina)
SYNOPSIS: Spock is put on trial for diverting the *Enterprise* to the forbidden planet of Talos IV.
KIRK POINTS: 1 (PB)
FRIENDS OF BILL: Malachi Throne (Commodore Mendez) played a doctor who treats Shatner in the *Outer Limits* TV episode "Cold Hands, Warm Heart" in 1964.

EPISODE 14: "Shore Leave"
ORIGINAL AIR DATE: 12/29/66
DIRECTOR: Robert Sparr; TELEWRITER: Theodore Sturgeon
GUEST CAST: Shirley Bonne (Ruth); Oliver McGowan (Caretaker)
SYNOPSIS: While on shore leave, the *Enterprise* crew finds their memories and nightmares brought to life by a mysterious caretaker.
KIRK POINTS: 4 (KGA, SO, KB, HHC)

EPISODE 15: "The Galileo Seven"
ORIGINAL AIR DATE: 1/5/67
DIRECTOR: Robert Gist; TELEWRITERS: Oliver Crawford and Shimon Wincelberg
GUEST CAST: John Crawford (High Commissioner Ferris); Don Marshall (Lieutenant Boma)

SYNOPSIS: Spock saves the crew of the shuttlecraft *Galileo* when it crash-lands on a planet populated by hostile ape creatures with spears.
KIRK POINTS: 1 (PB)

EPISODE 16 : "The Squire of Gothos"
ORIGINAL AIR DATE: 1/12/67
DIRECTOR: Don McDougall; TELEWRITER: Paul Schneider
GUEST CAST: William Campbell ("General" Trelane)
SYNOPSIS: The *Enterprise* crew encounters Trelane, a whimsical and impetuous alien child with strange powers and baroque taste in clothing.
KIRK POINTS: 1 (LMS)

EPISODE 17: "Arena"
ORIGINAL AIR DATE: 1/19/67
DIRECTOR: Joseph Pevney; TELEWRITER: Gene L. Coon
GUEST CAST: Carole Shelyne (Metron); Gary Coombs and Bobby Clark (Gorn)
SYNOPSIS: All-powerful aliens force Kirk to fight the Gorn, a hissing lizard-like creature.
KIRK POINTS: 10 (SO, KB, HHC, LMS, RTK + 5-point "nirvana" bonus)

EPISODE 18: "Tomorrow Is Yesterday"
ORIGINAL AIR DATE: 1/26/67
DIRECTOR: Michael O'Herlihy; TELEWRITER: D.C. Fontana
GUEST CAST: Roger Perry (Captain John Christopher)
SYNOPSIS: The *Enterprise* is thrown backward in time to late 1960s America, where they must deal with an incredulous Air Force pilot.
KIRK POINTS: 0

EPISODE 19: "Court-Martial"
ORIGINAL AIR DATE: 2/2/67
DIRECTOR: Marc Daniels; TELEWRITERS: Don M. Mankiewicz and Stephen W. Carabatsos
GUEST CAST: Richard Webb (Lt. Comdr. Benjamin Finney); Elisha Cook Jr. (Samuel T. Cogley)
SYNOPSIS: Kirk is court-martialed for allegedly causing the death of a crewmen.
KIRK POINTS: 2 (KGA, SO)

EPISODE 20: "The Return of the Archons"
ORIGINAL AIR DATE: 2/9/67
DIRECTOR: Joseph Pevney; TELEWRITER: Boris Sobelman
GUEST CAST: Charles Macaulay (Landru)
SYNOPSIS: The *Enterprise* visits the planet Beta III, run by the supercomputer Landru, whose inhabitants worship it as a god.
KIRK POINTS: 1 (SC)

EPISODE 21: "Space Seed"
ORIGINAL AIR DATE: 2/16/67
DIRECTOR: Marc Daniels; TELEWRITERS: Gene L. Coon and Carey Wilbur
GUEST CAST: Ricardo Montalban (Khan Noonien Singh); Madlyn Rhue (Lt. Marla McGivers)
SYNOPSIS: Kirk and company thaw out a cadre of cryogenically frozen ubermenschen led by Ricardo Montalban.
KIRK POINTS: 5 (special bonus for setting the stage for the ultimate battle of ham versus ham fifteen years later in *Star Trek II: The Wrath of Khan*).

EPISODE 22: "A Taste of Armageddon"
ORIGINAL AIR DATE: 2/23/67
DIRECTOR: Joseph Pevney; TELEWRITERS: Robert Hamner and Gene L. Coon
GUEST CAST: Gene Lyons (Ambassador Robert Fox)
SYNOPSIS: Kirk must talk some sense into the heads of a race that fights war cleanly, via computer.
KIRK POINTS: 3 (SC, LMS, PB)

EPISODE 23: "This Side of Paradise"
ORIGINAL AIR DATE: 3/2/67
DIRECTOR: Ralph Senensky; TELEWRITER: D.C. Fontana
GUEST CAST: Jill Ireland (Leila Kalomi)
SYNOPSIS: Spock and the rest of the crew are infected by alien spores that liberate repressed emotions. Kirk alone remains immune.
KIRK POINTS: 2 (KB, HHC)

EPISODE 24: "The Devil in the Dark"
ORIGINAL AIR DATE: 3/9/67
DIRECTOR: Joseph Pevney; TELEWRITER: Gene L. Coon

Guest Cast: Janos Prohaska (Horta)
Synopsis: Kirk and company investigate a series of mysterious deaths in an underground mining colony.
Kirk Points: 1 (RTK)

Episode 25: "Errand of Mercy"
Original Air Date: 3/23/67
Director: John Newland; Telewriter: Gene L. Coon
Guest Cast: John Colicos (Commander Kor)
Synopsis: Kirk acts to stem a Klingon invasion of Organia, a planet populated by passive, elderly men.
Kirk Points: 2 (LMS, EV)

Episode 26: "The Alternative Factor"
Original Air Date: 3/30/67
Director: Gerd Oswald; Telewriter: Don Ingalls
Guest Cast: Robert Brown (Lazarus)
Synopsis: The *Enterprise* takes in two versions of a man named Lazarus—each from different universes and unable to coexist without causing destruction.
Kirk Points: 0

Episode 27: "The City on the Edge of Forever"
Original Air Date: 4/6/67
Director: Joseph Pevney; Telewriter: Harlan Ellison
Guest Cast: Joan Collins (Sister Edith Keeler)
Synopsis: Kirk falls in love with doomed social worker Joan Collins while trapped on Earth in the 1930s.
Kirk Points: 6 (KGA + 5-point bonus for putting up with Harlan Ellison)

Episode 28: "Operation: Annihilate"
Original Air Date: 4/13/67
Director: Herschel Daugherty; Telewriter: Stephen W. Carabatsos
Guest Cast: Majel Barrett (Nurse Christine Chapel)
Synopsis: Kirk's brother and his family are wiped out by fuzzy flying bats that disrupt the central nervous system.
Kirk Points: 1 (DR, as Kirk and, in different hairpiece and false mustache, as his brother's corpse)

SECOND SEASON, 1967–68

(NBC-TV, each episode 60 minutes)

REGULAR CAST ADDITION: Walter Koenig (Ensign Pavel Chekov)

EPISODE 29: "Amok Time"

ORIGINAL AIR DATE: 9/15/67

DIRECTOR: Joseph Pevney; TELEWRITER: Theodore Sturgeon

GUEST CAST: Majel Barrett (Nurse Christine Chapel); Arlene Martel (T'Pring)

SYNOPSIS: Spock's sexual drive reasserts itself, forcing him to return to Vulcan for a marriage ceremony. Unfortunately, part of the festivities involves swinging a large axe at Kirk.

KIRK POINTS: 3 (KB, SO, HHC)

FRIENDS OF BILL: Larry Montaigne (Stonn) had appeared with Shatner in the *Outer Limits* episode "Cold Hands, Warm Heart" in 1964; Arlene Martel (T'Pring) went on to costar with Shatner in the 1974 TV movie *Indict and Convict.*

EPISODE 30: "Who Mourns for Adonais?"

ORIGINAL AIR DATE: 9/22/67

DIRECTOR: Marc Daniels; TELEWRITERS: Gilbert A. Ralston and Gene L. Coon

GUEST CAST: Michael Forest (Apollo); Leslie Parrish (Lt. Carolyn Palamas)

SYNOPSIS: The *Enterprise* is waylaid by the Greek god Apollo, an ancient space traveler now dwelling on the planet Pollux IV.

KIRK POINTS: 0

EPISODE 31: "The Changeling"

ORIGINAL AIR DATE: 9/29/67

DIRECTOR: Marc Daniels; TELEWRITER: John Meredyth Lucas

GUEST CAST: Majel Barrett (Nurse Christine Chapel); Vic Perrin (the voice of "Nomad")

SYNOPSIS: Nomad/Tan-Ru, a hybrid computer/alien probe, invades the *Enterprise* and mistakes Kirk for its creator.

KIRK POINTS: 6 (SC + 5-pont bonus for being the ultimate "Kirk destroys a supercomputer" episode)

EPISODE 32: "Mirror, Mirror"
ORIGINAL AIR DATE: 10/6/67
DIRECTOR: Marc Daniels; TELEWRITER: Jerome Bixby
GUEST CAST: Barbara Luna (Lt. Marlena Moreau)
SYNOPSIS: A transporter malfunction deposits an *Enterprise* away team in an alternate universe where Spock has a cool-looking goatee.
KIRK POINTS: 9 (KGA, KB, HHC, RTK + 5-point "tunic" bonus)

EPISODE 33: "The Apple"
ORIGINAL AIR DATE: 10/13/67
DIRECTOR: Joseph Pevney; TELEWRITERS: Max Ehrlich and Gene L. Coon
GUEST CAST: Celeste Yarnall (Yeoman Martha Landon)
SYNOPSIS: Kirk pulls the plug on a supercomputer that the inhabitants of Gamma Trianguli IV have been worshipping as a god.
KIRK POINTS: 1 (SC)

EPISODE 34: "The Doomsday Machine"
ORIGINAL AIR DATE: 10/20/67
DIRECTOR: Marc Daniels; TELEWRITER: Norman Spinrad
GUEST CAST: William Windom (Comdr. Matthew Decker)
SYNOPSIS: The *Enterprise* rescues a ruined starship and its half-cracked commander, Matthew Decker, who is ridden with guilt over the destruction of his vessel by a huge calzone-shaped "doomsday machine."
KIRK POINTS: 5 (special bonus for the debut appearance of Kirk's dress tunic)
FRIENDS OF BILL: William Windom (Decker) was Shatner's understudy on Broadway in *The World of Suzie Wong* (1958).

EPISODE 35: "Catspaw"
ORIGINAL AIR DATE: 10/27/67
DIRECTOR: Joseph Pevney; TELEWRITER: Robert Bloch
GUEST CAST: Antoinette Bower (Sylvia); Theo Marcuse (Korob)
SYNOPSIS: Kirk and company encounter two alien pipe cleaners in human form. Using a transmuter device, they turn Scott and Sulu into drooling, pasty-faced zombies.
KIRK POINTS: 0

EPISODE 36: "I, Mudd"
ORIGINAL AIR DATE: 11/3/67
DIRECTOR: Marc Daniels; TELEWRITERS: Stephen Kandel and David Gerrold
GUEST CAST: Roger C. Carmel (Harry Mudd); Kay Elliott (Stella Mudd)
SYNOPSIS: The *Enterprise* is hijacked by Harry Mudd and his army of androids.
KIRK POINTS: 1 (SC)

EPISODE 37: "Metamorphosis"
ORIGINAL AIR DATE: 11/10/67
DIRECTOR: Ralph Senensky; TELEWRITER: Gene L. Coon
GUEST CAST: Elinor Donahue (Ambassador Nancy Hedord); Glenn Corbett (Zefram Cochrane)
SYNOPSIS: The *Enterprise* crew encounters Zefram Cochrane, the 180-year-old inventor of warp drive, being kept young and healthy by a mysterious cloud entity known as "The Companion."
KIRK POINTS: 1 (PB)

EPISODE 38: "Journey to Babel"
ORIGINAL AIR DATE: 11/17/67
DIRECTOR: Joseph Pevney; TELEWRITER: D.C. Fontana
GUEST CAST: Majel Barrett (Nurse Christine Chapel); Mark Lenard (Ambassador Sarek); William O'Connell (Thelev)
SYNOPSIS: While en route to a Federation conference, the *Enterprise* plays host to a series of intrigues involving ambassadors both real and disguised.
KIRK POINTS: 1 (PB)

EPISODE 39: "The Deadly Years"
ORIGINAL AIR DATE: 12/8/67
DIRECTOR: Joseph Pevney; TELEWRITER: David P. Harmon
GUEST CAST: Charles Drake (Comm. George Stocker); Sarah Marshall (Dr. Janet Wallace); Beverly Washburn (Lt. Arlene Galway)
SYNOPSIS: The *Enterprise* becomes infected with a disease that accelerates the aging process.
KIRK POINTS: 1 (PB)

EPISODE 40: "Obsession"
ORIGINAL AIR DATE: 12/15/67
DIRECTOR: Ralph Senensky; TELEWRITER: Art Wallace
GUEST CAST: Majel Barrett (Nurse Christine Chapel); Stephen Brooks (Ensign Garrovick)
SYNOPSIS: Kirk goes nutzoid when the *Enterprise* is infiltrated by a hovering cloud creature that, years earlier, had decimated the crew of his first starship.
KIRK POINTS: o

EPISODE 41: "Wolf in the Fold"
ORIGINAL AIR DATE: 12/22/67
DIRECTOR: Joseph Pevney; TELEWRITER: Robert Bloch
GUEST CAST: John Fiedler (Commissioner Hengist)
SYNOPSIS: Scotty is implicated in a series of brutal knife murders on a pleasure planet.
KIRK POINTS: 1 (PB)

EPISODE 42: "The Trouble with Tribbles"
ORIGINAL AIR DATE: 12/29/67
DIRECTOR: Joseph Pevney; TELEWRITER: David Gerrold
GUEST CAST: Stanley Adams (Cyrano Jones); William Schallert (Nilz Baris)
SYNOPSIS: While on a mission to protect grain storehouses on Space Station K-7, the *Enterprise* crew is pestered by trader Cyrano Jones and his stock of purring, rapidly multiplying Tribbles.
KIRK POINTS: 1 (PB)
FRIENDS OF BILL: William Schallert (Nilz Barris) went on to play Shatner's father-in-law in the 1978 TV movie *Little Women*.

EPISODE 43: "The Gamesters of Triskelion"
ORIGINAL AIR DATE: 1/5/68
DIRECTOR: Gene Nelson; TELEWRITER: Margaret Armen
GUEST CAST: Joseph Ruskin (Galt); Angelique Pettyjohn (Shahna)
SYNOPSIS: Kirk, Uhura, and Chekov are forced to engage in gladiatorial combat by a race of oozy, brain-like beings called the Providers.
KIRK POINTS: 3 (KGA, SO, HHC)

EPISODE 44: "A Piece of the Action"
ORIGINAL AIR DATE: 1/12/68
DIRECTOR: James Komack; TELEWRITERS: David Harmon and Gene L. Coon
GUEST CAST: Anthony Caruso (Bela Oxmyx); Victor Tayback (Jojo Krako)
SYNOPSIS: Kirk and the crew get caught up in a mob war on a planet modeled after 1920s gangland Chicago.
KIRK POINTS: 0

EPISODE 45: "The Immunity Syndrome"
ORIGINAL AIR DATE: 1/19/68
DIRECTOR: Joseph Pevney; TELEWRITER: Robert Sabaroff
GUEST CAST: Majel Barrett (Nurse Christine Chapel)
SYNOPSIS: The *Enterprise* confronts a gigantic space virus that eats starships.
KIRK POINTS: 0

EPISODE 46: "A Private Little War"
ORIGINAL AIR DATE: 2/2/68
DIRECTOR: Marc Daniels; TELEWRITER: Gene Roddenberry
GUEST CAST: Majel Barrett (Nurse Christine Chapel); Michael Witney (Tyree); Nancy Kovack (Nona)
SYNOPSIS: Kirk interferes with life on an undeveloped planet in order to prevent the Klingons from interfering with life on an undeveloped planet.
KIRK POINTS: 1 (EV)

EPISODE 47: "Return to Tomorrow"
ORIGINAL AIR DATE: 2/9/68
DIRECTOR: Ralph Senensky; TELEWRITER: Gene Roddenberry
GUEST CAST: Majel Barrett (Nurse Christine Chapel); Diana Muldaur (Dr. Ann Mulhall)
SYNOPSIS: Three disembodied alien brains attempt to appropriate the forms of Kirk, Spock, and Dr. Anne Mulhall.
KIRK POINTS: 1 (SO)

EPISODE 48: "Patterns of Force"
ORIGINAL AIR DATE: 2/16/68

DIRECTOR: Vincent McEveety; TELEWRITER: John Meredyth Lucas
GUEST STAR: David Brian (John Gill); Skip Homeier (Melakon)
SYNOPSIS: Kirk and his crew join the resistance movement on a planet modeled after Nazi Germany.
KIRK POINTS: 1 (LMS)

EPISODE 49: "By Any Other Name"
ORIGINAL AIR DATE: 2/23/68
DIRECTOR: Marc Daniels; TELEWRITERS: D. C. Fontana and Jerome Bixby
GUEST CAST: Majel Barrett (Nurse Christine Chapel); Warren Stevens (Rojan)
SYNOPSIS: The *Enterprise* is subdued by the Kelvans, a race of emotionless aliens who enjoy turning people into little dodecahedrons.
KIRK POINTS: 1 (KGA)

EPISODE 50: "The Omega Glory"
ORIGINAL AIR DATE: 3/1/68
DIRECTOR: Vincent McEveety; TELEWRITER: Gene Roddenberry
GUEST CAST: Morgan Woodward (Captain Ronald Tracey); Roy Jensen (Cloude William)
SYNOPSIS: Kirk intervenes in a planetary conflict eerily similar to the Vietnam War.
KIRK POINTS: 7 (HHC, LMS + 5-point bonus because the long, moralizing speech is the Preamble to the Constitution)

EPISODE 51: "The Ultimate Computer"
ORIGINAL AIR DATE: 3/8/68
DIRECTOR: John Meredyth Lucas; TELEWRITER: D.C. Fontana
GUEST CAST: William Marshall (Dr. Richard Daystrom)
SYNOPSIS: Kirk bristles when he is relieved of command so that Dr. Richard Daystrom can test out his new starship-commanding computer on the *Enterprise*.
KIRK POINTS: 2 (SC, PB)

EPISODE 52: "Bread and Circuses"
ORIGINAL AIR DATE: 3/15/68
DIRECTOR: Ralph Senensky; TELEWRITERS: Gene L. Coon and Gene Roddenberry
GUEST CAST: William Smithers (Captain R. M. Merik/Merikus)

SYNOPSIS: Kirk and company are forced to engage in gladiatorial combat on a planet modeled after imperial Rome.
KIRK POINTS: 3 (KGA, HHC, EV)

EPISODE 53: "Friday's Child"
ORIGINAL AIR DATE: 3/22/68
DIRECTOR: Joseph Pevney; TELEWRITER: D.C. Fontana
GUEST CAST: Julie Newmar (Eleen); Tige Andrews (Kras); Michael Dante (Maab)
SYNOPSIS: Kirk and company meddle in the affairs of the planet Capella in order to prevent the Capellans from aligning with the Klingons.
KIRK POINTS: 1 (EV)

EPISODE 54: "Assignment: Earth"
ORIGINAL AIR DATE: 3/29/68
DIRECTOR: Marc Daniels; TELEWRITERS: Gene Roddenberry and Art Wallace
GUEST CAST: Robert Lansing (Gary Seven); Teri Garr (Roberta Lincoln)
SYNOPSIS: The *Enterprise* travels back in time to 1968 Earth to stop an interstellar super agent from sabotaging a rocket launch and altering history.
KIRK POINTS: 0

THIRD SEASON, 1968–69

(NBC-TV, each episode 60 minutes)
REGULAR CAST ADDITION: Majel Barrett (Nurse Christine Chapel)

EPISODE 55: "Spock's Brain"
ORIGINAL AIR DATE: 9/20/68
DIRECTOR: Marc Daniels; TELEWRITER: Lee Cronin
GUEST CAST: Marj Dusay (Kara)
SYNOPSIS: Amazon women swipe Spock's noodle and use it to power their planet.
KIRK POINTS: 0

EPISODE 56: "The *Enterprise* Incident"
ORIGINAL AIR DATE: 9/27/68
DIRECTOR: John Meredyth Lucas; TELEWRITER: D. C. Fontana
GUEST CAST: Joanne Linville (Romulan Commander)

SYNOPSIS: Kirk appears to be going nuts, but it's all part of a plan to get him on board a Romulan ship to steal their cloaking device.
KIRK POINTS: 1 (DR)

EPISODE 57: "The Paradise Syndrome"
ORIGINAL AIR DATE: 10/4/68
DIRECTOR: Jud Taylor; TELEWRITER: Margaret Armen
GUEST CAST: Sabrina Scharf (Maramanee); Rudy Solari (Salish)
SYNOPSIS: Kirk gets bonked on the noggin and thinks he's the chief of an alien Indian tribe.
KIRK POINTS: 10+ (KGA, SO, KB, HHC, DR, RTK, EV + 5-point "nirvana" bonus and Special Award for Excellence; this is the ultimate Kirk showcase)

EPISODE 58: "And the Children Shall Lead"
ORIGINAL AIR DATE: 10/11/68
DIRECTOR: Marvin Chomsky; TELEWRITER: Edward J. Lasko
GUEST CAST: Melvin Beli (Gorgan)
SYNOPSIS: A fat, evil angel named Gorgan uses a band of orphans to incapacitate the Enterprise crew and take over the ship.
KIRK POINTS: 1 (LMS)

EPISODE 59: "Is There in Truth No Beauty?"
ORIGINAL AIR DATE: 10/18/68
DIRECTOR: Ralph Senensky; TELEWRITER: Jean Lisette Aroeste
GUEST CAST: Diana Muldaur (Dr. Miranda Jones); David Frankham (Lawrence Marvick)
SYNOPSIS: Dr. Miranda Jones arrives on the Enterprise with a nefarious sidekick and a box containing a telepathic alien who makes Spock go blind.
KIRK POINTS: 0

EPISODE 60: "Spectre of the Gun"
ORIGINAL AIR DATE: 10/25/68
DIRECTOR: Vincent McEveety; TELEWRITER: Lee Cronin
GUEST CAST: Rex Holman (Morgan Earp); Ron Soble (Wyatt Earp); Charles Maxwell (Virgil Earp); Sam Gilman (Doc Holliday)
SYNOPSIS: After violating Melkotian space, the Enterprise crew is sentenced to participate in a reenactment of the Gunfight at the O. K. Corral.
KIRK POINTS: 1 (RTK)

EPISODE 61: "Day of the Dove"
ORIGINAL AIR DATE: 11/1/68
DIRECTOR: Marvin Chomsky; TELEWRITER: Jerome Bixby
GUEST CAST: Michael Ansara (Kang); Susan Howard (Mara)
SYNOPSIS: The crews of the *Enterprise* and a Klingon battle cruiser are set at odds by an invisible entity that feeds on hatred.
KIRK POINTS: 1 (RTK)
FRIENDS OF BILL: Michael Ansara (Kang) went on to play Diamond Jack Bassitter alongside Shatner in the 1975 TV movie pilot for *The Barbary Coast.*

EPISODE 62: "For the World Is Hollow and I Have Touched the Sky"
ORIGINAL AIR DATE: 11/8/68
DIRECTOR: Tony Leader; TELEWRITER: Rick Vollaerts
GUEST CAST: Kate Woodville (Natira)
SYNOPSIS: A terminally ill McCoy falls in love with a High Priestess who holds the key to curing his disease.
KIRK POINTS: 0

EPISODE 63: "The Tholian Web"
ORIGINAL AIR DATE: 11/15/68
DIRECTOR: Ralph Senensky; TELEWRITERS: Judy A. Burns and Chet L. Richards
GUEST CAST: Barbara Babcock (voice of the Tholians)
SYNOPSIS: Kirk is stranded on a "ghost ship" that rematerializes at regular intervals. A bickering Spock and McCoy must find a way to get him back.
KIRK POINTS: 0

EPISODE 64: "Plato's Stepchildren"
ORIGINAL AIR DATE: 11/22/68
DIRECTOR: David Alexander; TELEWRITER: Meyer Dolinsky
GUEST CAST: Michael Dunn (Alexander); Liam Sullivan (Parmen)
SYNOPSIS: Telekinetic Greeks in space force Kirk and his crew to hit one another and perform musical comedy.
KIRK POINTS: 10 (KGA, SO, HHC, LMS, RTK + 5-point "nirvana" bonus)

EPISODE 65: "Wink of an Eye"
ORIGINAL AIR DATE: 11/29/68
DIRECTOR: Jud Taylor; TELEWRITER: Arthur Heinemann

GUEST CAST: Kathie Browne (Deela, Queen of Scalos)
SYNOPSIS: Kirk drinks some tainted water that sends him into a weird, speeded-up dimension populated by gorgeous women who need reproductive partners.
KIRK POINTS: 1 (KGA)

EPISODE 66: "The Empath"
ORIGINAL AIR DATE: 12/6/68
DIRECTOR: John Erman; TELEWRITER: Joyce Muskat
GUEST CAST: Kathryn Hays (Gem); Willard Sage (Thann); Alan Bergmann (Lal)
SYNOPSIS: While investigating a planet about to be destroyed by a supernova, Kirk, Spock, and McCoy are subject to experimentation by two hydrocephalic aliens.
KIRK POINTS: 0

EPISODE 67: "Elaan of Troyius"
ORIGINAL AIR DATE: 12/20/68
DIRECTOR/TELEWRITER: John Meredyth Lucas
GUEST CAST: France Nuyen (Elaan); Jay Robinson (Lord Petri); Tony Young (Kryton)
SYNOPSIS: While transporting the beautiful Elaan to her marriage ceremony on the planet Troyius, Kirk falls in love with the alien queen.
KIRK POINTS: 1 (KGA, PB)
FRIENDS OF BILL: France Nuyen (Elaan) played Shatner's love interest on the New York stage in *The World of Suzie Wong* in 1958.

EPISODE 68: "Whom Gods Destroy"
Air Date: 1/3/69
DIRECTOR: Herb Wallerstein; TELEWRITER: Lee Erwin
GUEST CAST: Steve Ihnat (Garth of Izar); Yvonne Craig (Marta)
SYNOPSIS: A shapeshifting psychotic imprisons Kirk and Spock in a Federation insane asylum.
KIRK POINTS: 1 (DR, as Kirk and Garth-as-Kirk)

EPISODE 69: "Let That Be Your Last Battlefield"
ORIGINAL AIR DATE: 1/10/69
DIRECTOR: Jud Taylor; TELEWRITER: Oliver Crawford
GUEST CAST: Lou Antonio (Lokai); Frank Gorshin (Bele)

SYNOPSIS: The *Enterprise* picks up alien minstrel show oddities Bele and Lokai, who chase each other endlessly around the ship, teaching everyone a lesson about racism.

KIRK POINTS: 2 (LMS, PB)

FRIENDS OF BILL: Lou Antonio (Lokai) appeared with Shatner in the 1970 TV movie *Sole Survivor*.

EPISODE 70: "The Mark of Gideon"
ORIGINAL AIR DATE: 1/17/69
DIRECTOR: Jud Taylor; TELEWRITERS: George F. Slavin and Stanley Adams
GUEST CAST: Sharon Acker (Odona); David Hurst (Hodin)
SYNOPSIS: Attempting to beam down to an overpopulated planet, Kirk finds himself on what appears to be a completely empty *Enterprise*.
KIRK POINTS: 1 (KGA)

EPISODE 71: "That Which Survives"
ORIGINAL AIR DATE: 1/24/69
DIRECTOR: Herb Wallerstein; TELEWRITER: John Merdyth Lucas
GUEST CAST: Lee Meriwether (Losira)
SYNOPSIS: While exploring an uncharted planet, Kirk and his crew are hunted by a beautiful woman whose touch is deadly.
KIRK POINTS: 1 (SC)

EPISODE 72: "The Lights of Zetar"
ORIGINAL AIR DATE: 1/31/69
DIRECTOR: Herb Kenwith; TELEWRITERS: Jeremy Tarcher and Shari Lewis
GUEST CAST: Jan Shutan (Lt. Mira Romaine)
SYNOPSIS: A cloud of twinkling lights takes over the body of Scotty's main squeeze.
KIRK POINTS: 0

EPISODE 73: "Requiem for Methuselah"
ORIGINAL AIR DATE: 2/14/69
DIRECTOR: Murray Golden; TELEWRITER: Jerome Bixby
GUEST CAST: James Daly (Flint); Louise Sorel (Rayna Kapec)
SYNOPSIS: Kirk falls in love with the beautiful android ward (Rayna Kapec) of Flint, an immortal alien who has lived many past lives, such as Johannes Brahms and Leonardo Da Vinci.
KIRK POINTS: 1 (KGA)

EPISODE 74: "The Way to Eden"
ORIGINAL AIR DATE: 2/21/69
DIRECTOR: David Alexander; TELEWRITER: Arthur Heinemann
GUEST STAR: Skip Homeier (Dr. Thomas Sevrin); Mary-Linda Rapelye
(Irina Galliulin); Victor Brandt (Tongo Rad)
SYNOPSIS: The *Enterprise* allow aboard a band of space hippies who
attempt to commandeer the starship.
KIRK POINTS: 0

EPISODE 75: "The Cloud Minders"
ORIGINAL AIR DATE: 2/28/69
DIRECTOR: Jud Taylor; TELEWRITER: Margaret Armen
GUEST CAST: Jeff Corey (Plasus); Charlene Polite (Vanna); Diana Ewing
(Droxine); Fred 'The Hammer' Williamson (Anka)
SYNOPSIS: Kirk and his crew become embroiled in a labor dispute between
troglodyte miners and their overlords, who live in an ethereal cloud city.
KIRK POINTS: 2 (EV, PB)

EPISODE 76: "The Savage Curtain"
ORIGINAL AIR DATE: 3/7/69
DIRECTOR: Herschel Daugherty; TELEWRITERS: Gene Roddenberry and
Arthur Heinemann
GUEST CAST: Janos Prohaska/voice of Bart LaRue (Yarnek); Lee Begere
(Abraham Lincoln); Barry Atwater (Surak); Philip Pine (Colonel
Green); Carol Daniels Dement (Zora); Nathan Jung (Genghis Khan);
Robert Herron (Kahless)
SYNOPSIS: Yarnek, an alien rock, attempts to decide the issue of Good vs.
Evil by having Abraham Lincoln and Genghis Khan battle each other.
Yeah, that's a fair fight.
KIRK POINTS: 1 (HHC)

EPISODE 77: "All Our Yesterdays"
ORIGINAL AIR DATE: 3/14/69
DIRECTOR: Marvin Chomsky; TELEWRITER: Jean Lisette Aroeste
GUEST CAST: Ian Wolfe (Mr. Atoz); Mariette Hartley (Zarabeth)
SYNOPSIS: Spock and McCoy leap through a time portal and wind up
stranded in an ice age where Spock reverts to early Vulcan savagery.
KIRK POINTS: 0

EPISODE 78: "Turnabout Intruder"

ORIGINAL AIR DATE: 6/3/69

DIRECTOR: Herb Wallerstein; TELEWRITER: Arthur H. Singer

GUEST CAST: Sandra Smith (Dr. Janice Lester); Harry Landers (Dr. Arthur Coleman)

SYNOPSIS: Resentful Janice Lester uses a machine to place her mind in Kirk's body, and vice versa.

KIRK POINTS: 6 (DR + 5-point bonus for playing the ultimate dual role as a member of the opposite sex)

Appendix 3

~

Shatner Fan Club Information

It seems a cliché, but *Star Trek* truly is a worldwide phenomenon. Universal, even. Just ask the millions of fans who lobbied to have America's first space shuttle christened the *Enterprise*. And as if the world needed further proof of the TV program's galactic reach, Gene Roddenberry's ashes were scattered in outer space by a space shuttle crew in 1992. So it's no surprise that there are Shatner and *Star Trek* affinity groups in every corner of the globe. Word has it they may even be close to a quorum on *Mir*. Here are a few of the more prominent ones, with contact information, for your perusal:

Organia fan club and fanzine
http://organia.skynet.com.br/

Queensland Star Trekkers (Quest)
GPO Box 2084,
Brisbane 4001, Australia

Star Trek : The Official Fan Club
P.O. Box 111000
Aurora, CO 80042
Toll Free : 1-800-true-fan/1-800-878-3326
Fax : 1 (303) 574-9442

Star Trek: The Official Fan Club of Australia
GPO Box 2067, Sydney 2001, Australia
Toll Free : 1-800-67-1701
Phone : (02) 9311-3841
International : + 61 (2) 9311-3841
Fax : (02) 9311 3697

Star Trek Unofficial Fan Club
http://www.comox.island.net/events/duncan/duncan-a18078.html

Starfleet International Star Trek [A Fan Association]
http://www.sfi.org/

U.S.S. Powhatan
http://hampton.worldreach.net/powhatan/

U.S.S. Rubicon
http://www.ncw.net/~myrddin/agenda.html

The William Shatner Connection
7059 Atoll Ave
North Hollywood, CA 91605

Appendix 4

~

Shatner-related Internet Newsgroups

Usenet newsgroups are the front lines of high-tech fandom. Shatner's name often crops up on these cyber bulletin boards. A recent Deja News search on the actor's name received 595 hits. Some of the more prominent Shatner-related newsgroups on the Internet include:

alt.org.starfleet
alt.starfleet
alt.startrek
alt.startrek.binaries
alt.startrek.creative
alt.startrek.creative.erotica
alt.startrek.klingon
alt.startrek.romulan
alt.startrek.vulcan
alt.tv.star-trek
alt.tv.star-trek.tos
aus.sf.star-trek
rec.arts.startrek.current
rec.arts.startrek.fandom
rec.arts.startrek.info
rec.arts.startrek.misc
rec.arts.startrek.reviews
rec.arts.startrek.tech
uk.media.tv.sf.startrek

Appendix 5

~

Shatner-related Internet Web Sites

It has been said that everyone will be famous for fifteen minutes. "But Andy Warhol had it wrong," William Shatner has said. "Everyone will be famous for fifteen minutes and have their own Web page."

The Web presence of the various *Star Trek* series is strong and growing stronger. Shatner himself is currently in negotiations to establish numerous Trek-related Web sites. "I am especially intrigued by Trek on the Internet," he has said. "I like the exchange among the fans and the endless web sites devoted to the endless minutiae. As far as I'm concerned, nothing but good can come of it."

To list all of the official and unofficial Web sites devoted to *Star Trek* would be a monumental task. Presented here are just a few of the many sites devoted to William Shatner and Shatner projects:

The First Church of Shatnerology
http://www.fastlane.net/homepages/hattan/
Billing itself as a "lunatic millenium cult with a difference," this elaborate Web site features comics, a filmography, and generous helping of Shatner-related links, including places where you can buy the great man's album.

The Official William Shatner Fan Club Web site
http://www.shatner.com/
A reverent page featuring news about Shatner's public appearances and an exhaustive calendar of events. If you're stalking Shatner, this is the place to start.

278 THE ENCYCLOPEDIA SHATNERICA

The Second National Church of Shatnerology
http://www.geocities.com/Hollywood/Set/1931/shatner.html
The inevitable second church is a pale shadow of the first, but where else could you find the James T. Kirk Macarena Page? Can you say "cease and desist letter"?

The Shatner Page
http://www.tp.net/tp/users/lewser/ShatnerPage.htm
A site almost entirely devoted to Shatner's toupee. It includes several doctored photographs of a bald Shatner. This is what we have the First Amendment for.

The Temple of Shatner
http://comp.uark.edu/~breed/shatner.html
Why do so many Shatner pages have a religious theme? This site is driven by pictures of Shatner, many of them quite amusing.

The William Shatner Experience
http://www.geocities.com/Area51/Zone/8865/
Not much content here, but if you're looking for digitized images of Shatner as T. J. Hooker (and who isn't really?) this is the place for you.

The William Shatner Fan Club Page
http://users.aol.com/maxnova/shatner.htm
This unofficial fan page is woefully thin on content and insufficiently irreverent in its approach. For completists only.

Quiz Answers

~

Answers to **The Shatnerific Trivia Challenge**
Part One: *Star Trek*

1. The *S.S. Yorktown*

2. Stun. Kill.

3. Leonard Nimoy and Majel Barrett

4. DeForest Kelley

5. Gary Lockwood, in *2001: A Space Odyssey* (1968)

6. Warp 12

7. Seventy-two officers and a crew of 428

8. Communicator signal

9. Twelve seconds

10. William Shatner and James Doohan

11. Majel Barrett

12. Khan Noonian Singh

13. The Russian writer Anton Chekhov (1860–1904)

14. Hikaru

15. Scotty is Montgomery, McCoy is Leonard

16. James Tiberius Kirk

17. Spock

18. The *S.S. Valiant*

19. Bird of Prey

20. A woman inhabiting Captain Kirk's body

Answers to **Is There in Truth No Booty?**:

Kirk enjoyed a piece of the action with B, C, E, G, AND L

Answers to **The Shatnerific Trivia Challenge**
Part Two: The Life and Career of William Shatner

1. The "Cold Hands, Warm Heart" episode of *The Outer Limits* (1964)

2. Harold Sakata: with Shatner in *Want a Ride, Little Girl?* (1972); with Sean Connery in *Goldfinger* (1964)

3. Tinnitus—that's the ringing in Shatner's ears

4. His acclaimed TV series *For the People* (1965) was not renewed, so Shatner was available for *Star Trek*

5. On the *Studio One* anthology TV series presentation of Reginald Rose's "The Defender" (2/15/57 and 3/4/57), which became the basis for the TV series

6. a. Judy Garland, in *Judgment at Nuremberg* (1961)
   b. Yul Brynner, in *The Brothers Karamazov* (1958)
   c. Paul Newman, in *The Outrage* (1964)
   d. Marlene Dietrich, in *Judgment at Nuremberg* (1961)
   e. Edward G. Robinson, in *The Outrage* (1964)
   f. John Travolta, in *The Devil's Rain* (1975)
   g. Ava Gardner, in *The Kidnapping of the President* (1980)
   h. Sonny Bono, in *Airplane II: The Sequel* (1982)

7. False. Before *Star Trek*, he appeared in *Twilight Zone* and *The Outer Limits*

8. He appeared on *all* of these game shows, and more

9. a. Eva Marie Friedrick, ex-girlfriend, sued for palimony
   b. Nerine Kidd, wife

   c. Marcy Lafferty, ex-wife

   d. Vira Montes, ex-girlfriend, also sued for palimony

   e. Gloria Rand, ex-wife

10. They both have beloved homes/estates named Belle Reve (beautiful dream)

11. Operation Lazarus was a 1983 covert military operation into Laos to rescue American P.O.W.s—an undertaking partially financed by Shatner

12. *The Outrage* (1964), from Akira Kurosawa's *Rashomon* (1951). *The Magnificent Seven* (1960) is based on Kurosawa's *Seven Samurai* (1954).

13. Promise margarine

14. 1-D, 2-G, 3-A, 4-F, 5-C, 6-E, 7-B

15. Jack Lord

16. Melanie Shatner, who appeared in *Star Trek VI: The Undiscovered Country* (1991)

17. a-2, b-3, c-5, d-1, e-4

18. Ricardo Montalban and Hervé Villechaize

19. *The Hound of the Baskervilles* (1972)

20. They're three of Shatner's favorite Doberman pinschers

Bibliography

〜

PERIODICALS

"Beamed Up Again." *Variety* (January 10, 1994).

Beauregard, Sue-Ellen. Review of the Videotape *Ultimate Survivors: Winning Against Incredible Odds*. *Booklist* (January 1, 1992): 845.

Bianculli, David. "'Tek' Another Look." *New York Daily News* (January 5, 1995).

Boulton, Marsha. "Shatner Keeps on Trekkin.'" *Maclean's* (December 10, 1979): 14.

Brady, James. "In Step with William Shatner." *Parade* (March 2, 1986): 19.

Brooke, Jill. "Shatner Captains Real Life Drama." *New York Post* (April 18, 1989): 89.

Brown, Peter H. "Embattled Enterprise." *Washington Post* (December 18, 1986).

Buchalter, Gail. "Star Trek's Straight Arrow..." *People* (July 5, 1982): 50.

Buckler, Grant. "Star Trek's Kirk Beams Up to CEO Role." *Newsbytes News Network* (February 21, 1995).

"The Captains." *TV Guide* (August 24, 1996): 20.

Castro, Peter. "Chatter: Star Search." *People* (July 10, 1989): 108.

Challender, Mary. "Captain Kirk Has Lost Faith, but *Star Trek* Has Its Faithful." *Gannett News Service* (August 22, 1996).

"Chatter column: 'Walking Tall.'" *People* (April 5, 1982): 142.

Chidley, Joe. "Captain of Enterprise." *Maclean's* (November 28 1994).

_____. Review of the Television Movie *TekWar*. *Maclean's* (May 2, 1994).

Cohen, Charles E. "The Trek to *Tek*." *TV Guide* (January 15, 1994): 16.

Dick, Jeff. Review of the Video *I Am Become Death*. *Booklist* (August 1997).

Eisenberg, Lawrence. "William Shatner Finds Heroism a Touchy Enterprise." *TV Guide* (December 16, 1989): 26.

Engel, Joel. "Bad News for Captain Kirk in the 24th Century." *New York Times* (July 25, 1994).

Fessier, Michael. "No One Ever Upsets the Star." *TV Guide* (October 15, 1966): 30.

Finn, Robin. "Star's Trek: Spaceship to Show Ring." *New York Times* (November 8, 1986): 15.

Flamm, Matthew. "Maiden Voyage for Kirk." *New York Post* (June 4, 1989): 28.

Fowler, James E. "Dammit Jim, I'm Just a Cowboy." *Los Angeles Times* (April 18, 1996).

"A Galaxy of Trek Stars." *TV Guide* (November, 1997): 7.

Gardella, Kay. "Riding Herd on Troublemakers." *New York Daily News* (November 12, 1985).

_____. "Shatner Takes Weighty Approach to New Role." *New York Daily News* (1966).

Graham, Jefferson. "Shatner Finds a New Frontier as Director of *Star Trek V*." *USA Today* (June 8, 1989).

Green, Roland. Review of the Book *Delta Search*. *Booklist* (January 1, 1997).

_____. Review of the Book *Tek Money*. *Booklist* (September 15, 1995).

_____. Review of the Book *Tek Net*. *Booklist* (August 1997).

Green, Tom. "Even Kirk Won't Tell Spock's Fate." *USA Today* (1984).

Greppi, Michelle. "Series Planned for Shatner's 'TekWar.'" *New York Post* (July 29, 1994).

Gross, Ben. "Science Fiction and Reality." *New York Daily News* (1967).

Hammond, Sally. "CBS Prosecutor Won't Win 'Em All." *New York Post* (January 3, 1965).

Higgins, Robert. "The Intergalactic Golden Boy." *TV Guide* (June 22, 1968): 12.

Hill, Sandy. "At 63, Shatner Has All Systems Engaged." *Knight-Ridder/Tribune News Service* (April 21, 1994).

Hughes, Mike. "Shatner Finds New Space." *Gannett News Service* (January 20, 1994).

Jones, Steven. "Shatner's 'Trek.'" *USA Today* (November 9, 1993).

Keck, William. "Celebrities' Pets Get Star Treatment." *National Enquirer* (October 21, 1997): 37.

Kempley, Rita. "*Star Trek VI* Boldly Going." *Washington Post* (December 4, 1991).

Kenny, Glenn. Review of the Book *Star Trek Memories*. *Entertainment Weekly* (February 16, 1996).

_____. Review of the Movie *Star Trek: Generations*. *Entertainment Weekly* (July 14, 1995).

Kiester, Edwin, Jr. "A Star's Trek." *TV Guide* (August 14, 1982): 18.

Koltnow, Barry. "Shatner Looks Back on 30 Years as Kirk." *Knight-Ridder/Tribune News Service* (November 17, 1994).

Lee, Luaine. "Now An Admiral, Shatner Hopes to Keep on Trekkin.'" *New York Daily News* (June 20, 1982).

Marin, Rick. "Warp Speed Ahead." *TV Guide* (July 24, 1993): 21.

Monthly Film Bulletin. (February 1975).

_____. (February 1980).

Neuhaus, Cable. "Geek Love." *Entertainment Weekly* (March 11, 1994).

Noth, Dominique Paul. "Star Trek Hero a Busy Man." *Biography News* (August, 1974): 952.

Oldenburg, Ann. "Kirk Out?" *USA Today* (October 26, 1994).

"Out of This World!" *Globe* (December 12, 1997).

Peck, Harvey. "Shatner on Stage." *New York Daily News* (May 18, 1969).

"Power Rangers item." *National Enquirer* (October 7, 1997): 13.

Prevetti, C.A. Review of the Video *It Didn't Have to Happen: Drinking and Driving*. *School Library Journal* (March 1995): 165.

Queenan, Joe. Review of the Television Movie *Prisoner of Zenda, Inc.* *People* (September 30, 1996).

Raddatz, Leslie. "*Star Trek* Wins the Ricky Schwarz Award." *TV Guide* (November 15, 1967): 25.

Rensin, David. "A Farewell to Kirk." *TV Guide* (October 8, 1994): 25.

_____. "20 Questions." *Playboy* (July 1989): 141.

Review of the Book "Voice of the Planet" by Michael Tobias. *People* (February 18, 1991).

Review of the Television Movie *TekWar*. *People* (March 20, 1995).

Richter, Erin. "Counterfeit Bills." *Entertainment Weekly* (October 13, 1995).

Roush, Matt. "*TekWar* Treks To Future-Cop Territory." *USA Today* (January 17, 1994).

Sanz, Cynthia. "Beam Him Down." *People* (November 28, 1994): 179.

Schnaufer, Jeff. "Coping: Sound of Silence..." *People* (May 19, 1997).

Shatner, William. "What I Watch." *TV Guide* (April 10, 1993): 2.

"Shatner in Palimony Suit," *Los Angeles Times* (January 26, 1990).

Shepard, Richard F. "A Tale of Two Media." *New York Times* (August 10, 1958).

Simonetti, Karen. Review of the Book *Ashes of Eden. Booklist* (May 1, 1995).

"Star Trek: The Geritol Generation." *Entertainment Weekly* (November 20 1992).

"Star Trek's Stars Trek." *People* (July 20, 1992): 40.

Steffens, Daneet. "The Pen Is Mightier Than the Phaser." *Entertainment Weekly* (June 23, 1995).

Svetky, Benjamin. "I'm Typing As Fast As I Can." *Entertainment Weekly* (January 15, 1993).

Swertlos, Frank. "Did Shatner Finance Raid into Laos?" *TV Guide* (February 12 1983): A-3.

Teubner, Greg. "Beam Me *Out*, Scotty." *New York Post* (February 4, 1994).

Towle, Patricia and Alan Smith. "William Shatner Branded a Sex Maniac." *National Enquirer* (October 10, 1995): 37.

TV Teletype Feature: "New Star Trek series planned." *TV Guide* (February 7, 1981): 46.

Variety (September 3, 1980).

Viens, Stephen and Melissa Key. "Beam Me Up." *Star* (December 2, 1997): 10.

"We're Having a Ball." *Web Magazine* (December, 1997).

"What's Up with William." *TV Guide* (May 5, 1990).

Wilkins, Mike. "It May Be Music to Your Ears . . . . But Not Mine." *TV Guide* (October 3, 1987): 12.

"William Shatner Treks Down the Aisle." *National Enquirer* (December 12, 1997): 40.

Wilson, David S. "Captain Kirk Comes Down to Earth." *TV Guide* (October 13, 1990): 10.

Witchel, Alex. "Contemplating Death and the Sequel." *New York Times* (November 23, 1994).

Books

Alexander, David. *Star Trek Creator: The Authorized Biography of Gene Roddenberry*. New York: Penguin Books, 1994.

Beckley, Timothy Greene. *UFOs Among the Stars*. New York: Global Communications, 1992. pp. 8-11.

Berlin, Joey. *Toxic Fame: Celebrities Speak on Stardom*. Detroit: Visible Ink, 1996. pp. 171 and 499.

Bly, Robert W. *The Ultimate Unauthorized Star Trek Quiz Book*. New York: HarperPerrenial, 1994.

Contemporary Theatre, Film, and Television, vol. 3. Detroit: Gale Research, 1983. pp. 336-38.

Current Biography Yearbook. New York: H.W. Wilson, 1987. pp. 504-507.

Engel, Joel. *Gene Roddenberry: The Myth and the Man Behind Star Trek*. New York: Hyperion, 1994.

Funt, Marilyn. *Are You Anybody?* New York: Dial Press, 1979. pp. 292-310.

Gould, Jodie. *Heather! An Unabashed, Unauthorized Celebration of All Things Locklear*. New York: Citadel Press, 1995.

Gross, Edward and Mark A. Altman. *Captain's Logs*. Boston: Little, Brown, 1995.

Hauck, Dennis William. *Captain Quirk*. New York: Pinnacle Books, 1995.

_____. *William Shatner: A Bio-Bibliography*. Westport, CT: Greenwood Press, 1994.

Hill, Marilyn and Rabbi Jerome Cutler, editors. *Celebrity Kosher Cookbook*. New York: Parker, 1975. p.16.

Koenig, Walter. *Warped Factors: A Neurotic's Guide to the Universe*. New York: Taylor, 1998.

Nemecek, Larry. *The Star Trek: The Next Generation Companion*. (rev. ed.) New York: Pocket Books, 1995.

Nichols, Nichelle. *Beyond Uhura*. New York: G. P. Putnam's Sons, 1994.

Nimoy, Leonard. *I Am Not Spock*. New York: Hyperion, 1975.

_____. *I Am Spock*. New York: Hyperion, 1995.

Okuda, Michael and Denise Okuda. *The Star Trek Encyclopedia* (revised edition). New York: Pocket Books, 1997.

Parish, James Robert and Vincent Terrace. *The Complete Actors' Television Credits, 1948-1988*. Metuchen, NJ & London: Scarecrow Press, 1989. pp. 437-39.

Robbins, Ira A. *The Trouser Press Record Guide*. New York: Macmillan, 1991.

Sachs, Margaret. *UFO Encyclopedia*. New York: G. P. Putnam's Sons, 1980. p. 289.

Shatner, Lisabeth with William Shatner. *Captain's Log: William Shatner's Personal Account of the Making of Star Trek V*. New York: Pocket Books, 1989.

Shatner, William with Christ Kreski. *Star Trek Memories*. New York: HarperCollins, 1993.

_____. *Star Trek Movie Memories*. New York: HarperCollins, 1994.

Shatner, William, Sondra Marshak, and Myra Culbreath. *Shatner: Where No Man*. New York: Grosset & Dunlap, 1979.

Solow, Herbert and Robert Justman. *Inside Star Trek: The* Real *Story*. New York: Pocket Books, 1996.

Takei, George. *To the Stars!* New York: Pocket Books, 1994.

Trimble, Bjo. *Star Trek Concordance*. New York: Citadel Press, 1995.

PRESS RELEASES

December 1, 1959. *Sunday Showcase* (NBC)

October 8, 1963. *Man of Decision* (ABC)

January 13, 1965. *For the People* (CBS)

April 10, 1967. *William Shatner's Trek to Stardom* (NBC)

August 31, 1968. *William Shatner: Captain James Kirk in* Star Trek (NBC)

February 2, 1968. *Shatner and Captain Kirk Share Common Traits* (NBC)

November 11, 1968. *William Shatner Cuts a Different Kind of Record* (NBC)

March 28, 1972. *William Shatner, Host of the ABC Sports series "Challenge"* (ABC)

July 14, 1976. *The Tenth Level* (CBS)

October 19, 1977. *William Shatner Joins Guest Star Cast of "How the West Was Won"* (ABC)

February 6, 1980. *William Shatner Signed for Second Six Programs in "This Was America" Series* (BBI)

June 30, 1981. *Shatner to Appear on "Over Easy"* (Over Easy)

1983. *William Shatner, Sgt. T. J. Hooker in the ABC Television Network's "T. J. Hooker"* (ABC)

December 11, 1986. *William Shatner Host on Dec. 20 Edition of NBC's "Saturday Night Live"* (NBC)

April, 1989. *William Shatner: A Biography* (Rogers & Cowan, Inc.)

October 25, 1993. *William Shatner to Be a Guest on CNBC's "Tom Snyder" Oct. 26* (CNBC)

January 17, 1994. *William Shatner Guest Stars on "seaQuest DSV" on NBC* (NBC)

November, 1994. *William Shatner, Executive Producer/Director/Guest Star "TekWar" action dramas* (Showtime)

November 30, 1994. *William Shatner in "Eek the Cat Christmas Special Airing December 5 on Fox* (Fox)

December 22, 1994. *William Shatner Stars As Columbo's Crafty Adversary Jan. 10 1995* (ABC)

March 8, 1995. *Beam Me Up Scotty.... William Shatner on CNBC's "Charles Grodin"* (CNBC)

June 5, 1995. *William Shatner on A-T Show "Straight Forward with Roger Ailes"* (NBC)

Index

About the Author

~

ROBERT E. SCHNAKENBERG has followed William Shatner's career since, at the age of six, he first saw Captain Kirk whip the pants off the Gorn. He has written extensively about television and popular culture for a variety of traditional and non-traditional media outlets.

Formerly an editor at New York's Museum of Television & Radio, Schnakenberg is the author of *Star Trek: The Episode Guides*, a two-volume illustrated guide to *Star Trek* issued in comic book form. He has written unauthorized comic book biographies of Leonard Nimoy, DeForest Kelley, and Grace Lee Whitney, among many others.

A squat, puckish man with a rakish twinkle in his eye, Schnakenberg is beloved by children and animals everywhere. He was educated by the state of New York, for which he is eternally grateful. He lives in New York City and owns all of Shatner's albums.

Also available from
<small>RENAISSANCE BOOKS</small>

Hercules & Xena: The Unofficial Companion
by James Van Hise
ISBN: 1-58063-001-4 · $15.95

Alien Nation: The Unofficial Companion
by Ed Gross
ISBN: 1-58063-002-2 · $14.95

Party of Five: The Unofficial Companion
by Brenda Scott Royce
ISBN: 1-58063-000-6 · $14.95

Pufnstuf & Other Stuff
The Weird and Wonderful World of Sid & Marty Krofft
by David Martindale, Foreword by Marty Krofft & Afterword by Sid Krofft
ISBN: 1-58063-007-3 · $16.95

The Ultimate Marilyn
by Ernest W. Cunningham
ISBN: 1-58063-003-0 · $16.95

Rock Stars Do the Dumbest Things
by Margaret Moser & Bill Crawford
ISBN: 1-58063-023-5 · $12.95

Law and Order: The Unofficial Companion
by Kevin Courrier & Susan Green
ISBN: 1-58063-022-7 · $16.95

Reel Gags
by Bill Givens
ISBN: 1-58063-042-1 · $9.95

The Girl's Got Bite: An Unofficial Guide to Buffy's World
by Kathleen Tracy
ISBN: 1-58063-035-9 · $14.95

The Ultimate Barbra
by Ernest W. Cunningham
ISBN: 1-58063-041-3 · $16.95

To order please call
1-800-452-5589